Adeline Klam
with Eriko Toureau-Kond

Origami for the Absolute Beginner

Over 40 super-easy projects

Styled photography by Adeline Klam
Step-by-step photography by Richard Boutin
Illustrations by Lucy Tézier

SEARCH PRESS

For Ulysse

Introduction

I created this book to be a simple and enjoyable tool that would make the art of origami accessible to everyone – the most important thing is that it should be fun.

By sticking to the essentials, I have provided a method that is very visual and uncluttered. There is a photograph of each step, and the more complex steps also have Lucy's illustrations to clarify exactly where you position your hands and what you do at each step of the process.

Simply follow the diagrams, and you will be amazed to see an object or animal coming to life in your hands. You can then use your origami creations as decorative invitations, to embellish wrapping paper or to brighten up a room or a party table.

Origami is my passion, and I am absolutely delighted to share it with you and help you discover the magic of paper folding.

I hope you get as much enjoyment from seeing your beautiful paper creations come to life as I did in designing this book for you!

Adeline Klam

Contents

Goldfish
page 28

Cup
page 30

Butterfly
page 32

Tulip
page 36

Cat
page 40

Hedgehog
page 44

Fan
page 48

Fox
page 50

Daisy
page 54

Parrot
page 56

Turtle dove
page 60

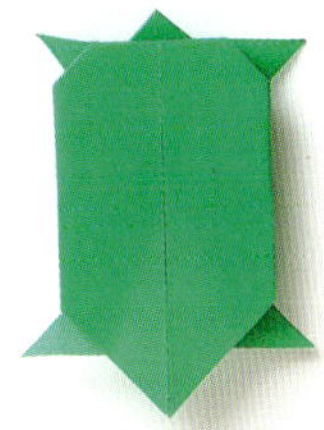

Turtle
page 62

Panda
page 66

Autumn leaf
page 72

Tatou envelope
page 76

Four-leaf clover
page 80

Heart
page 84

Star
page 88

Lion
page 92

Owl
page 96

Shirt
page 100

Dove
page 104

Ceremonial kimono
page 108

Scallop shell
page 112

Dress
page 116

Hydrangea
page 122

Simple kimono
page 126

Frog
page 130

Snail
page 134

Cherry blossom
page 140

Mouse
page 144

Rabbit
page 148

Ginkgo leaf
page 152

Morning glory
page 156

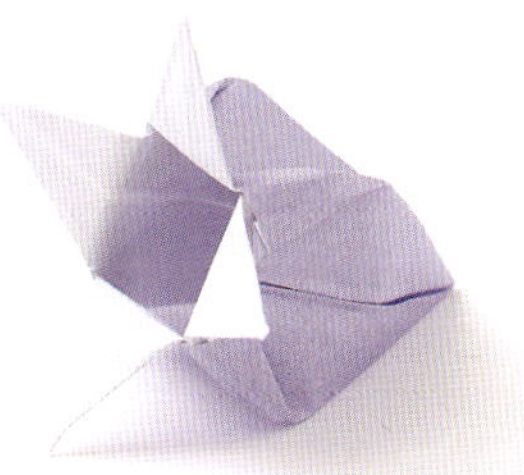

Campanula
page 160

Cockerel
page 164

Seated crane
page 170

Dragonfly
page 176

Marguerite
page 182

Christmas tree
page 188

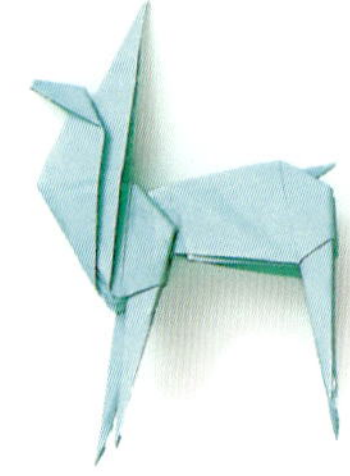

Stag
page 194

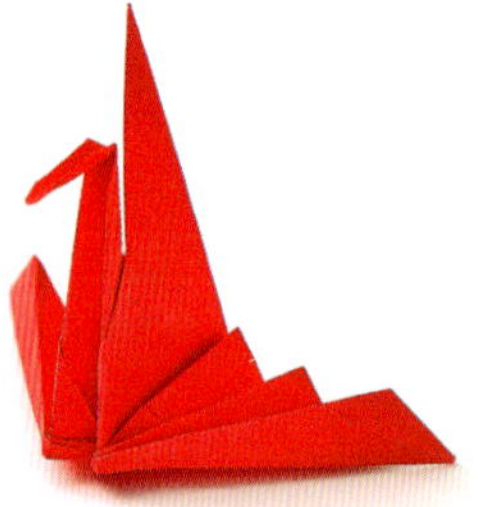

Majestic crane
page 200

Lily
page 208

Techniques

The squares of paper used in this book are coloured on the front and white on the back. This makes it easier to see where you are when folding.

The colours used in the photos and diagrams will help you to distinguish the coloured front of the paper from the white back.

Here are the ten key folding techniques used in origami. Look carefully at how they work and take some time
to practise. You will find they come up regularly in the instructions.

1. Flip over
This arrow tells you to flip the paper onto the other side.

2. Rotate
This arrow tells you to rotate the paper. The number of degrees rotation
is specified in the instructions.

3. Glue
These symbols show you where you need to put a spot of glue.

4. Cut
This line tells you where you need to cut using a pair of scissors.

5. Mark the diagonal lines
The diagonals are the two creases forming an X on a square of paper. To
make good diagonal creases, bring the two opposite corners together
and mark the crease that is formed. Unfold, bring the two other corners
together and mark the second crease.

6. Mark the central horizontal and vertical lines
The central horizontal and vertical lines are the two creases that form
a straight cross on a square of paper. To make creases, bring two opposite
edges together and mark the crease that is formed. Unfold and bring
the two other edges together and mark the second crease.

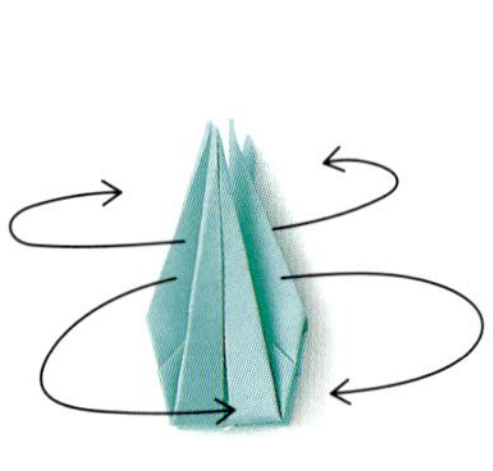 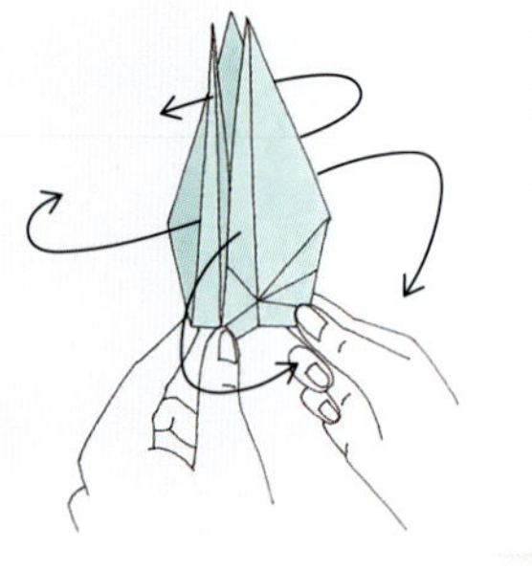 

7. Fold/unfold the flaps

The photos and this diagram demonstrate how to fold two flaps together. To unfold the flaps, you basically reverse the direction of the fold.

 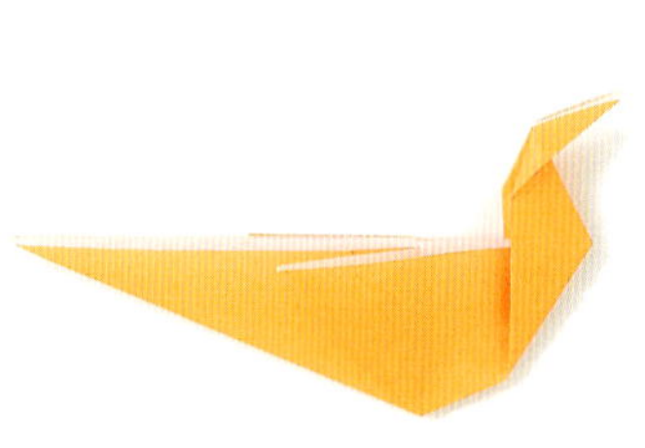

8. Outside reverse fold

The photos and this diagram demonstrate how to make an outside reverse fold to form heads and beaks, or animals' hindquarters and tails.

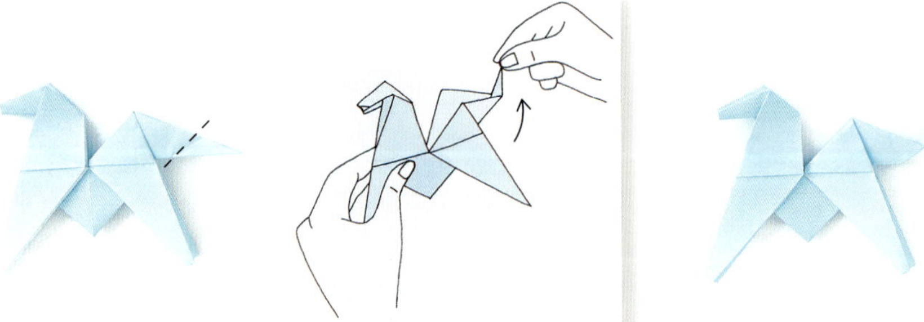

9. Inside reverse fold

The photos and this diagram demonstrate how to make an inside reverse fold, to form heads, beaks, or animals' hindquarters and tails.

10. Invert the fold

The photos and this diagram demonstrate how to invert a fold, following the solid black lines.

If you are new to origami, it is best to use plain paper. When you're more experienced, you can bring some variety to your projects by using patterned paper such as these Japanese papers.

Majestic crane, page 200

Seated crane, page 170 • Fan, page 48

Heart, page 84

Dress, page 116 • Shirt, page 100

Lily, page 208

Cockerel, page 164

Goldfish, page 28

Tulip, page 36

Rabbit, page 148

Butterfly, page 32

Hydrangea, page 122

Marguerite, page 182

Owl, page 96 • Lion, page 92

Simple kimono, page 126 • Ceremonial kimono, page 108

Campanula, page 160

Star, page 88

Stag, page 194

Autumn leaf, page 72

Ginkgo leaf, page 152 • Fox, page 50

Cherry blossom, page 140

Cup, page 30

Hedgehog, page 44 • Autumn leaf, page 72

Daisy, page 54 · *Tatou* envelope, page 76

Campanula, page 160

Mouse, page 144

Goldfish

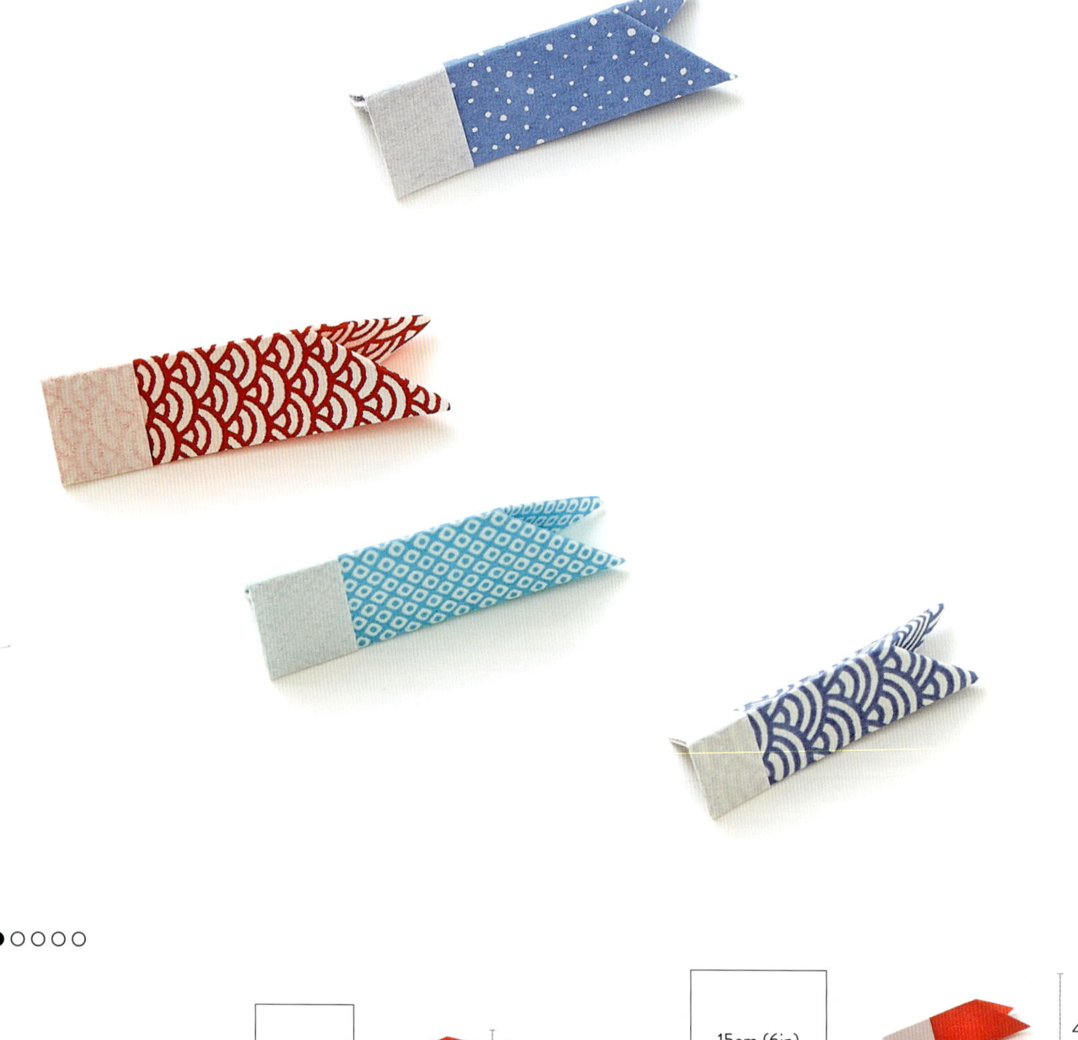

Level ●○○○○

Size

6cm (2¼in)		1.5cm (⅝in)
10cm (4in)		2.5cm (1in)
15cm (6in)		4cm (1½in)

4.5cm (1¾in)

7.5cm (3in)

11cm (4¼in)

Tip

Use a pen or pencil to personalize your fish. The 6 × 6cm (2¼ × 2¼in) paper is ideal if you want to use them as chopstick holders.

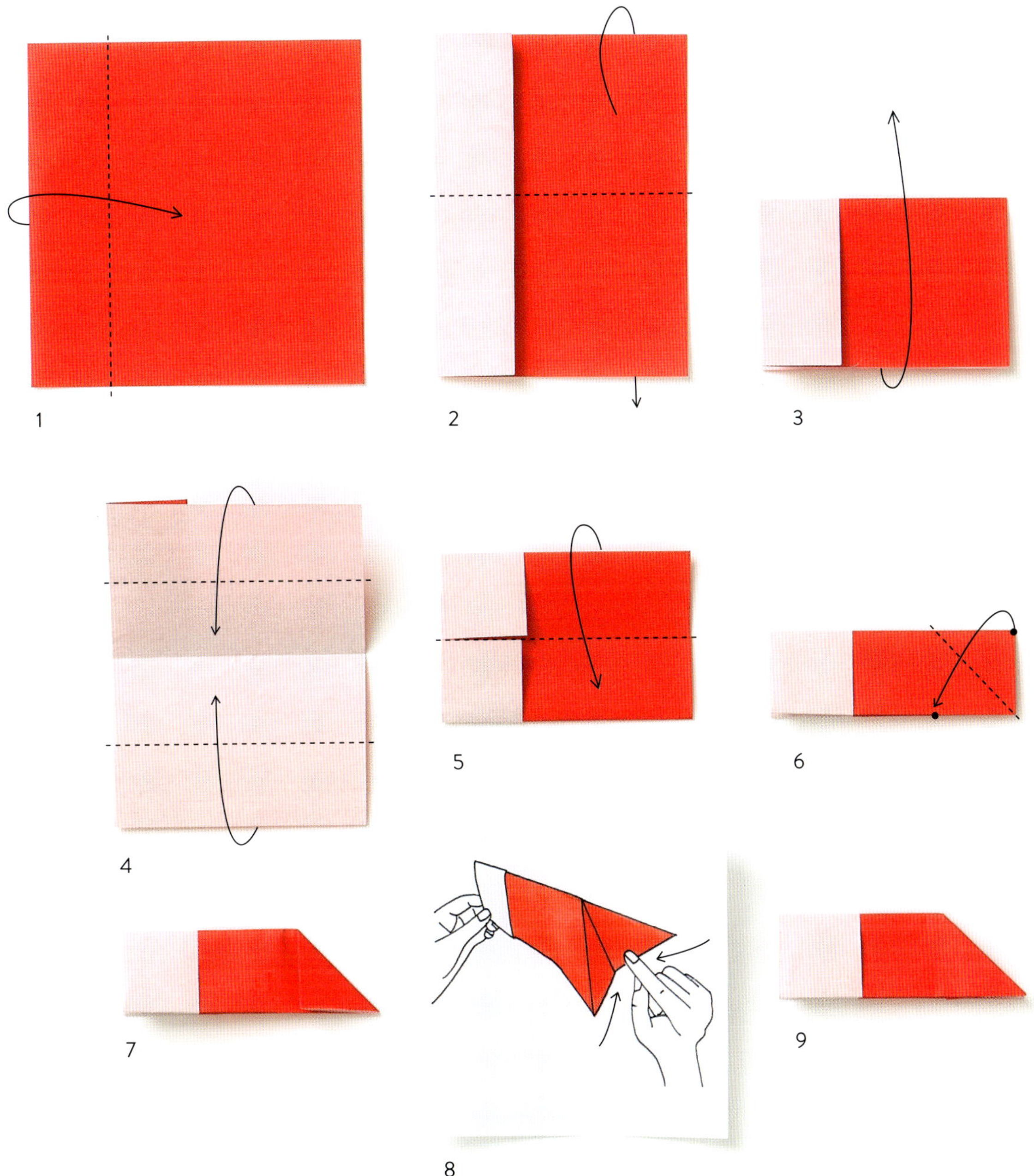

1. Place your paper coloured side up and fold along the dotted line (approximately a quarter of the way along the sheet). **2.** Fold in half behind along the dotted line. **3.** Open the white side towards you. **4.** Fold to the central line along the dotted lines. **5.** Fold in half along the dotted line. **6.** Fold the right-hand (RH) point along the dotted line. **7. 8. 9.** Unfold, open out the fold, invert and squash flat. You have formed the tail. Your goldfish is complete. Time to personalize it!

Cup

Level ●○○○○

Size

10cm (4in)

5.5cm (2¼in) — 4.5cm (1¾in)

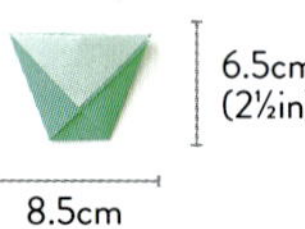
15cm (6in) — 8.5cm (3⅜in) — 6.5cm (2½in)

20cm (8in) — 11.5cm (4½in) — 8.5cm (3⅜in)

Tip

This design can be used as a little candy bag, a finger puppet or for a stacking component in a game! You can see this design on pages 24, 25 and 43.

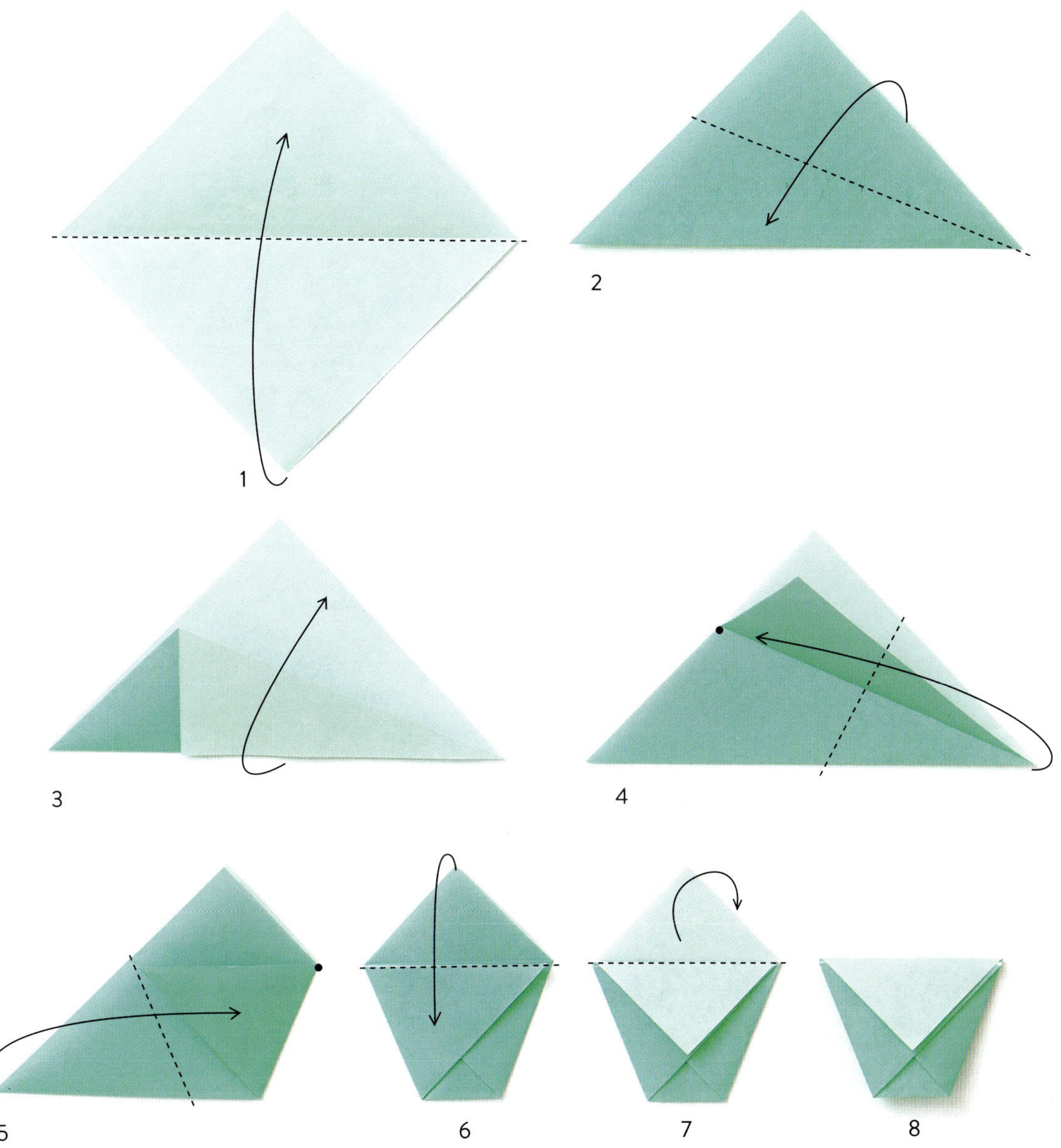

1. Place your square white side up. Rotate on to one corner and fold in half to form a triangle. **2.** Fold the top layer along the dotted line. **3.** Unfold the fold made in the previous step. **4.** Fold the RH (right-hand) point to the dot and mark the crease. **5.** Fold the LH (left-hand) point to the dot and mark the crease. **6.** Fold the top layer to the front along the dotted line. **7.** Fold the bottom layer behind along the dotted line. **8.** Your cup is complete.

Butterfly

Level ● ○ ○ ○ ○

Size

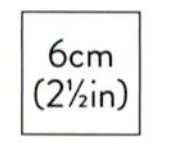
6cm
(2½in)

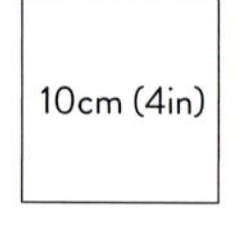
4.5cm
(1¾in)

6cm
(2½in)

10cm (4in)

7.5cm
(3in)

10cm (4in)

15cm (6in)

11.5cm
(4½in)

15cm (6in)

Tip

For this design, you will need two squares of paper. You will also need some quick-drying glue to stick the two parts together.

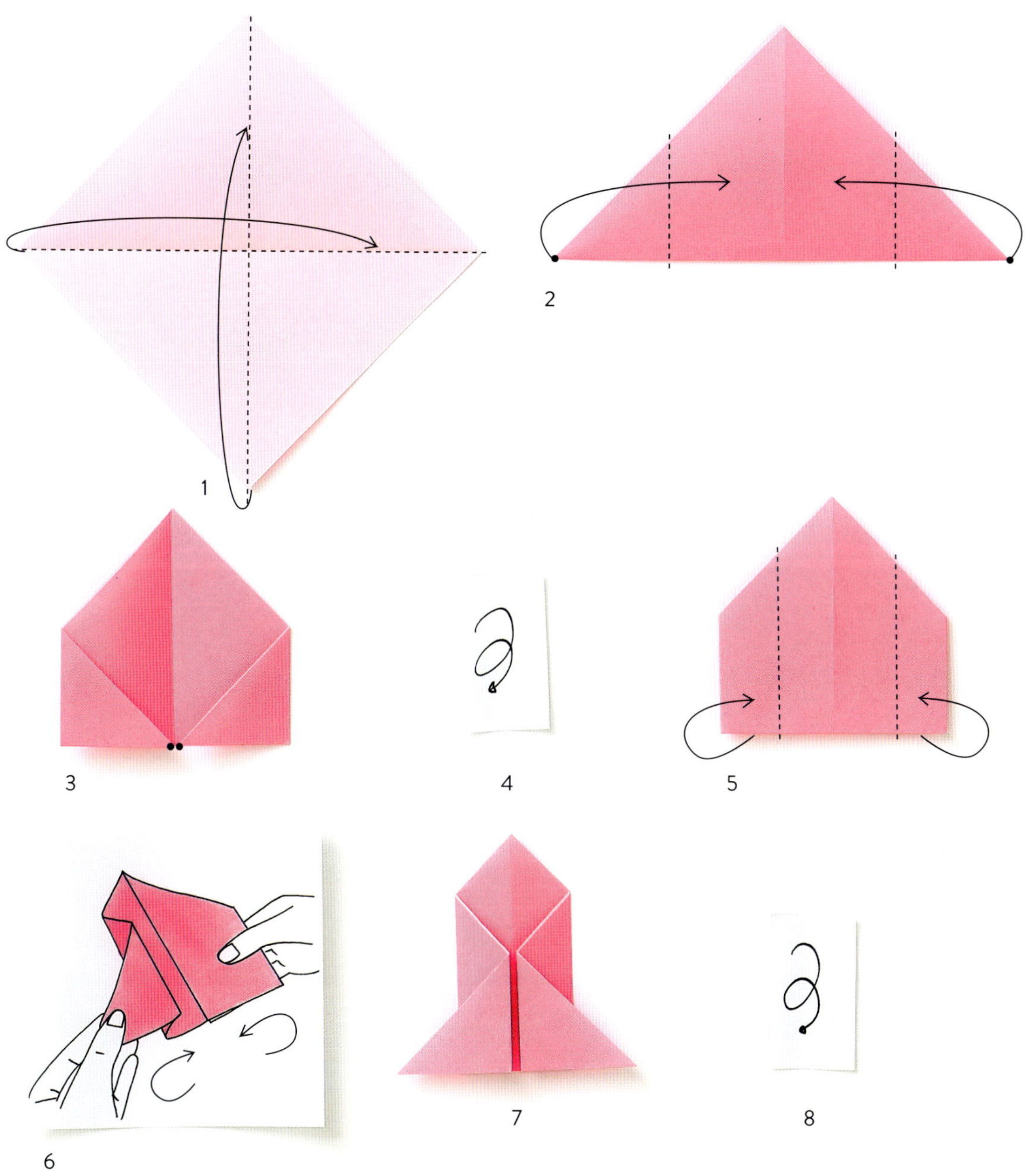

1. Place your square white side up. Rotate the square on to one corner and mark the crease of the diagonal line. Fold in half to form a triangle. Unfold, rotate the square 90° and repeat. **2.** Fold the points to the central line along the dotted lines. **3.** You now have this shape. **4.** Flip over. **5. 6. 7.** Fold along the dotted lines to fold the points to the front. **8.** Flip over.

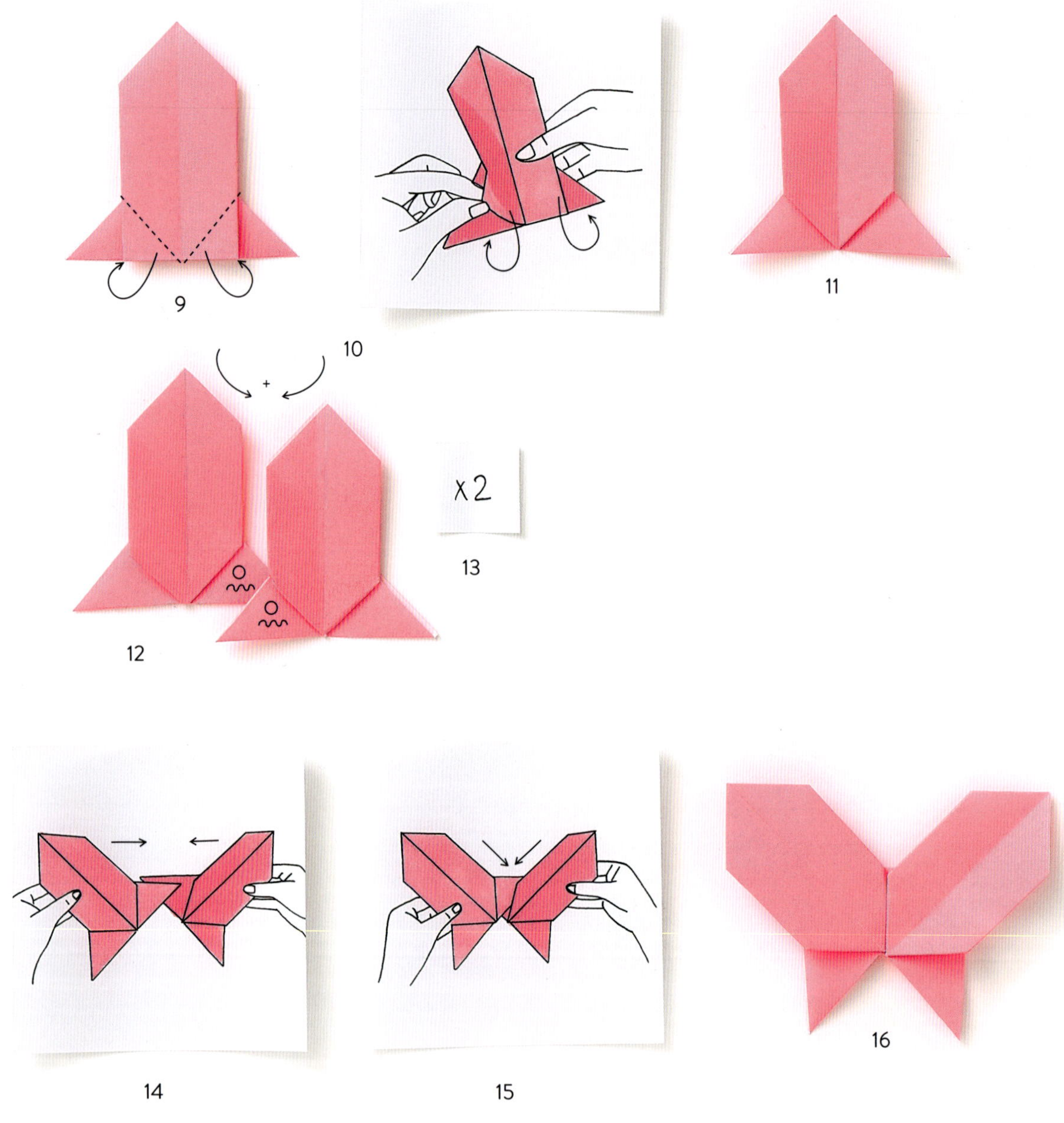

9. 10. 11. Fold along the dotted lines. Unfold and reverse the fold to tuck the LH flap inside. Do the same with the RH fold. **12.** Repeat steps 1 to 11 with the second piece of paper to create the other half of the butterfly. **13.** Add two dabs of glue where shown. **14. 15. 16.** Slot the two parts together, one inside the other, ensuring that the two glued triangles are aligned. Your butterfly is complete.

Tulip

Level ●○○○○

Size

FLOWERS

| 8cm (3¼in) | Version 1: 5.5cm (2¼in) / 6cm (2½in) | Version 2: 5.5cm (2¼in) / 5.5cm (2¼in) | Version 3: 5.5cm (2¼in) / 4cm (1½in) |

LEAVES

| 6cm (2½in) | Version 1: 8.5cm (3⅜in) / 3.5cm (1½in) | Version 2: 8.5cm (3⅜in) / 2cm (¾in) |

Tip
You can make several versions of the tulip and its leaves to create an attractive springtime picture.

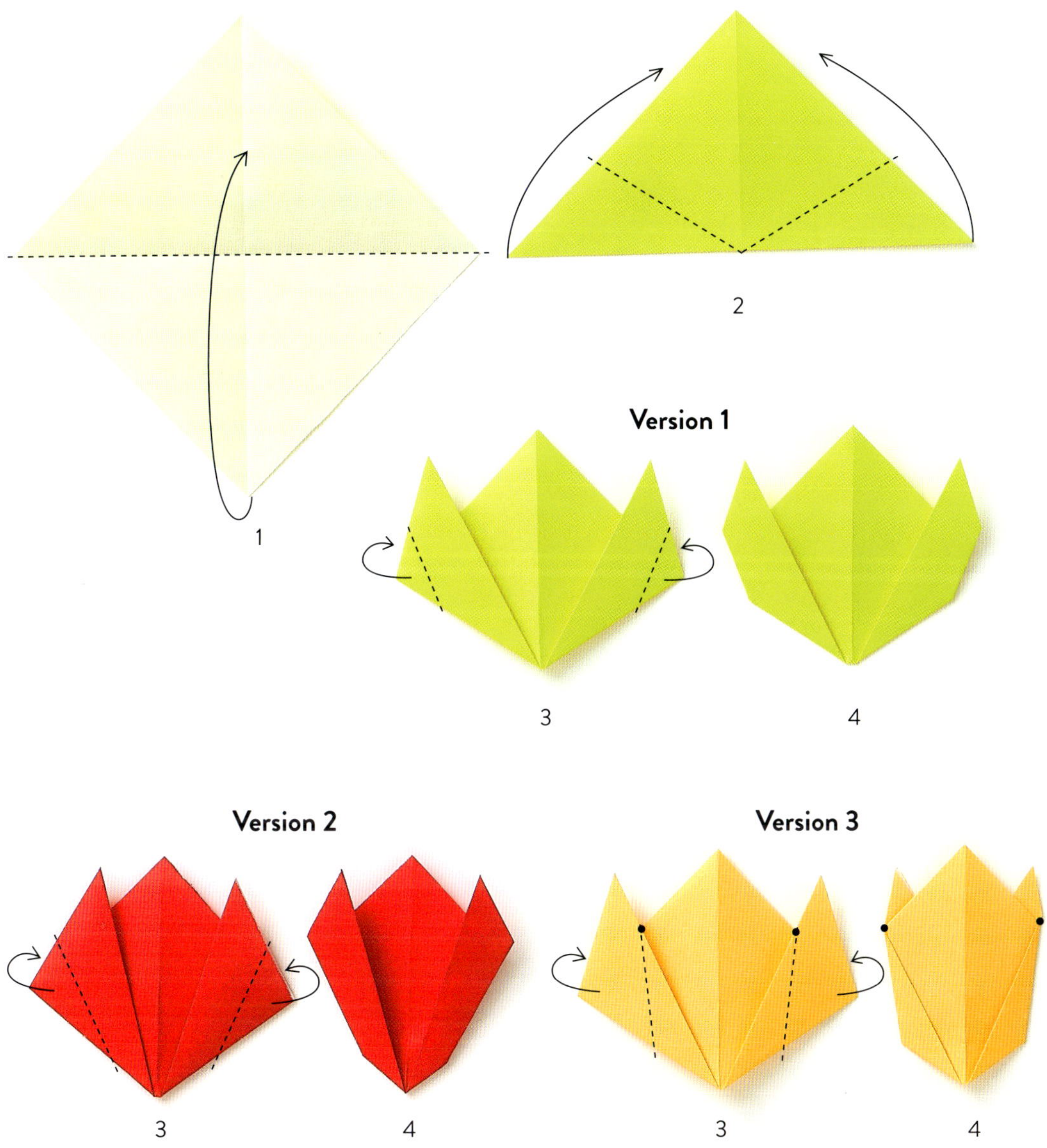

FLOWER

1. Place your square white side up. Rotate the square on to one corner and mark the creases of the diagonal lines. Fold in half. **2.** Fold the LH and RH points of the triangle upwards, a third of the way up the side.

Version 1: 3. 4. Fold behind along the dotted lines.

Version 2: 3. 4. Fold behind along the dotted lines.

Version 3: 3. 4. Fold behind along the dotted lines.

Version 1

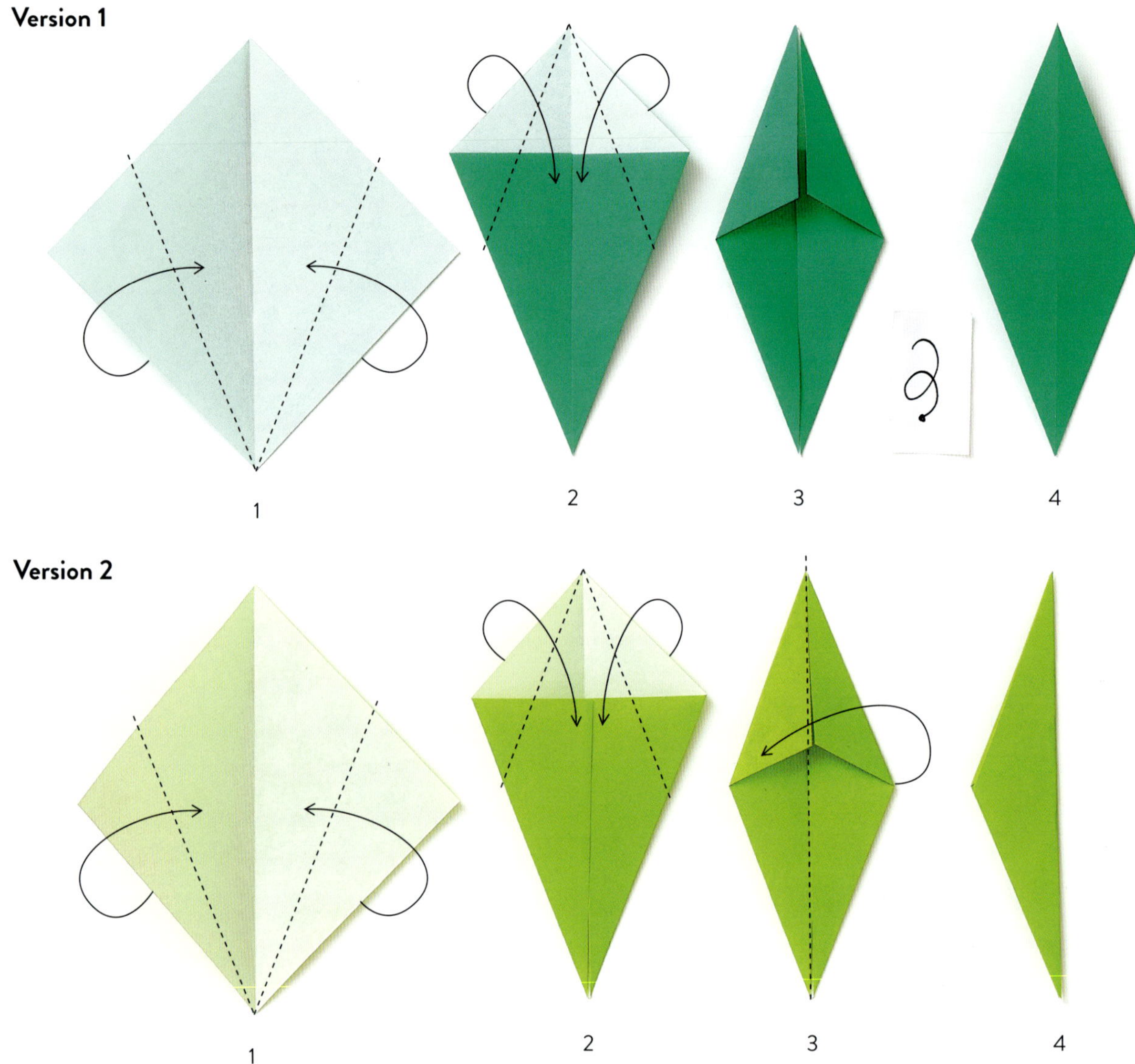

Version 2

LEAVES
Version 1
1. Place your square white side up. Rotate the square on to one corner and mark the crease of the diagonal line. Fold to the central line along the dotted lines. **2.** Fold to the central line along the dotted lines.
3. You now have this shape. **4.** Flip over. Your leaf is complete.
Version 2
1. Place your square white side up. Rotate the square on to one corner and mark the crease of the diagonal line. Fold to the central line along the dotted lines. **2.** Fold to the central line along the dotted lines.
3. 4. Fold in half. Your leaf is complete.

Cat

Level ● ● ○ ○ ○

Size

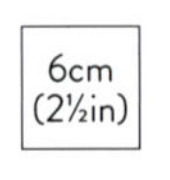 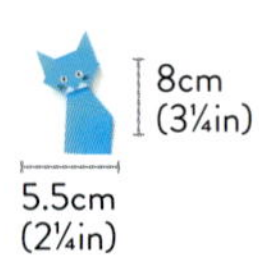

6cm (2½in) · 8cm (3¼in) · 5.5cm (2¼in)

10cm (4in) · 13cm (5⅛in) · 9.5cm (3¾in)

15cm (6in) · 19.5cm (7¾in) · 14cm (5½in)

Tip

For this design, you will need two squares of paper. You will also need some quick-drying glue and some pens or pencils so you can personalize your cat.

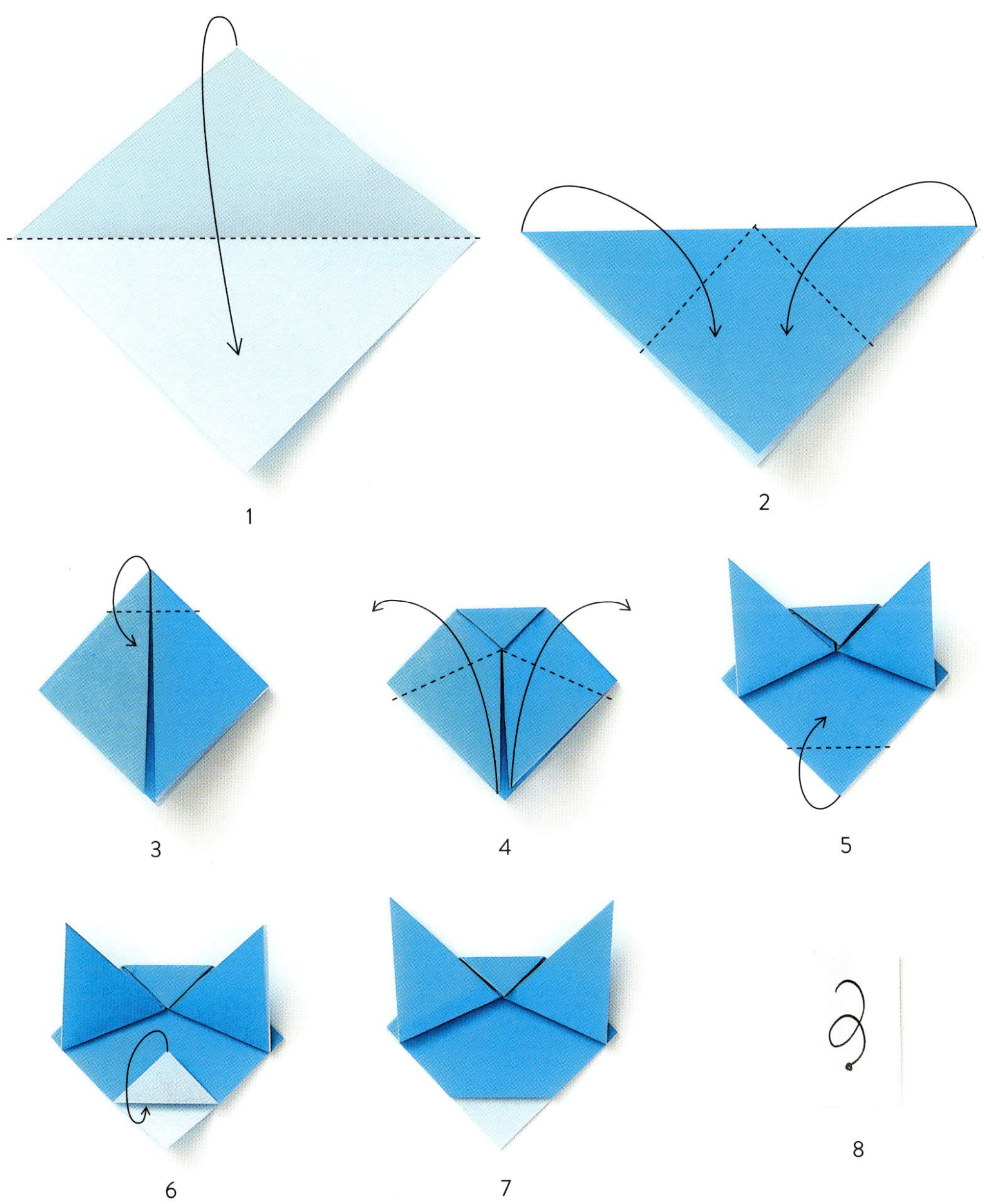

1. Place your square white side up. Rotate on to one corner and fold in half to form a triangle. **2.** Fold the two points down along the central line. Squash flat. **3.** Fold the top point down along the dotted line at the approximate point marked. **4.** Fold along the dotted lines, aligning with the sides of the top triangle.
5. Fold the point on the top layer along the dotted line at the approximate point marked. **6.** Unfold and fold the point inside. **7.** You now have this shape. **8.** Flip over.

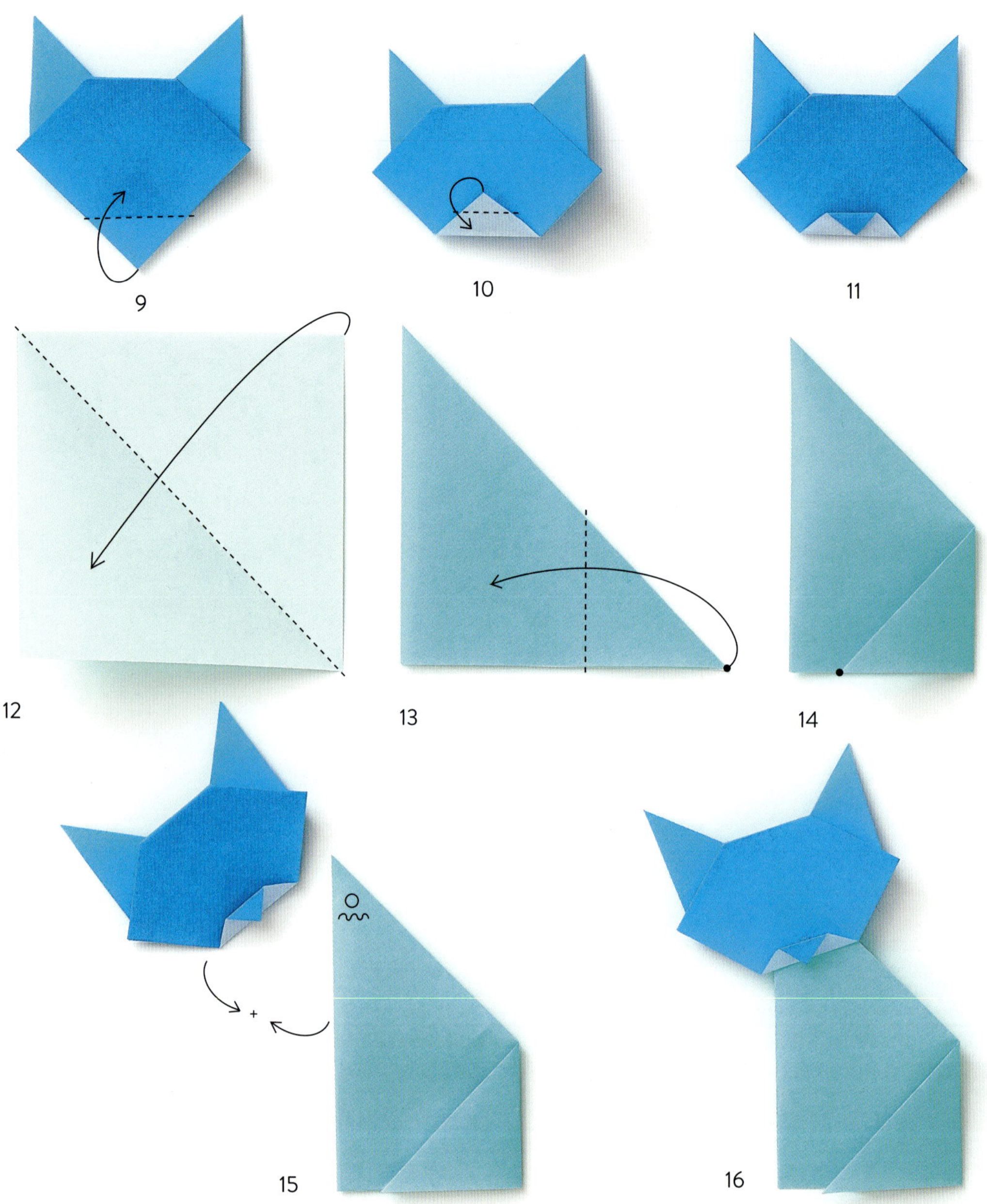

9. Fold along the dotted line. **10. 11.** Fold along the dotted lines. You now have this shape. The cat's head is complete. **12.** Fold the second square in half to form a triangle. **13. 14.** Fold the RH point to the left along the dotted line at the approximate point marked. The body is complete. **15. 16.** Apply a dab of glue as shown and slip the cat's body inside the head. Press. Your cat is complete. You can now personalize it.

POSTCARD

Hedgehog

Level ●●○○○

Size

7.5cm
(3in)

2.5cm
(1in)

5.5cm
(2¼in)

10cm (4in)

3.5cm
(1½in)

7cm
(2¾in)

15cm (6in)

5.5cm
(2¼in)

10.5cm (4⅛in)

Tip

You will need a pen or pencil to personalize your hedgehog.

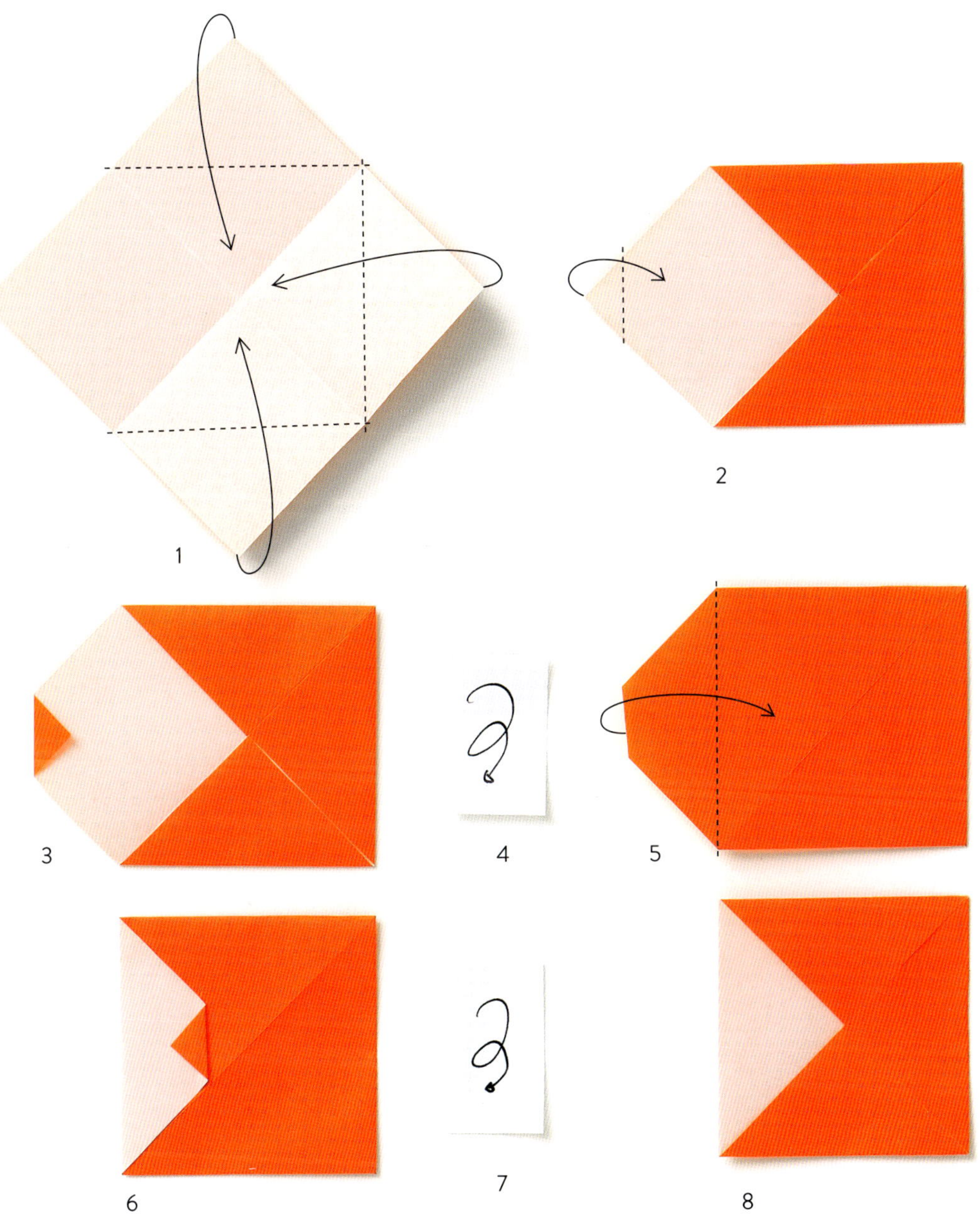

1. Place your square white side up and mark the creases of the central horizontal and vertical lines. Rotate on to one corner then fold the three points to the centre. **2. 3.** Fold along the dotted line. You now have this shape. **4.** Flip over. **5. 6.** Fold along the dotted line. You now have this shape. **7. 8.** Flip over. You now have this shape.

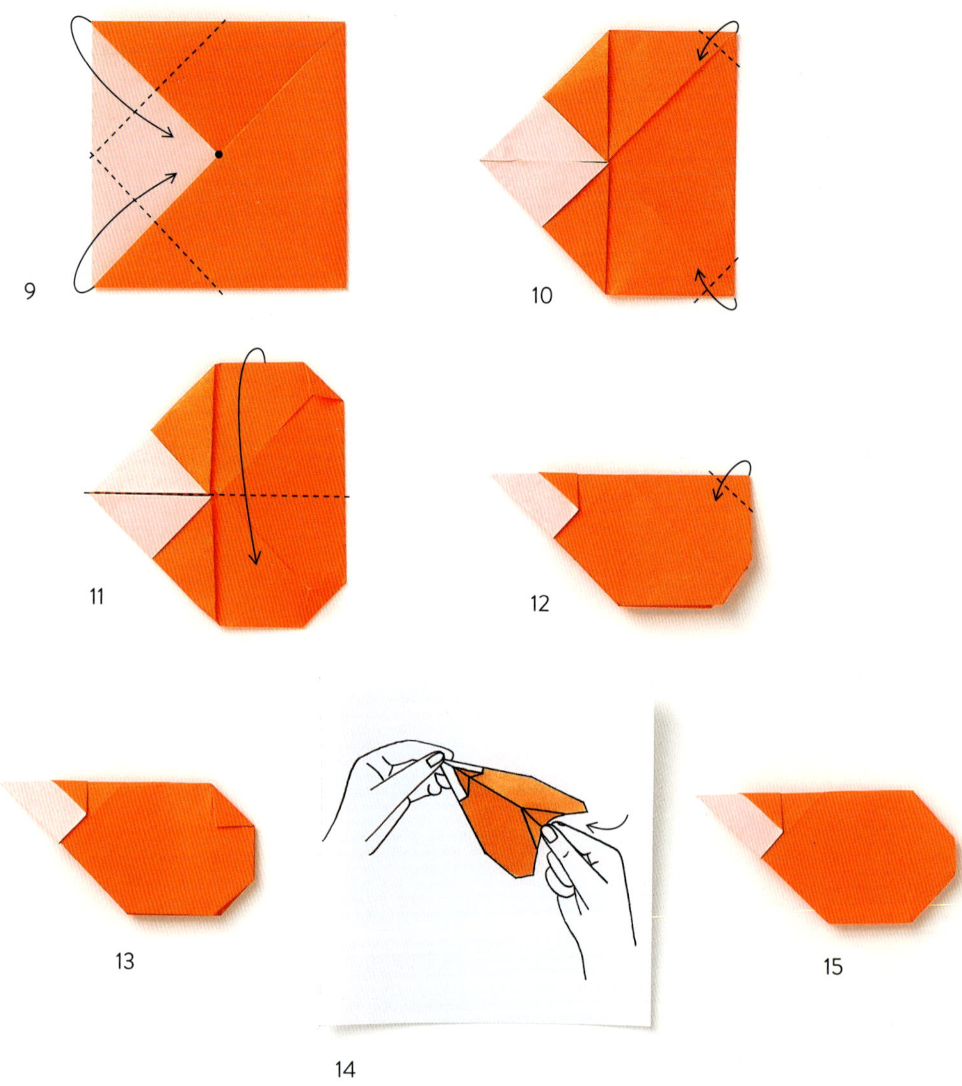

9. Fold to the central dot along the dotted lines. **10.** Fold along the dotted lines. **11.** Fold in half along the dotted line. **12.** Fold along the dotted line. **13. 14. 15.** Open out the fold of the small triangle and invert. Squash flat. This forms the hedgehog's back. You can now customize the head.

Adeline Klam

Fan

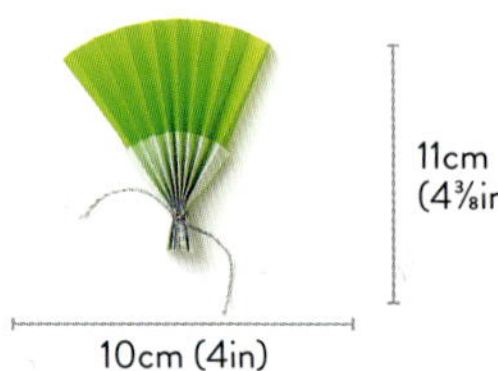

Level ● ○ ○ ○ ○

Size

 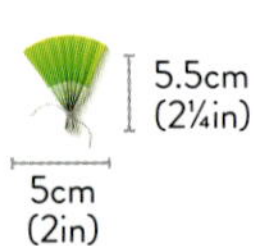

7.5cm (3in)

5.5cm (2¼in)

5cm (2in)

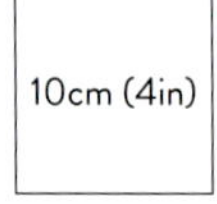 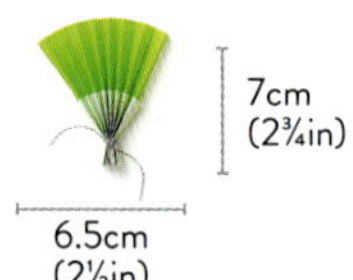

10cm (4in)

7cm (2¾in)

6.5cm (2½in)

15cm (6in)

11cm (4⅜in)

10cm (4in)

Tip

You will need a short length of yarn or thread.

1. Place your square coloured side up. Fold up approximately the lower third. **2.** Fold in half along the dotted line. **3.** Fold in half. **4.** Fold in half. **5.** Fold in half. **6. 7.** Unfold. **8.** Form accordion pleats by inverting every other fold. **9.** Gather the pleats at the bottom together. **10.** Tie the bottom together with a length of yarn or thread. Your fan is complete.

Fox

Level ●●○○○

Size

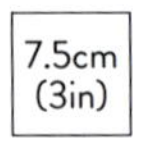

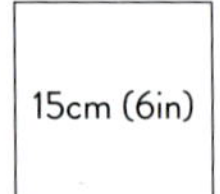

Tip

You will need a pen or pencil to personalize your fox.

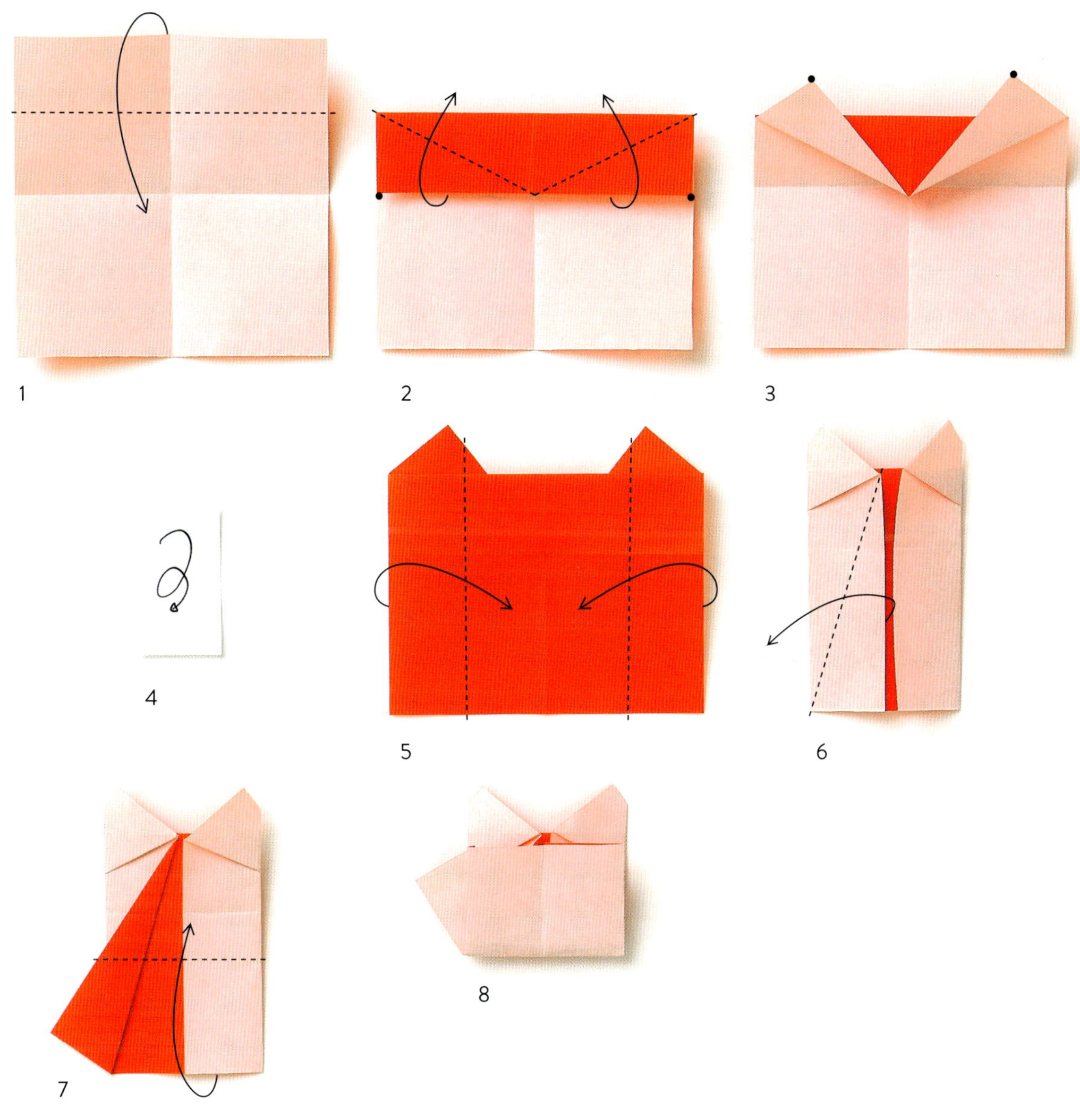

1. Place your square white side up and mark the creases of the central horizontal and vertical lines. Fold to the central line along the dotted line. **2. 3.** Fold the two dots upwards along the dotted lines **4.** Flip over.
5. Fold along the dotted lines. **6.** Fold the LH part at an oblique angle as shown. **7. 8.** Fold the bottom section upwards along the dotted line. You now have this shape.

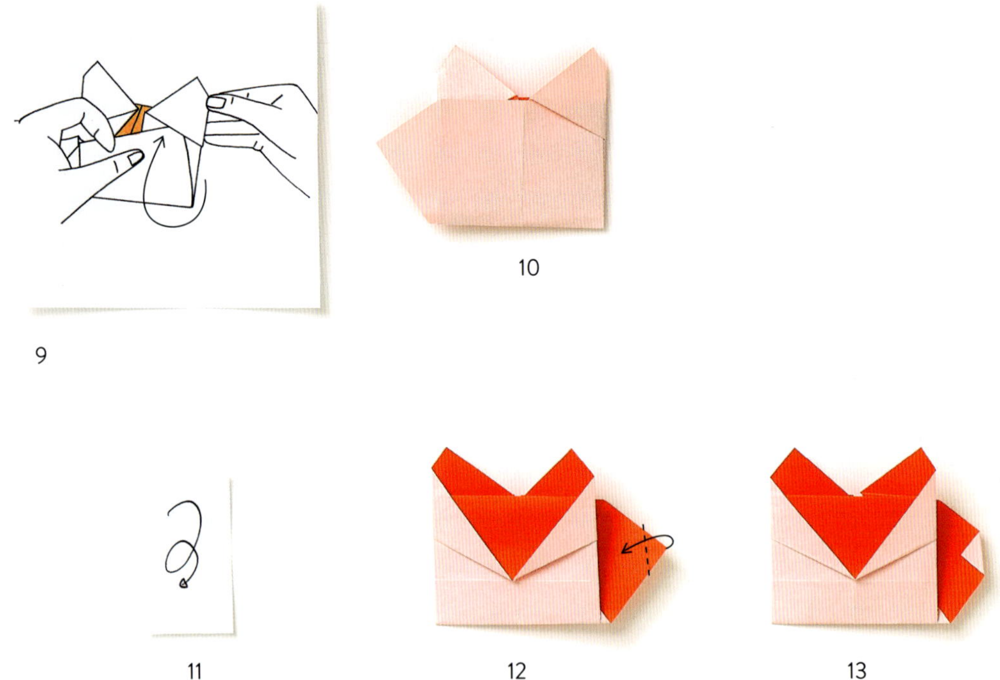

9

10

11

12

13

9. 10. Tuck the RH point under the RH ear. You now have this shape. **11.** Flip over. **12.** Fold along the dotted line. **13.** Your fox is complete. You can now personalize it.

Daisy

Level ● ● ○ ○ ○

Size

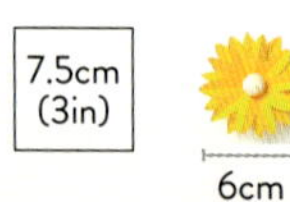

7.5cm
(3in)

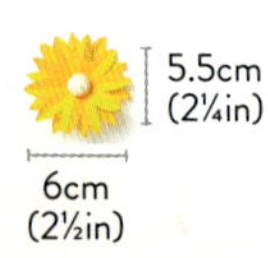

5.5cm
(2¼in)

6cm
(2½in)

10cm (4in)

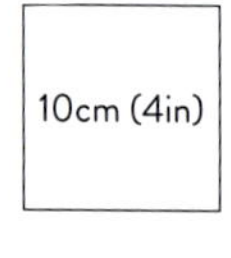

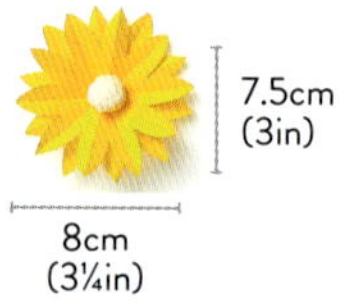

7.5cm
(3in)

8cm
(3¼in)

15cm (6in)

11.5cm
(4½in)

12cm (4¾in)

Tip
You will need a polystyrene ball, a small piece of crêpe paper, some quick-drying glue and a pair of scissors.

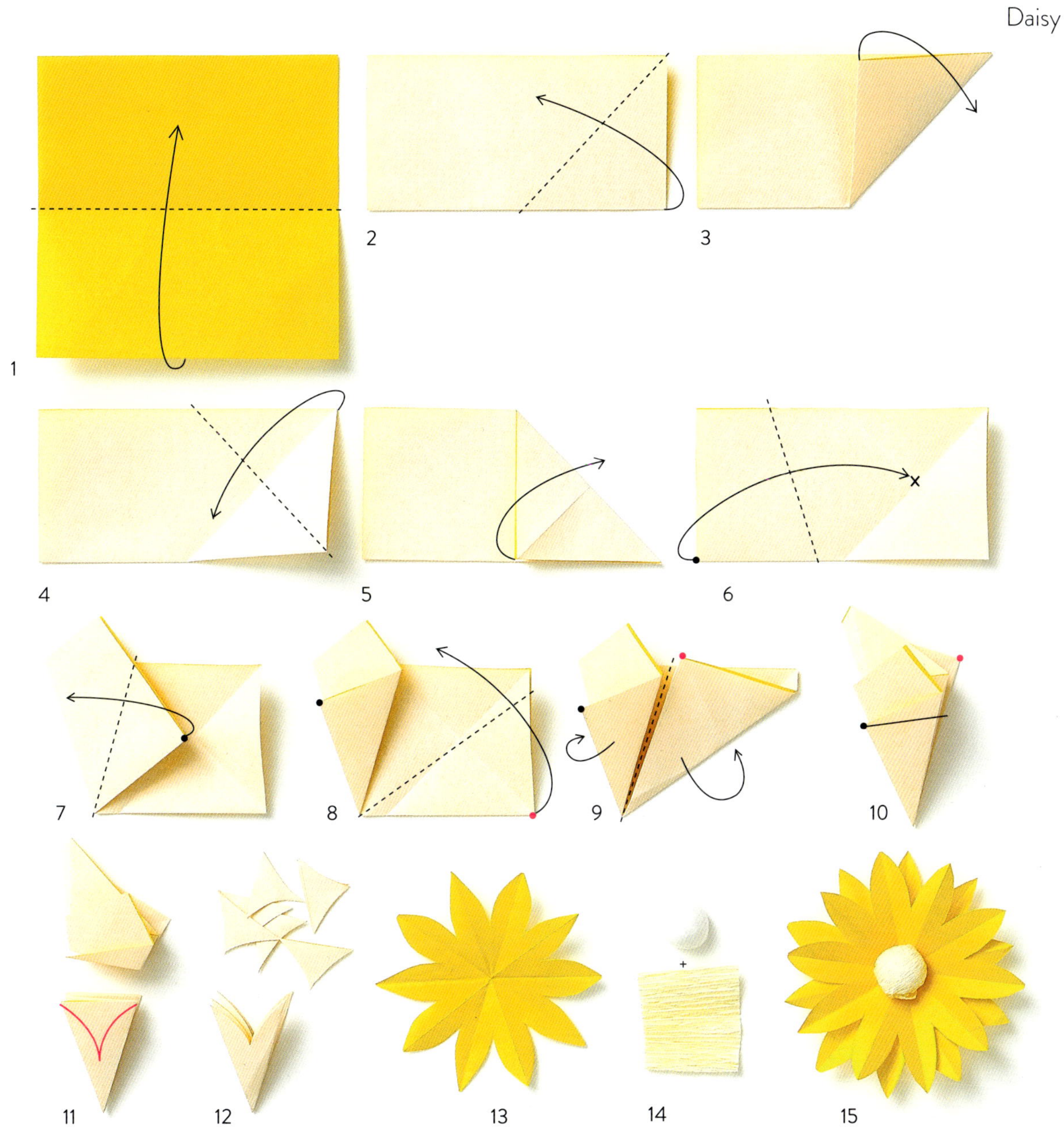

1. Place your square coloured side up and fold in half. **2. 3.** Fold the RH edge along the diagonal, following the dotted line. Unfold. **4. 5.** Fold the RH edge along the other diagonal. Unfold. **6.** Fold the dot to the cross marked in the centre. **7.** Fold the dot along the dotted line. **8.** Fold along the dotted line. **9.** Fold behind. **10.** Cut along the solid line. **11. 12.** Draw the outline of the petal in pencil. Cut along the lines through all the layers. **13.** Gently unfold. Repeat steps 1 to 13 so you have two flowers. **14.** Cut a polystyrene ball in half and wrap one half in a scrap of crêpe paper for the centre. **15.** Use a dab of glue to stick one flower to the other, staggering the petals slightly. Apply a dab of glue to the middle of the daisy and stick on the centre. Your daisy is complete.

Parrot

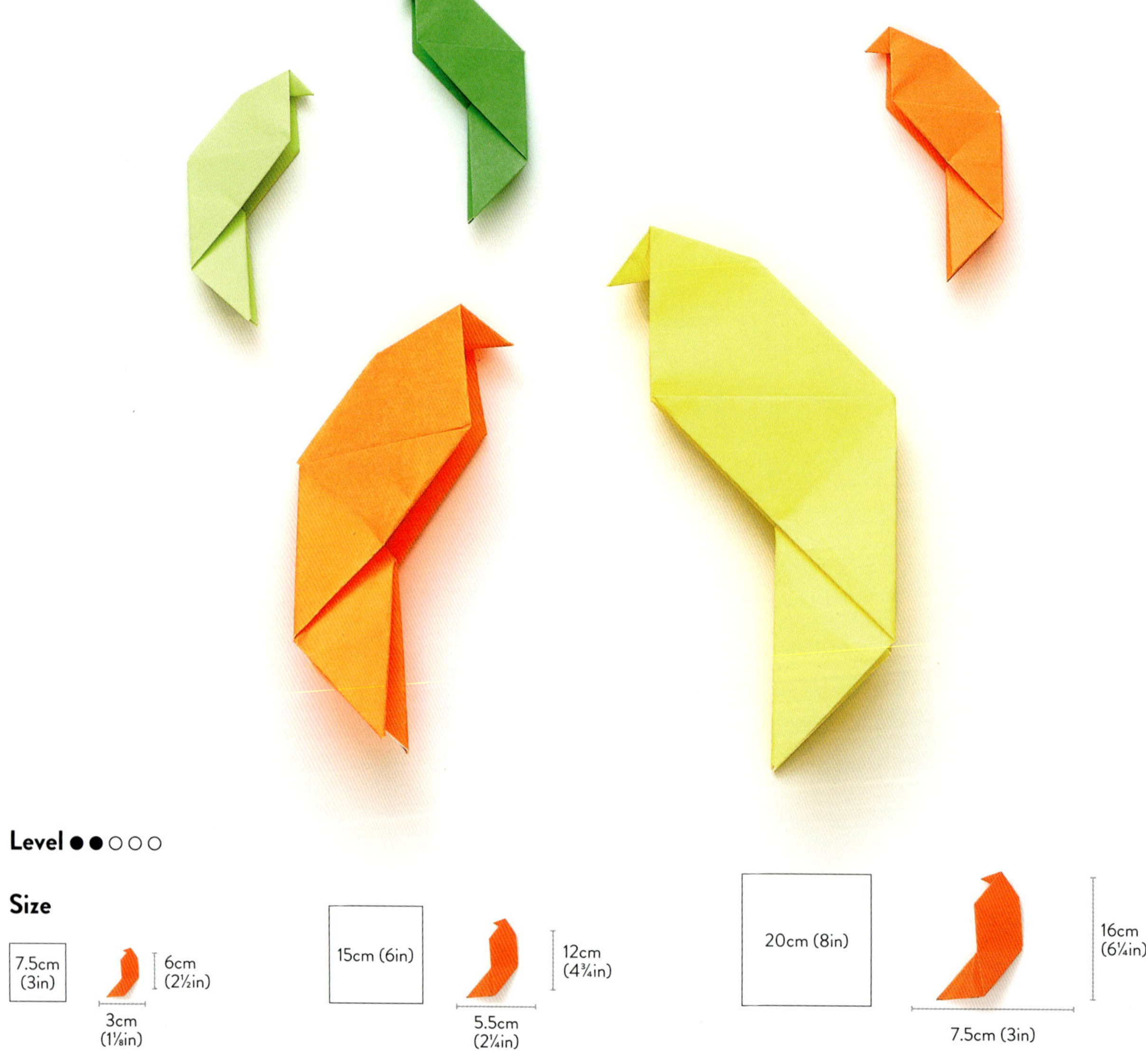

Level ● ● ○ ○ ○

Size

7.5cm
(3in)

6cm
(2½in)

3cm
(1⅛in)

15cm (6in)

12cm
(4¾in)

5.5cm
(2¼in)

20cm (8in)

16cm
(6¼in)

7.5cm (3in)

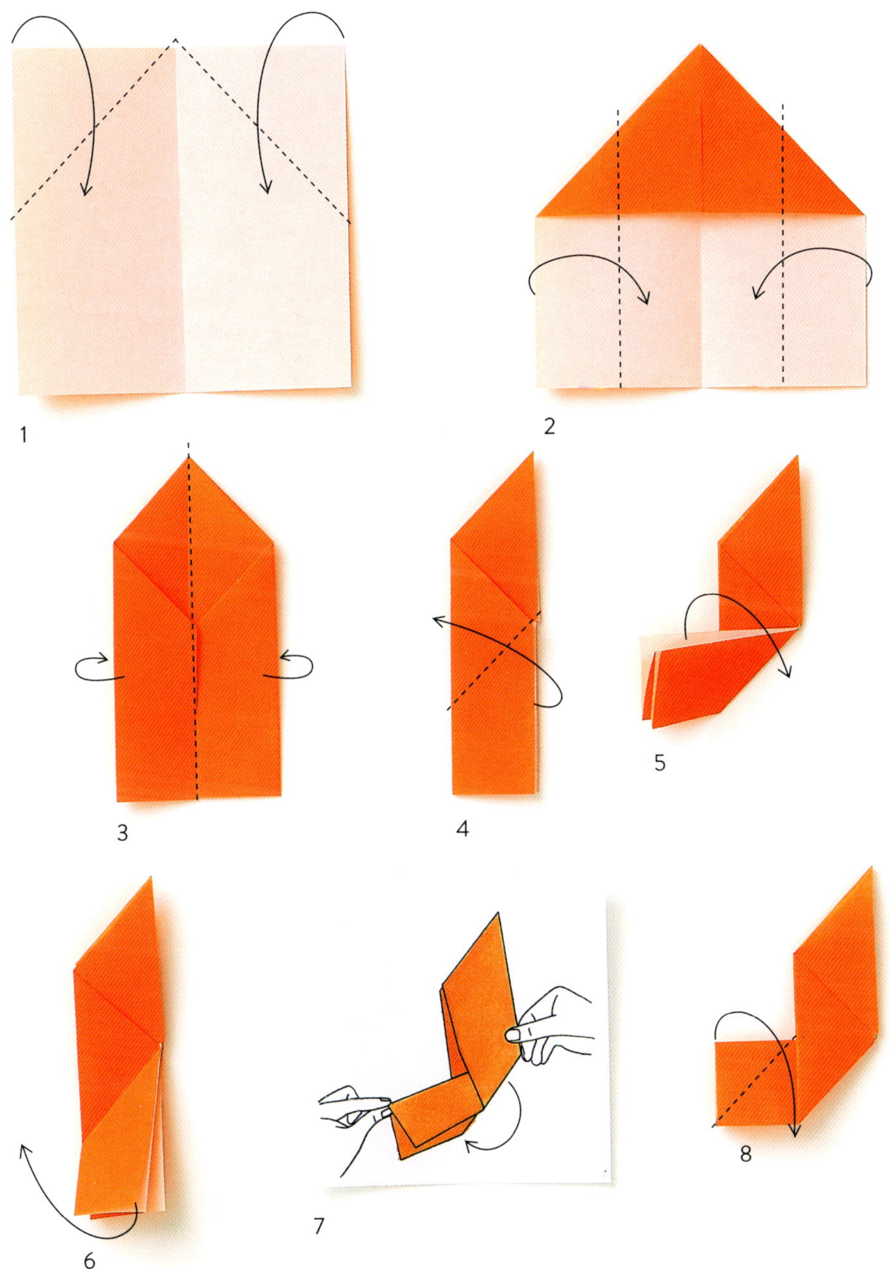

1. Place your square white side up and mark the crease of the central vertical line. Fold along the dotted lines.
2. Fold the edges to the central line along the dotted lines. **3.** Fold in half behind along the central vertical crease. Squash flat. **4.** Fold all layers along the dotted line. **5.** Unfold. **6. 7.** Invert the fold. Squash flat.
8. Fold along the dotted line.

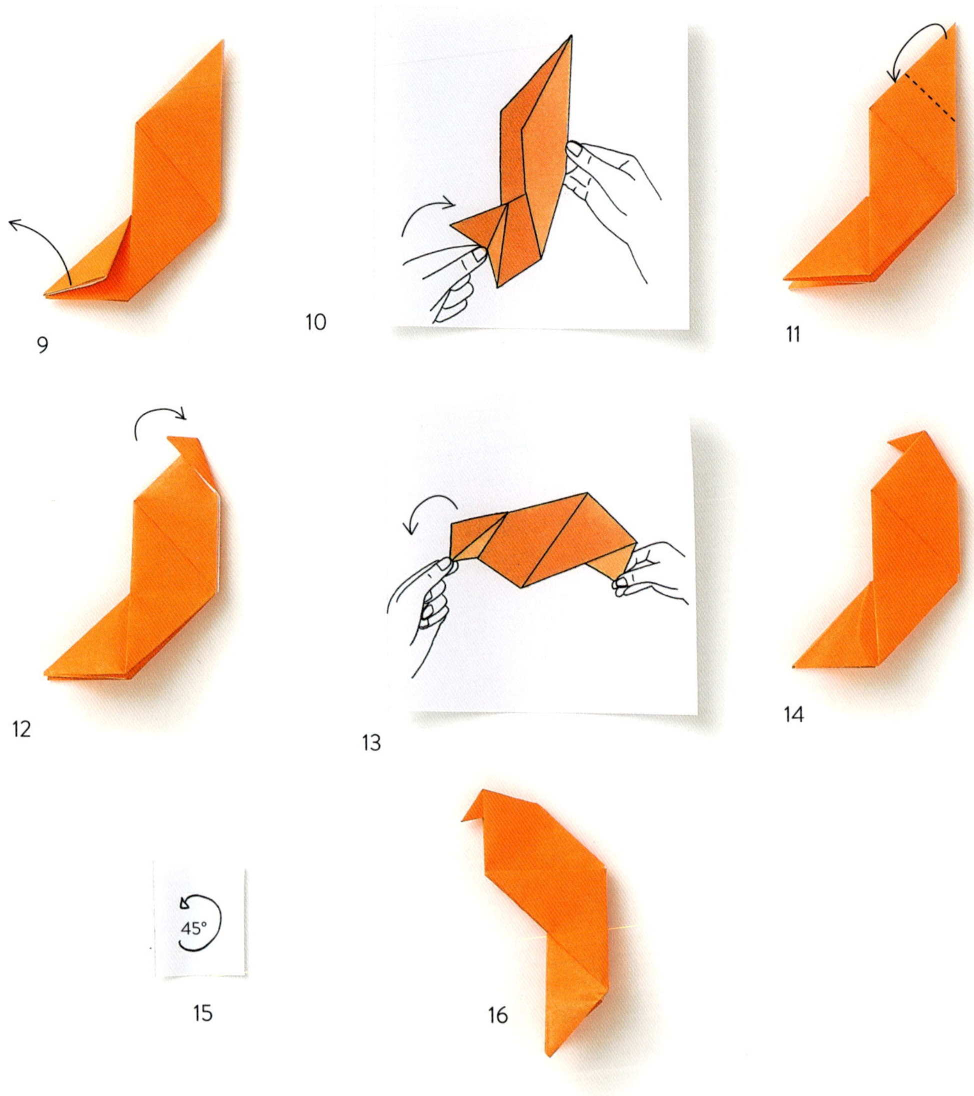

9. Unfold. **10.** Open the fold and invert. Squash flat. You have formed the parrot's tail. **11.** Fold along the dotted line. **12. 13. 14.** Unfold and invert the fold. Squash flat. You have formed the parrot's beak. **15.** Rotate the parrot by 45°. **16.** Your parrot is complete.

Turtle dove

Level ●●○○○

Size

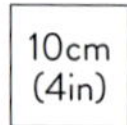
10cm
(4in)

4.5cm
(1¾in)

6.5cm
(2½in)

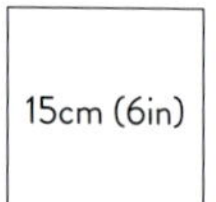
15cm (6in)

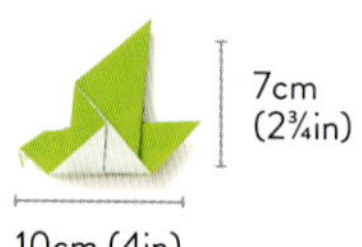
7cm
(2¾in)

10cm (4in)

20cm (8in)

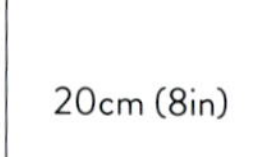

9.5cm
(3¾in)

13.5cm (5½in)

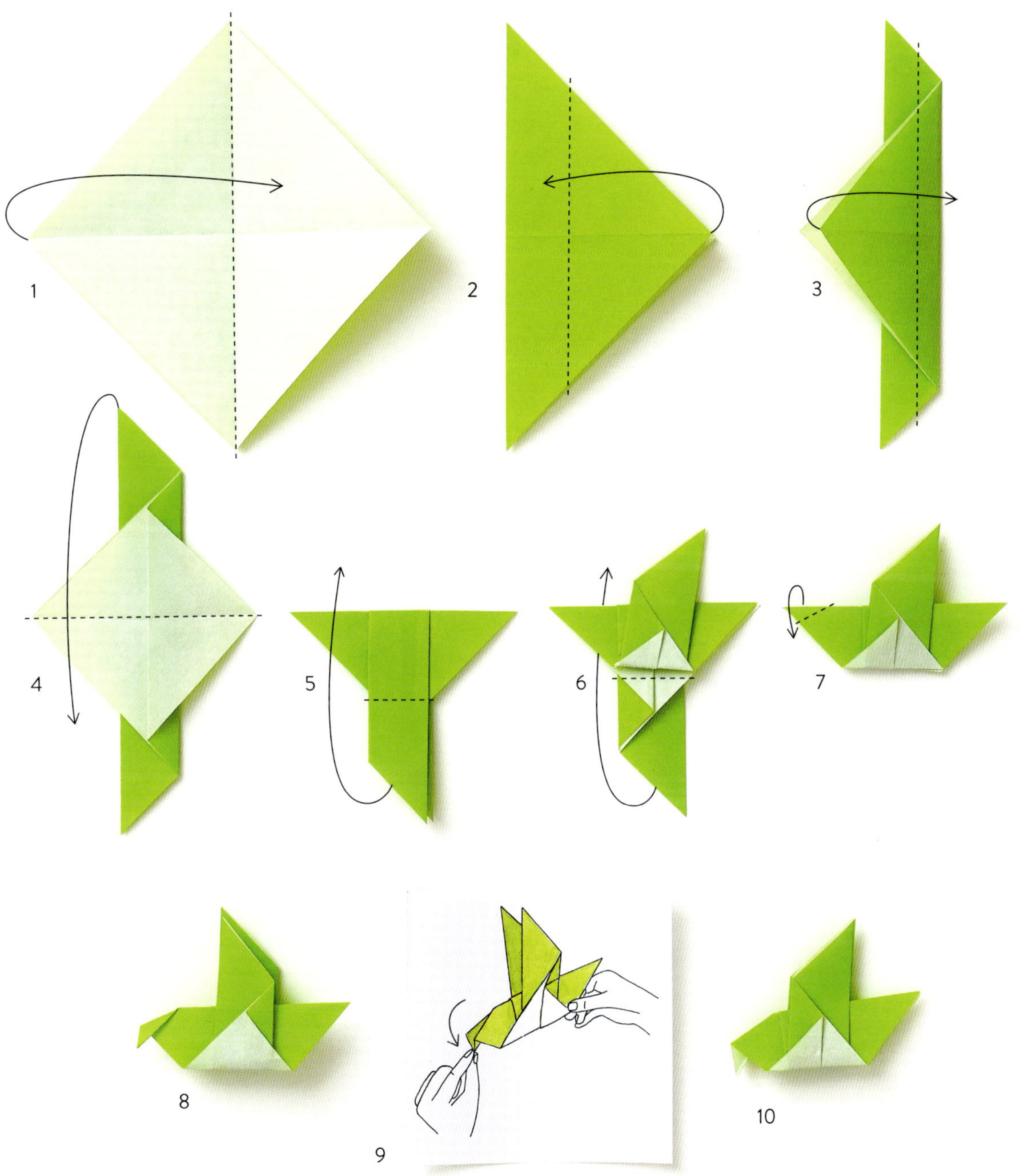

1. Place your square white side up and mark the creases on the diagonal. Rotate on to one corner. Fold in half to form a triangle. **2. 3.** Fold the two layers together along the dotted line. Unfold and refold the top layer along the dotted line. **4.** Fold in half along the dotted line. **5.** Fold the top layer upwards and mark the crease. **6.** Fold the bottom layer behind and mark the crease. **7.** Fold along the dotted line. **8. 9. 10.** Unfold, open out and invert. Squash flat. You have formed the beak. Your turtle dove is complete.

Turtle

Level ●●○○○

Size

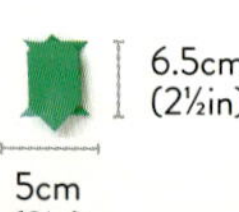 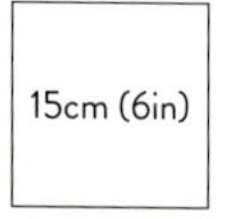

10cm
(4in)

6.5cm
(2½in)

5cm
(2in)

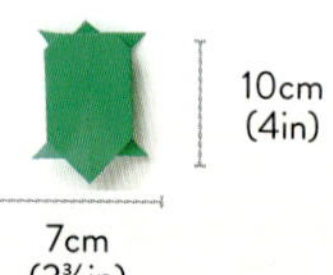

15cm (6in)

10cm
(4in)

7cm
(2¾in)

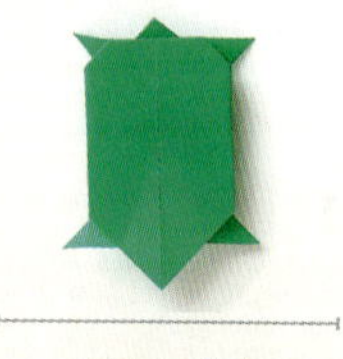

20cm (8in)

13cm
(5⅛in)

10cm (4in)

Tip
You will need a pair of scissors.

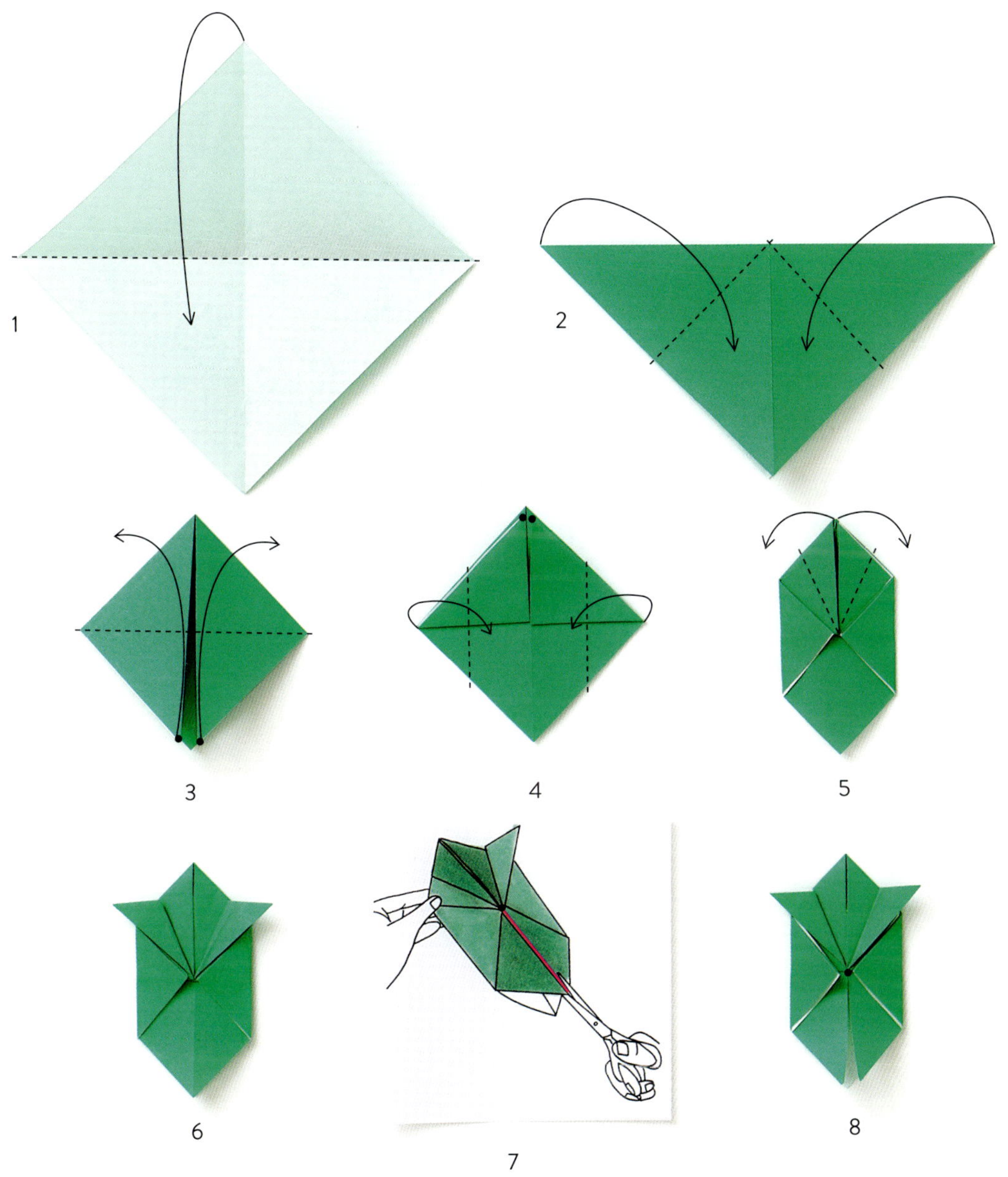

1. Place your square white side up and mark the creases of the diagonal lines. Rotate on to one corner and fold in half to form a triangle. **2.** Fold the two top points down to the bottom point to form a diamond. **3.** Fold the two bottom points up to the top point, along the dotted line. **4.** Fold the points to the central line along the dotted lines. **5. 6.** Fold along the dotted lines. You now have this shape. **7. 8.** Cut along the centre line of the top layer as far as the dot. You now have this shape.

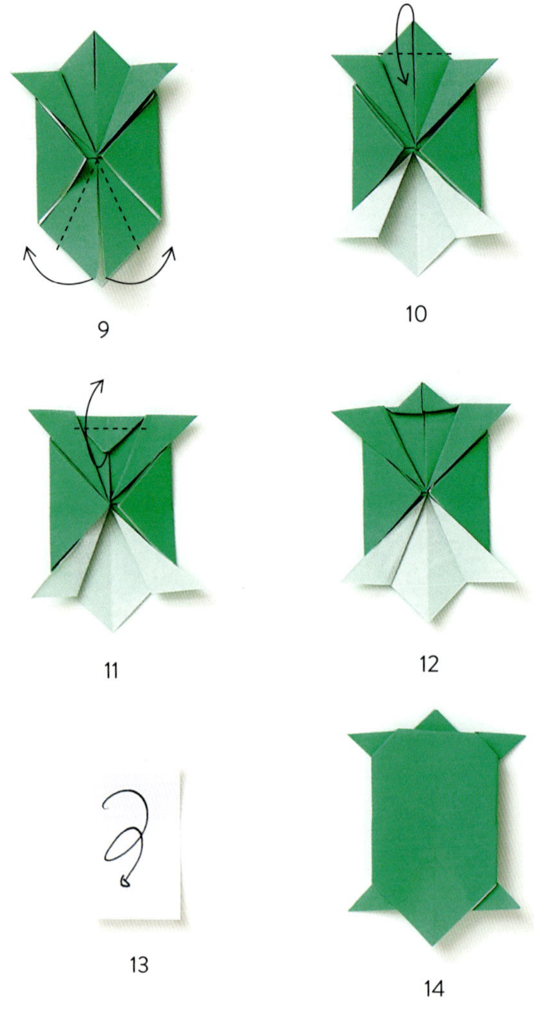

9. Fold along the dotted lines. **10.** Fold along the dotted line. **11. 12.** Fold along the dotted line. You now have this shape. **13.** Flip over. **14.** Your turtle is complete.

Panda

Level ●●●○○

Size

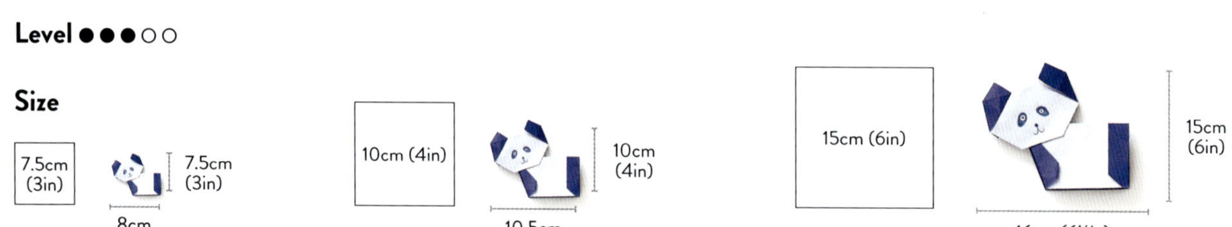

Tip

For this design, you will need two squares of paper. You will also need some quick-drying glue and a pen or pencil so you can personalize your panda. You can make the panda stand up or sit down simply by changing the position of its head.

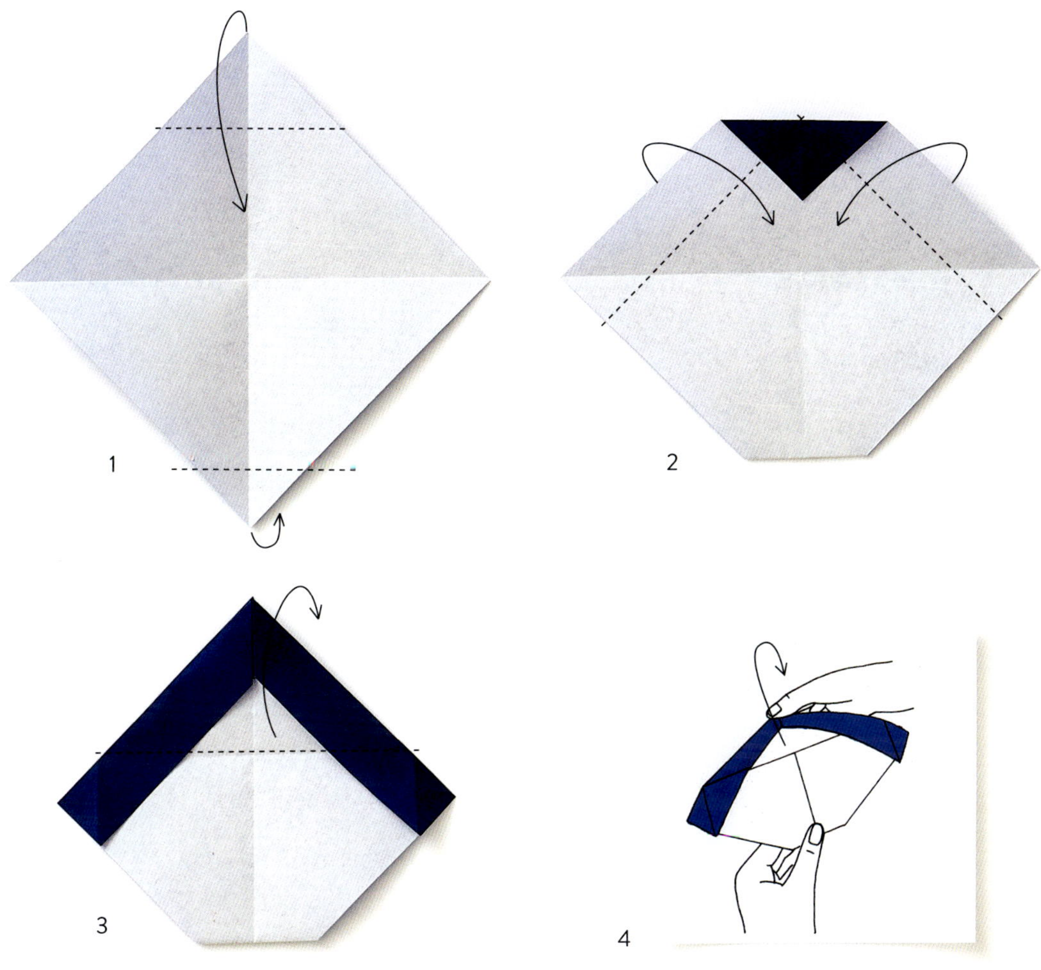

1. Place your square white side up and mark the creases on the diagonals. Rotate on to one corner. Fold the top point down along the dotted line. Fold the bottom point behind along the dotted line. **2.** Fold the top two edges along the dotted lines. **3. 4.** Fold behind along the dotted line, approximately two thirds of the way down from the point.

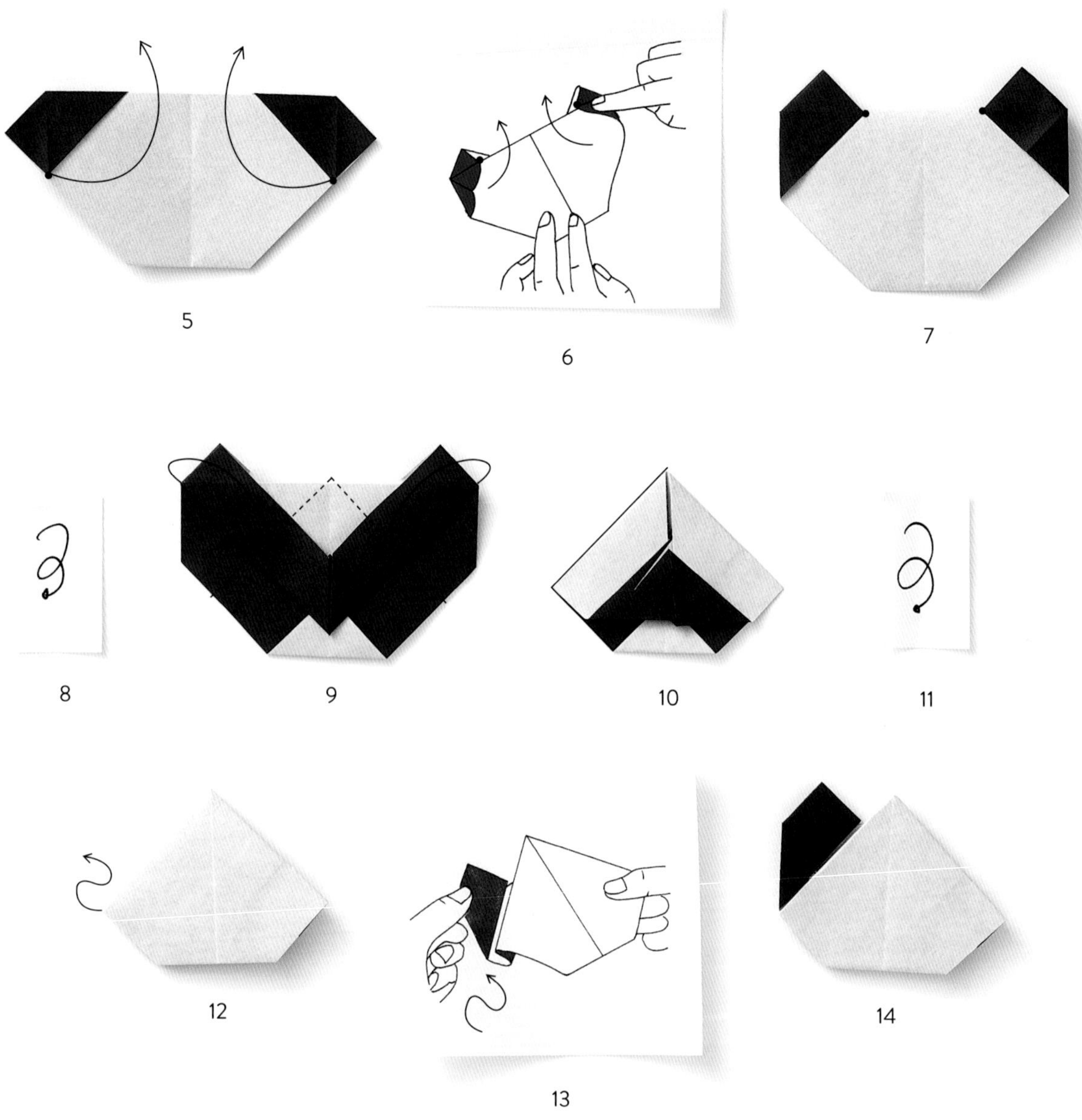

5. 6. 7. Pinch the dots and pull upwards to the top edge. Squash flat. **8.** Flip over. **9. 10.** Fold to the central line along the dotted lines. You now have this shape. **11.** Flip over. **12. 13.** Fold the back LH flap to the front as shown, forming a fold on the reverse side. **14.** You now have this shape.

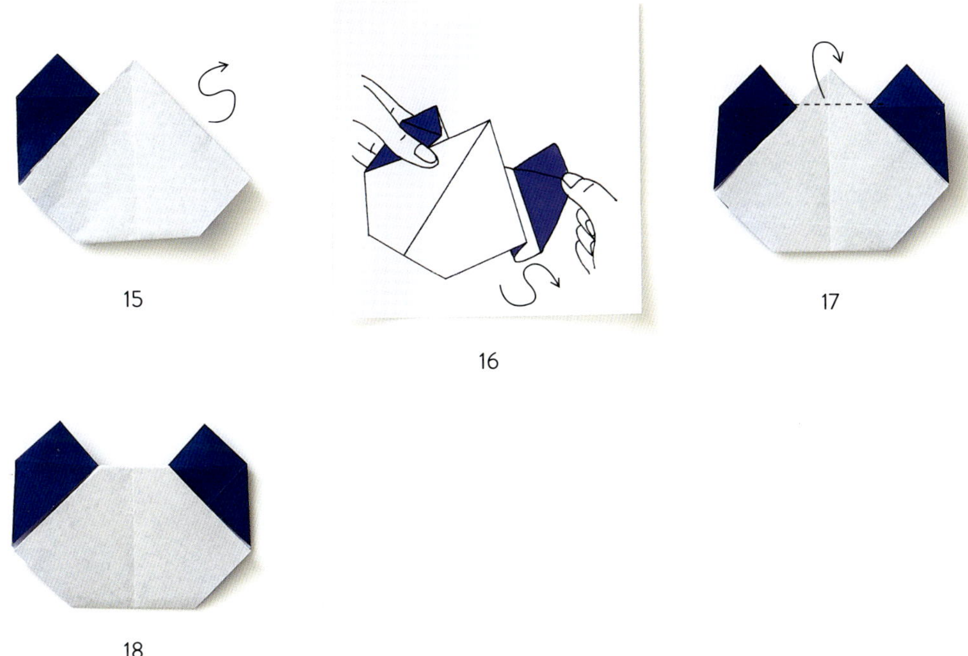

15

16

17

18

15. 16. Repeat with the RH flap. **17.** Fold behind along the dotted line. **18.** The panda's head is complete.

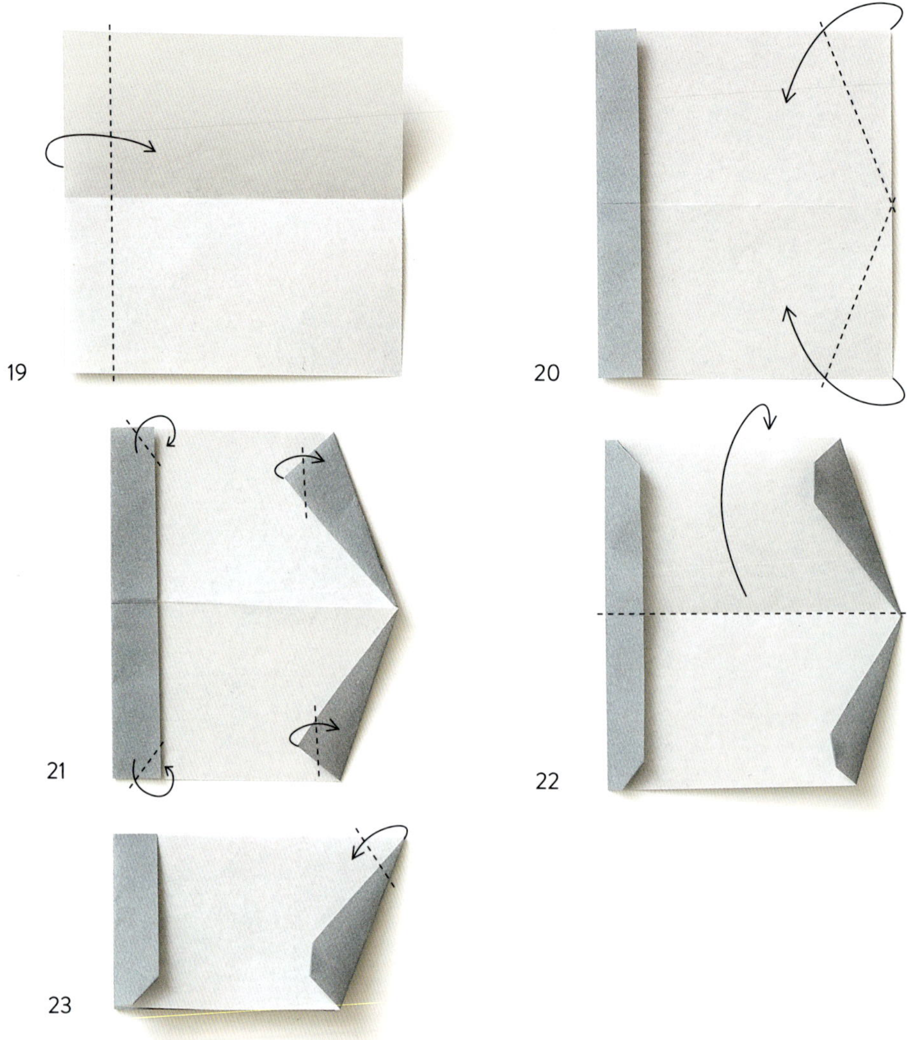

19. Place your second square white side up and mark the crease of the central horizontal line. Fold along the dotted line at the approximate point marked. **20.** Fold along the dotted lines at the approximate point marked. **21.** Fold the four small points inside. **22.** Fold the top half behind. **23.** Fold along the dotted line.

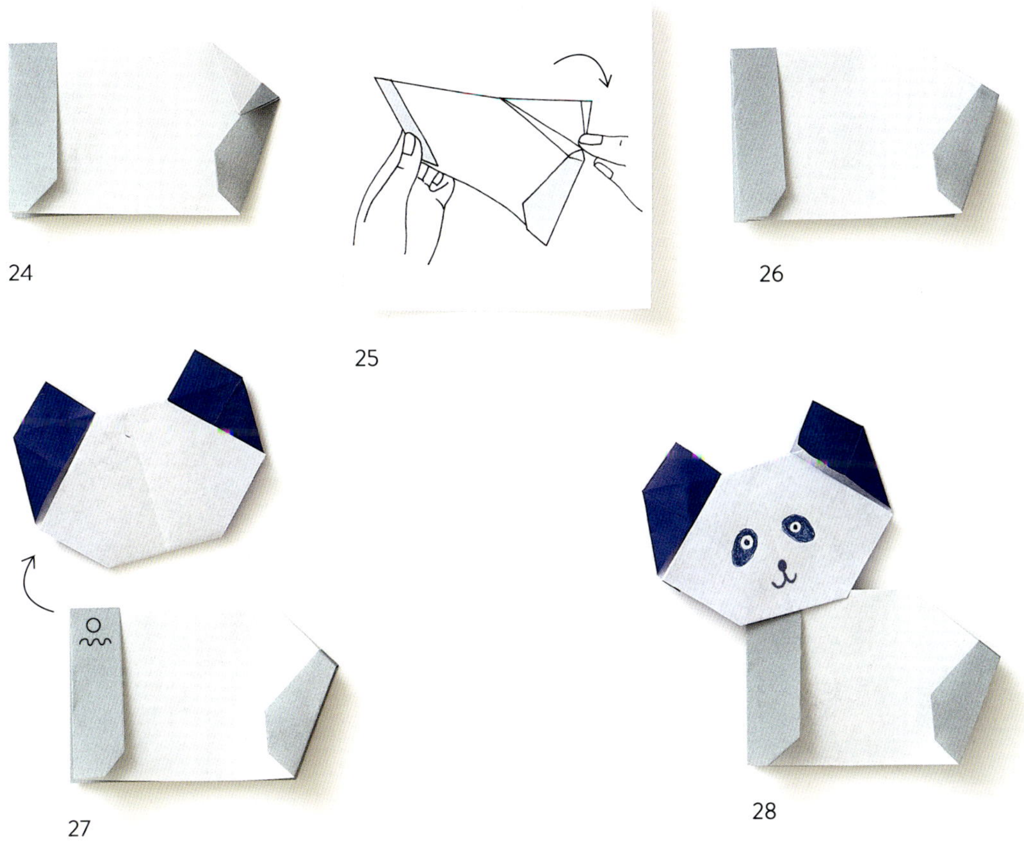

24

25

26

27

28

24. 25. 26. Open the fold and invert. Squash flat. The panda's body is complete. **27.** Apply a dab of glue as shown, then stick the two parts together. **28.** Your panda is complete. You can now personalize it.

Autumn leaf

Level ● ● ○ ○ ○

Size

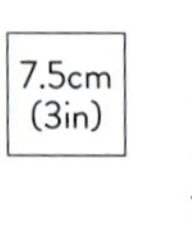

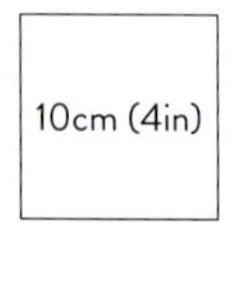

Tip
You need to mark the creases very firmly in steps 4 to 7 to obtain attractive veins.

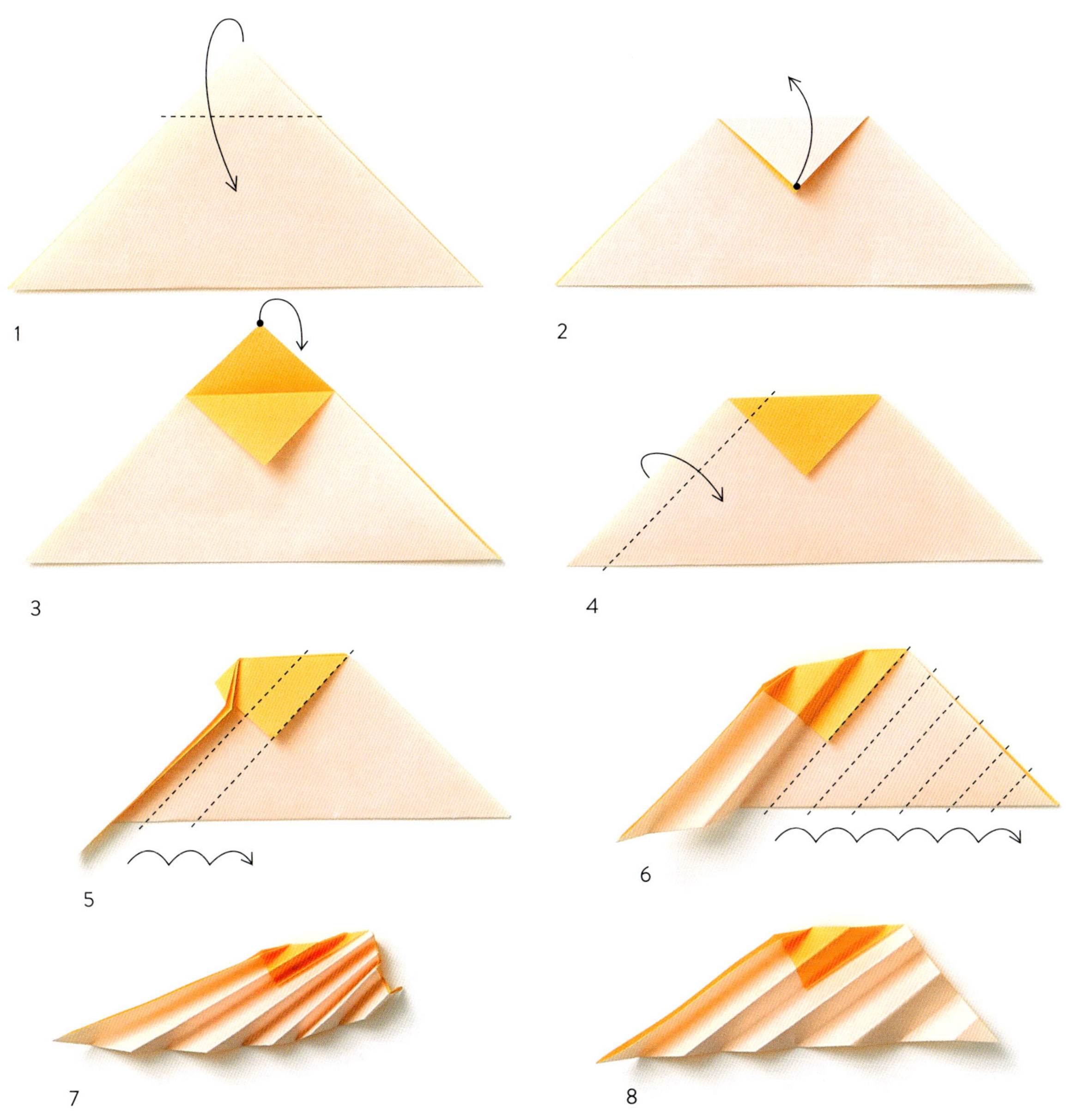

1. Place your square coloured side up. Rotate on to one corner and fold in half to form a triangle. Fold down the top of the triangle along the dotted line. **2.** Pinch the dot on the top layer. **3.** Fold behind and press in the crease. **4.** Fold along the dotted line (parallel to the LH edge). **5. 6. 7.** Create folds of the same width as the one in step 4, forming accordion pleats to the end. You now have this shape. **8.** Gently unfold.

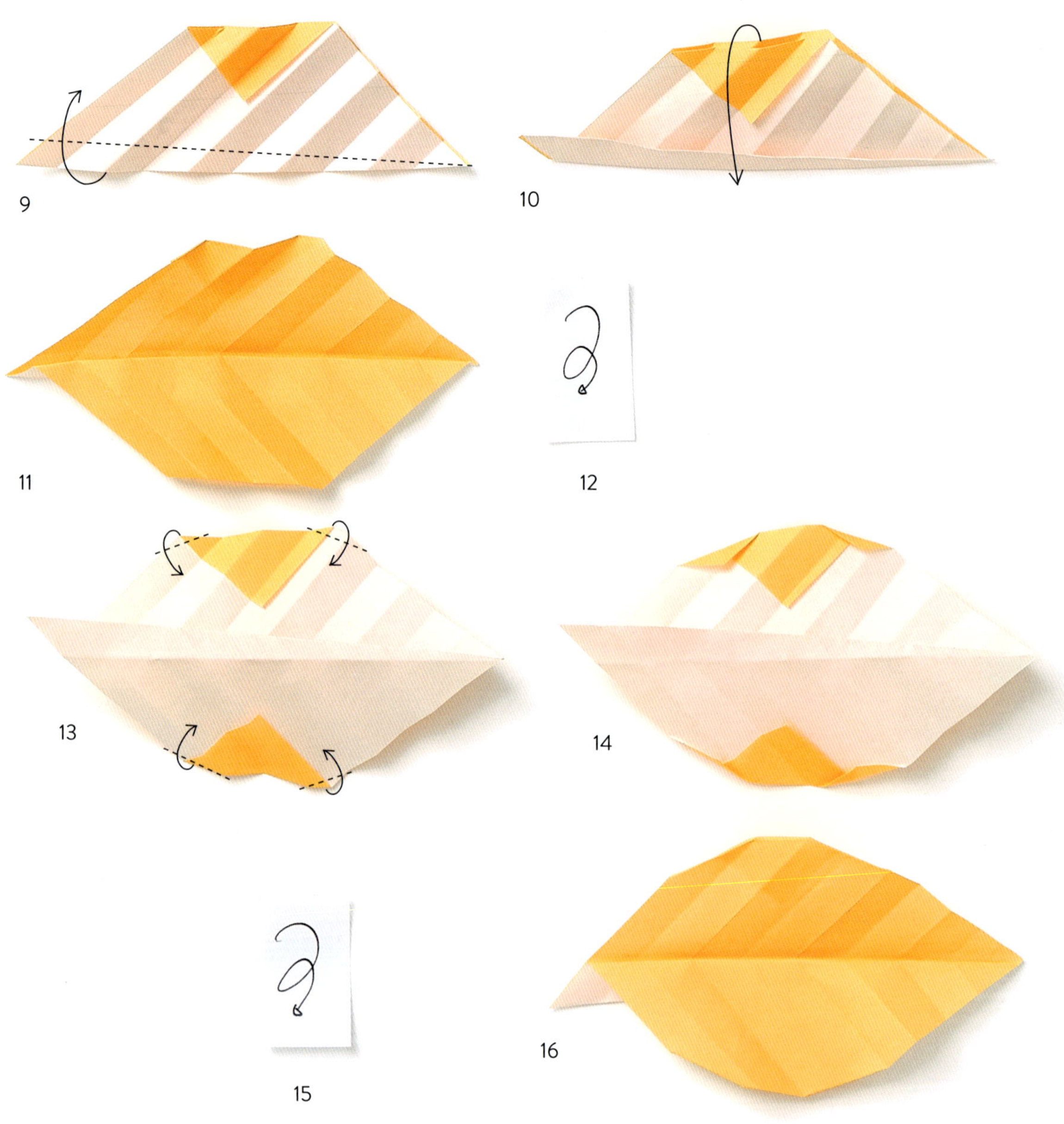

9. Fold the bottom edge along the dotted line. **10. 11.** Fold the top edge along the dotted lines. You now have this shape. **12.** Flip over. **13. 14.** Fold along the dotted lines to round off the points. You now have this shape. **15.** Flip over. **16.** Your autumn leaf is complete.

Tatou envelope

Size

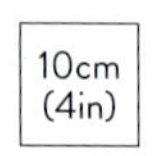
10cm
(4in)

5.5cm
(2¼in)

5.5cm
(2¼in)

15cm (6in)

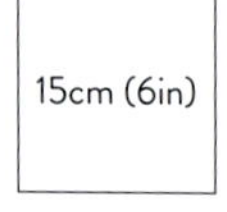
8cm
(3¼in)

8cm
(3¼in)

20cm (8in)

11cm
(4⅜in)

11cm (4⅜in)

Tip

This design can be used as wrapping for a very small gift, or as an envelope.

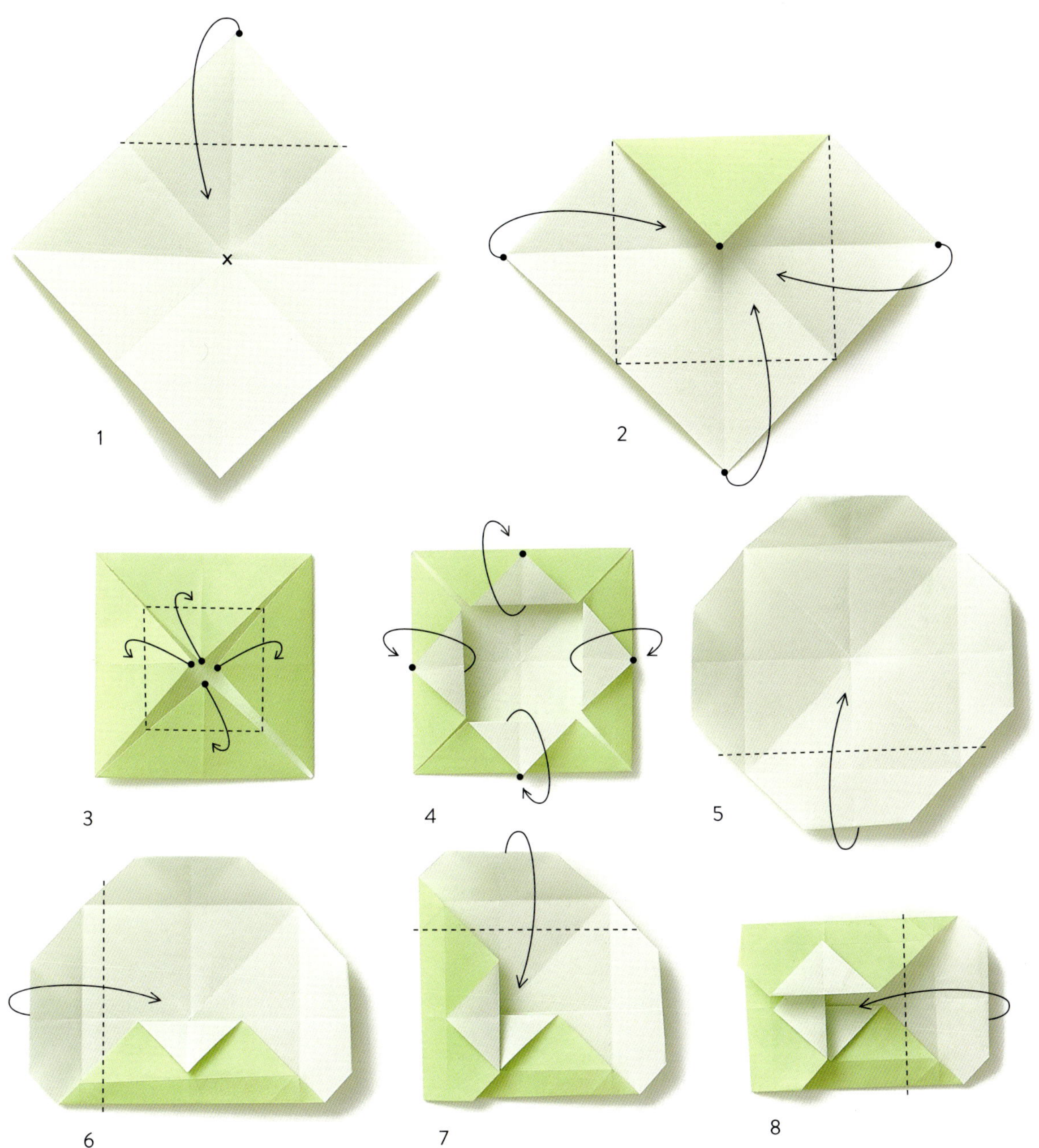

1. Place your square white side up. Mark the creases of the central diagonal, horizontal and vertical lines. Fold the top point to the centre. Squash flat. **2.** Fold the other three points in the same way. **3.** Fold the four points along the dotted lines. **4.** Unfold all the flaps. **5.** Fold the bottom edge to the central line. Squash flat. **6. 7. 8.** Rotating clockwise, fold the other edges to the centre in the same way.

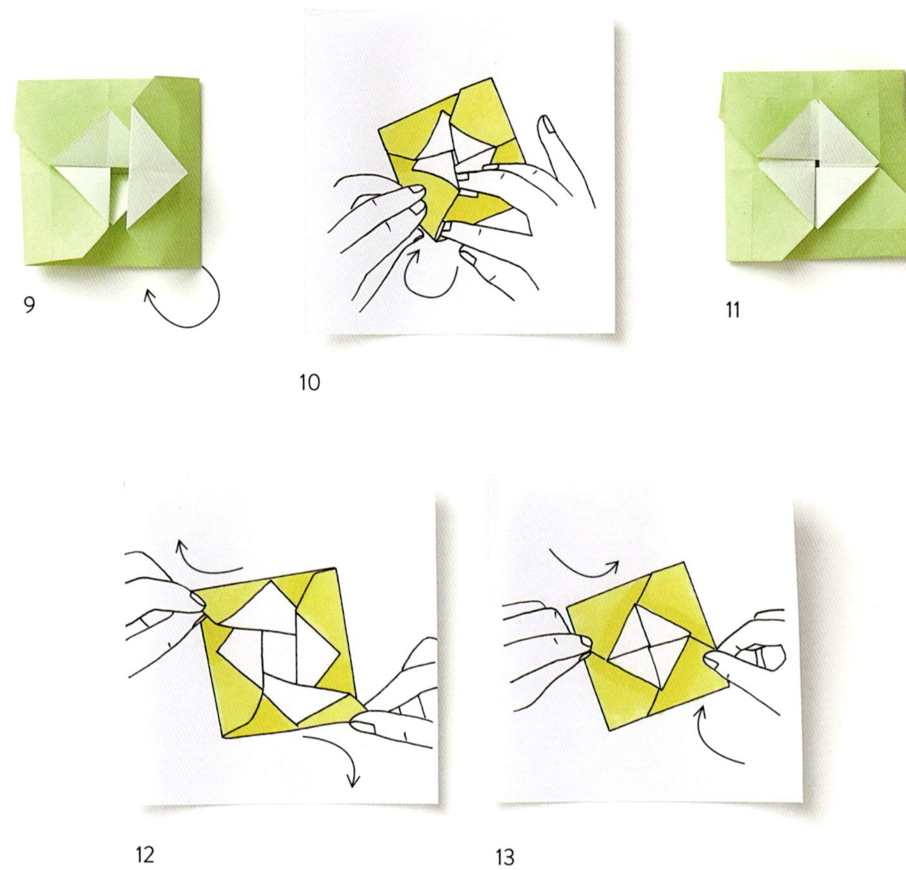

9. 10. 11. Tuck the RH flap under the bottom flap, inverting the fold. Your envelope is complete.
12. Pull gently on these two flaps to open the envelope. **13.** Push back into position to close.

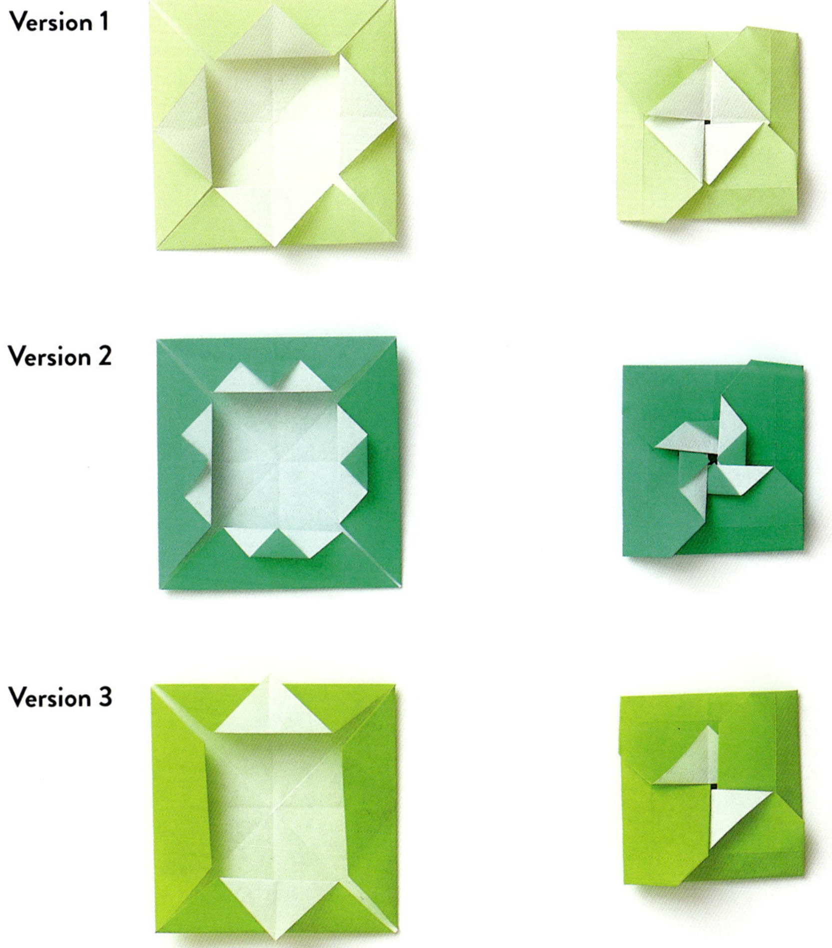

Version 1, the traditional version: this is the envelope you have just made, known in Japan as a *tatou* envelope.
Version 2, the windmill version: after step 8, fold a little triangle on the four flaps.
Version 3, the butterfly version: after step 3, invert the folds on the left and right.

Four-leaf clover

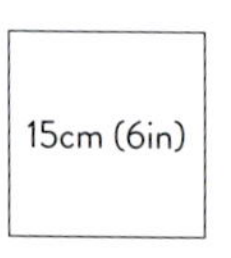

Level ●●○○○

Size

10cm (4in) — 9.5cm (3¾in) × 9.5cm (3¾in)

15cm (6in) — 14cm (5½in) × 14cm (5½in)

20cm (8in) — 18.5cm (7½in) × 18.5cm (7½in)

Tip

You will need a pencil and a pair of scissors.

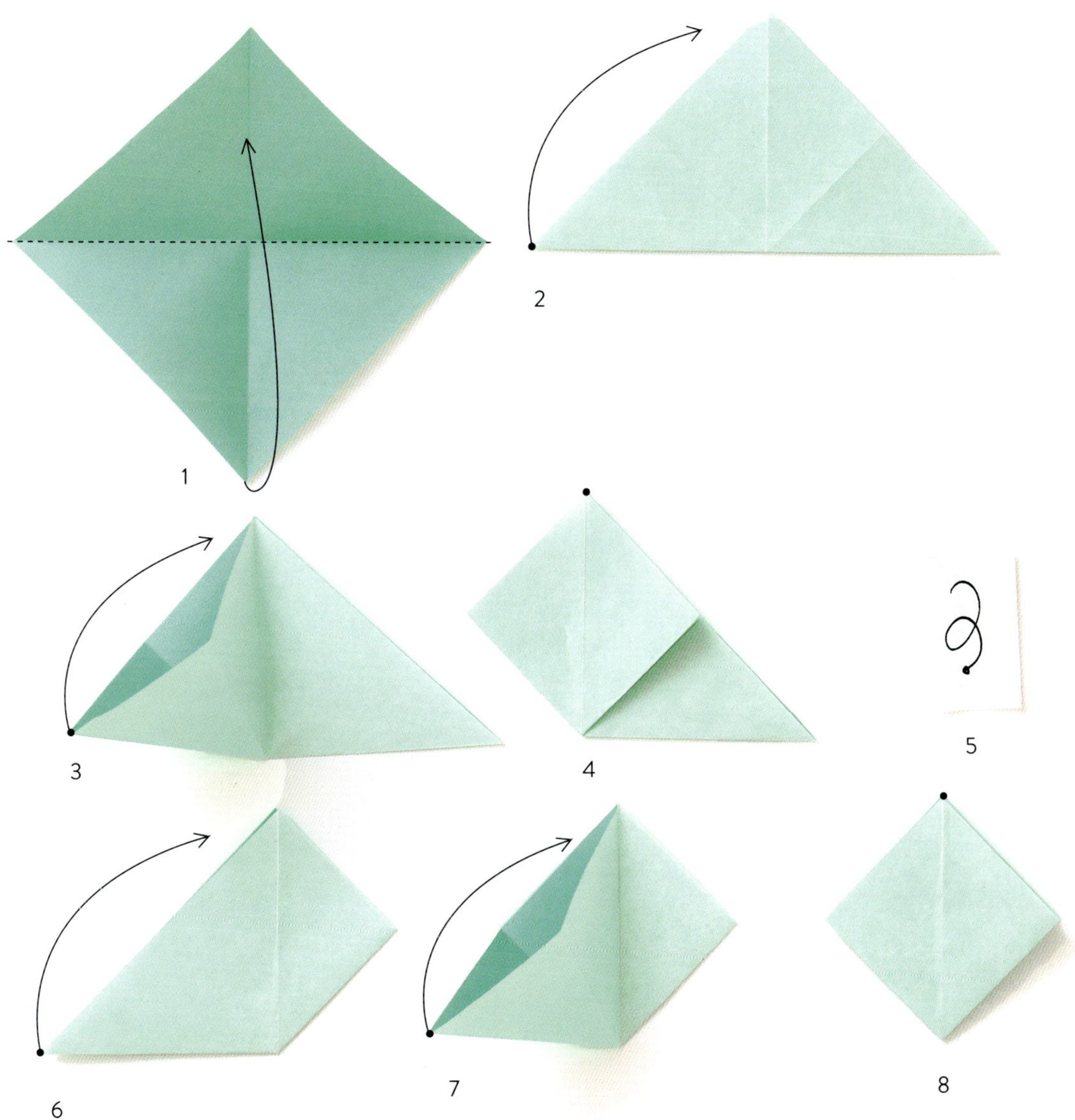

1. Place your square coloured side up. Mark the creases of the central diagonal, horizontal and vertical lines. Rotate on to one corner and fold in half to form a triangle. **2. 3. 4.** Fold the LH point to the top, opening out the fold to form a diamond. Squash flat. **5.** Flip over. **6. 7. 8.** Fold the LH point to the top, opening out the fold to form a diamond. Squash flat.

9. 10. Fold in half. You now have this shape. **11. 12.** Draw the marked line with a pencil. Cut out and open flat. **13.** Fold the bottom upwards. **14. 15. 16.** Unfold carefully without pulling on the centre too much. **17.** Squash flat. **18.** Your four-leaf clover is complete.

Heart

Level ●●○○○

Size

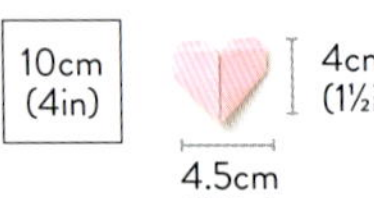

10cm (4in) — 4.5cm (1¾in) — 4cm (1½in)

15cm (6in) — 7.5cm (3in) — 6.5cm (2½in)

20cm (8in) — 10cm (4in) — 8.6cm (3⅜in)

Tip

You can use this design as a bookmark.

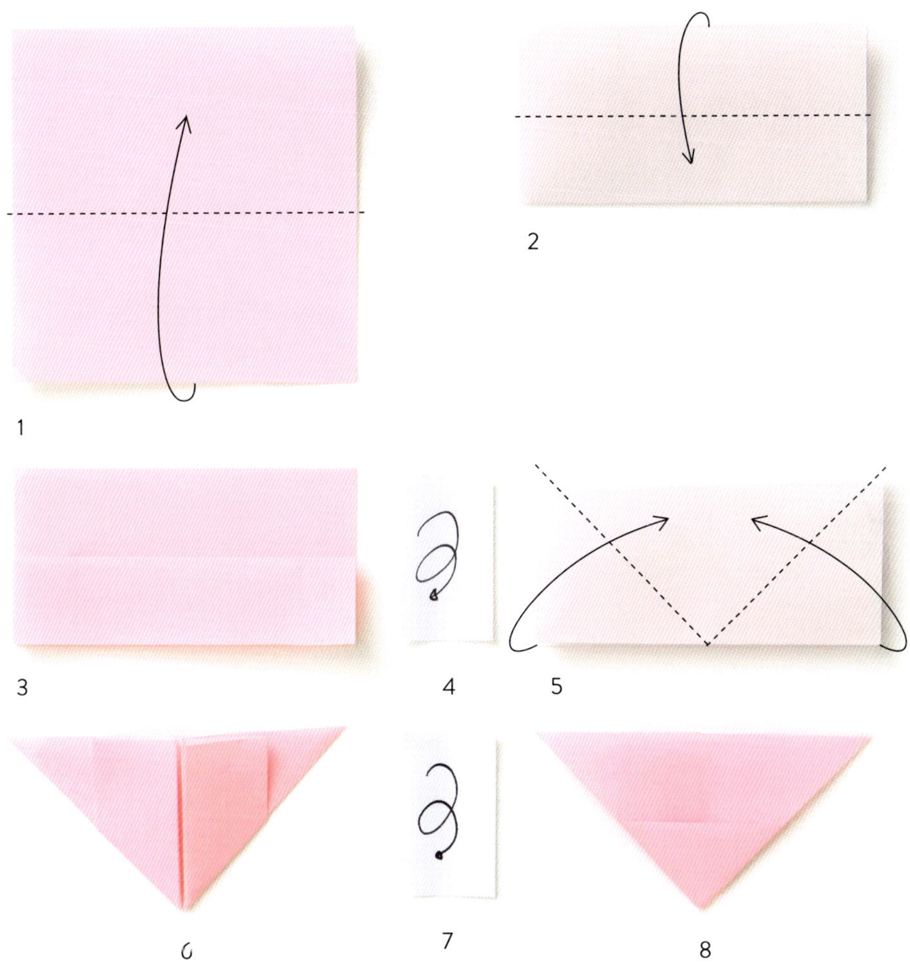

1. Place your square coloured side up. Fold in half. **2. 3.** Fold the top layer in half. You now have this shape.
4. Flip over. **5. 6.** Fold to the central line along the dotted lines. You now have this shape. **7.** Flip over.
8. You now have this shape.

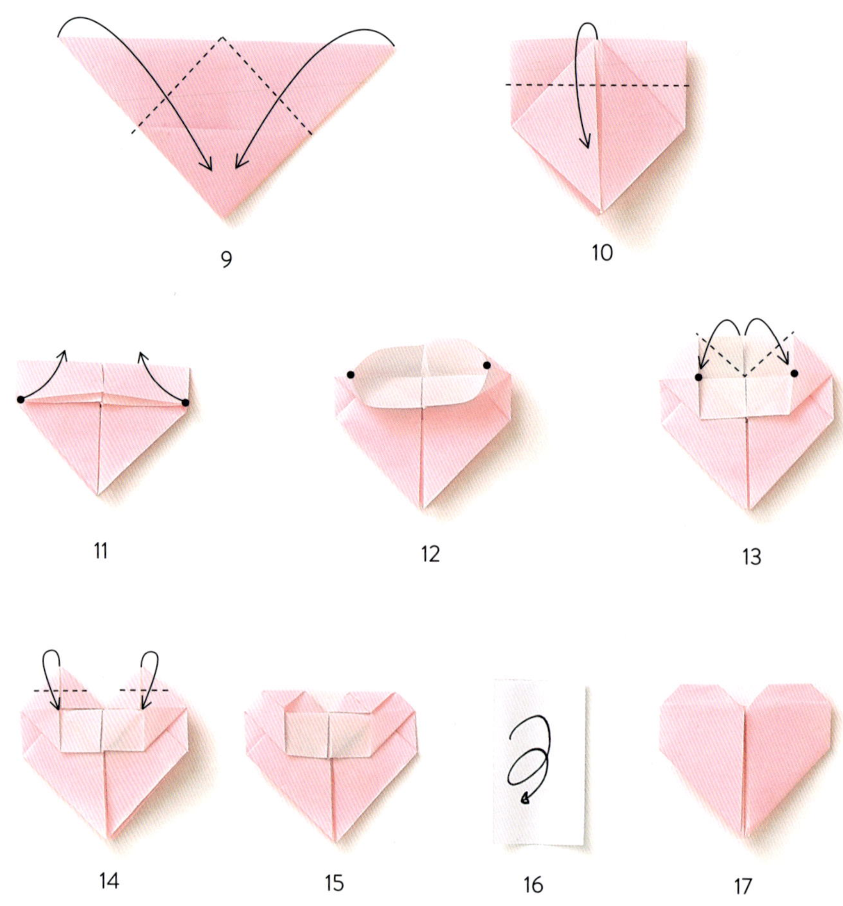

9. Fold the LH and RH flaps of the top layer to the central line along the dotted lines. Squash flat.
10. Fold downwards along the dotted line. **11. 12.** Unfold carefully and press down at the dots to open the folds and squash flat. **13.** Fold along the dotted lines. **14. 15.** Fold along the dotted line. You now have this shape. **16.** Flip over. **17.** Your heart is complete.

Star

Level ●●●○○

Size

10cm (4in)	6cm (2½in)
15cm (6in)	9cm (3½in)
20cm (8in)	12cm (4¾in)

6cm (2½in)

9cm (3½in)

12cm (4¾in)

Tip

You can make several stars and string them up to make a pretty garland.

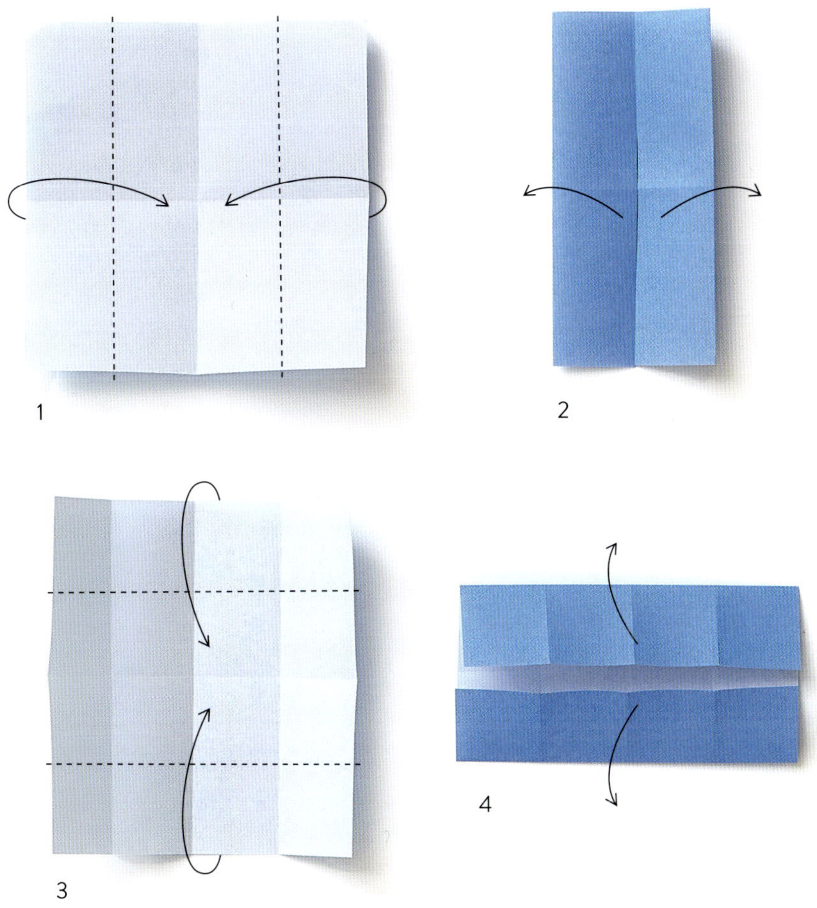

1. Place your square white side up and mark the creases of the central horizontal and vertical lines. Fold to the central line along the dotted lines. **2.** Open out the two flaps. **3. 4.** Fold to the central line then open out the two flaps.

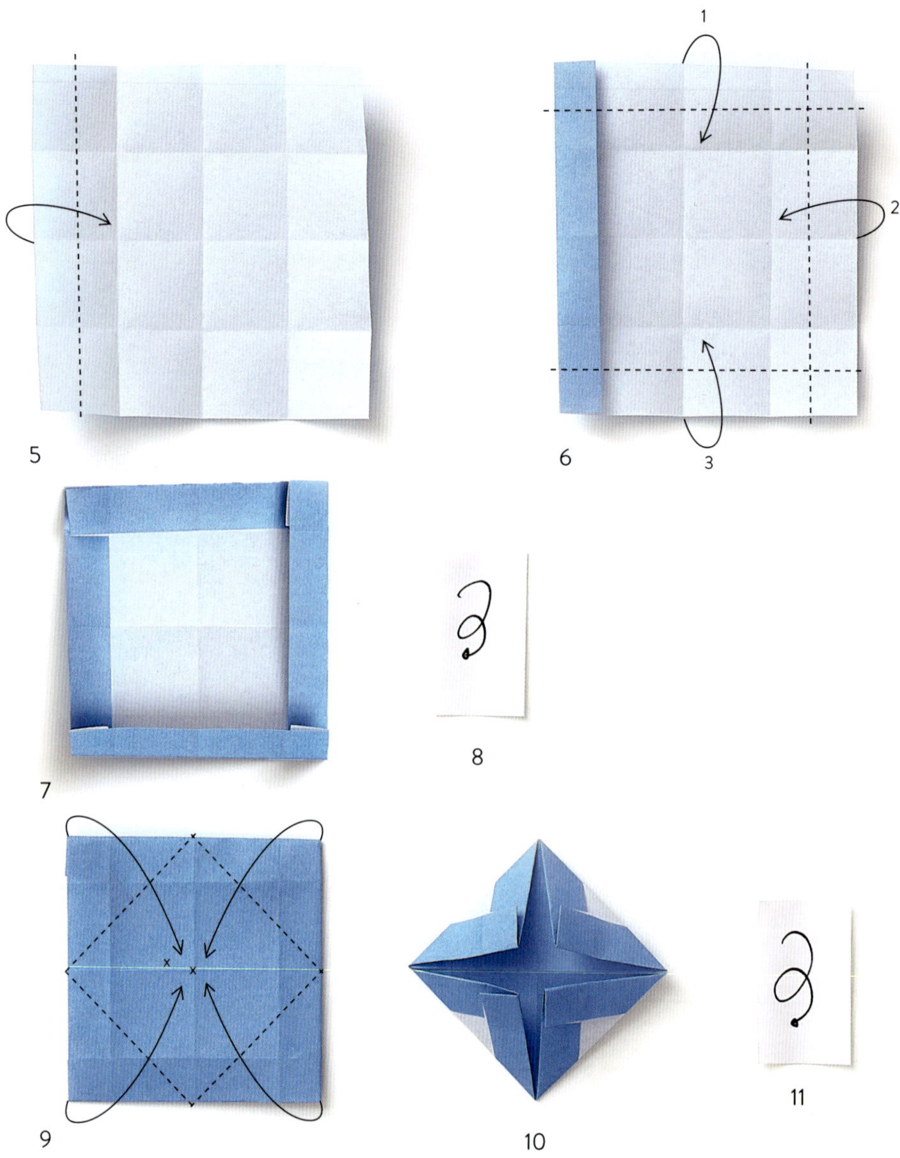

5. Fold inwards to the first fold line along the dotted line. **6. 7.** Fold the other edges in the same way, along the dotted lines, working in order 1 to 3. **8.** Flip over. **9. 10.** Fold to the central cross along the dotted lines. You now have this shape. **11.** Flip over.

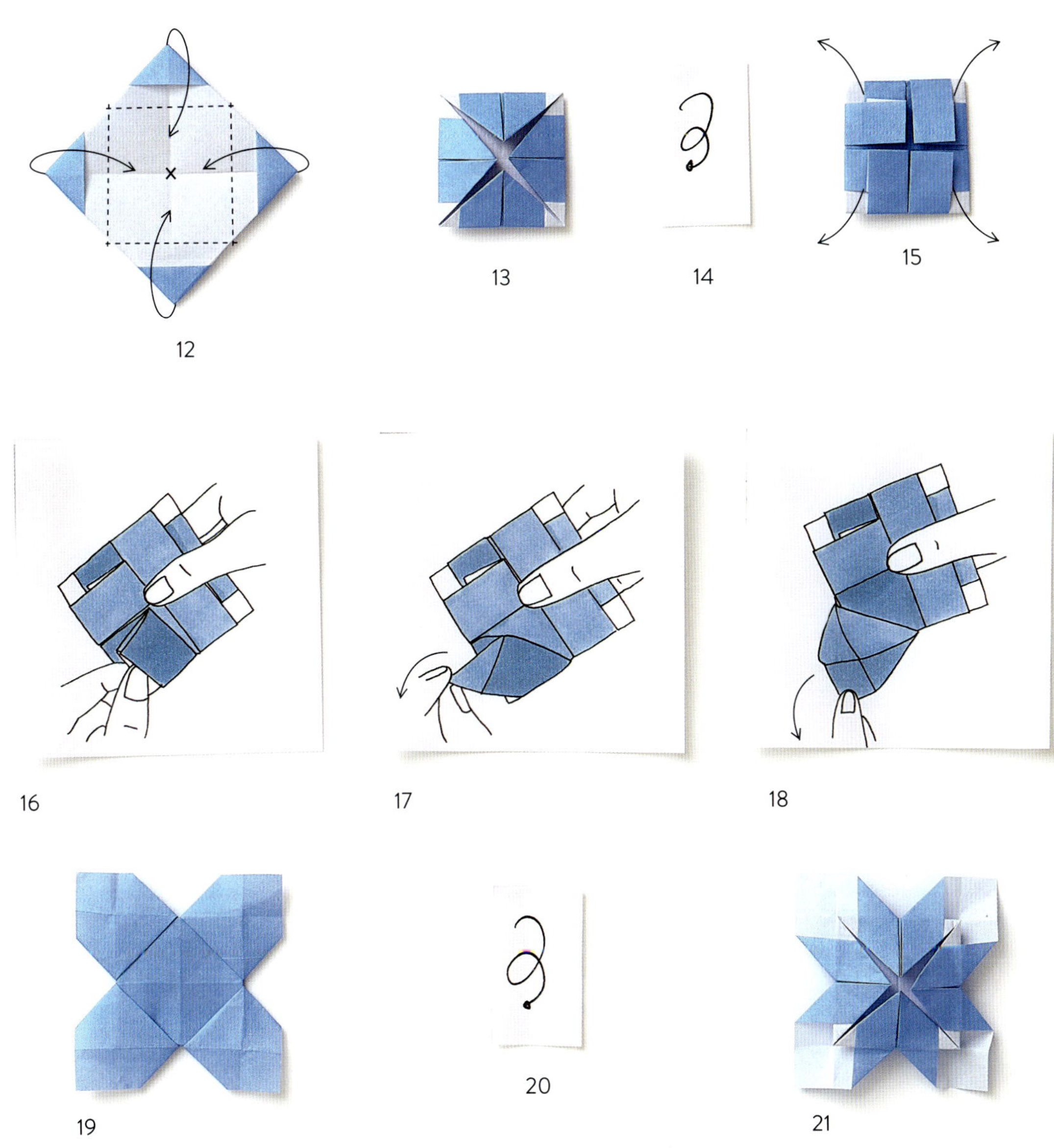

12. 13. Fold to the central cross along the dotted lines. You now have this shape. **14.** Flip over.
15. 16. 17. 18. 19. Pinch the inside point of each corner and carefully open out the folds. Squash flat. You now have this shape. **20.** Flip over. **21.** Your star is complete.

Lion

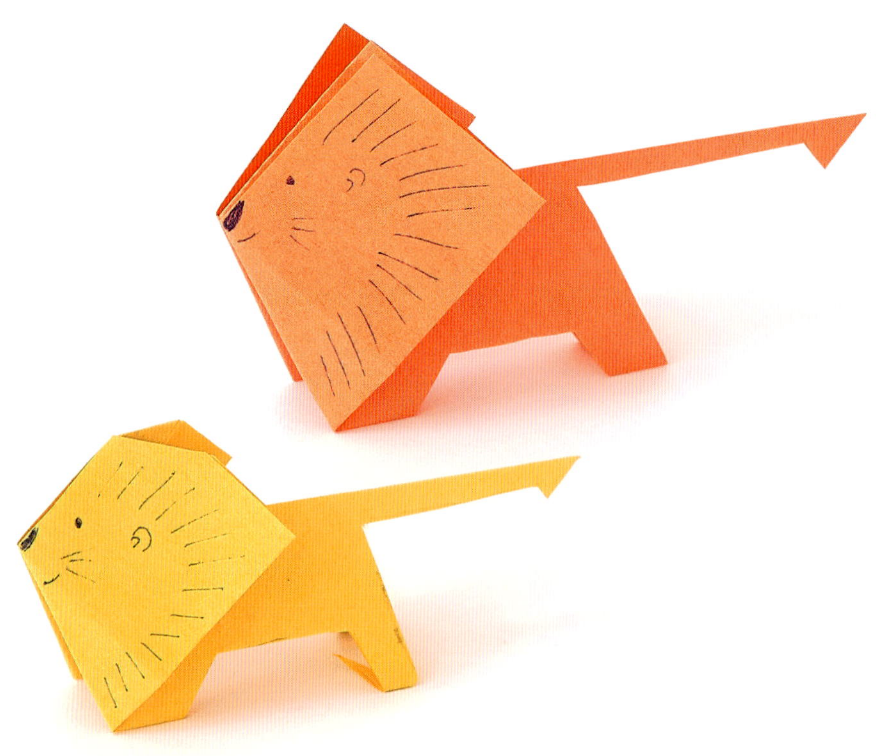

Level ●●○○○

Size

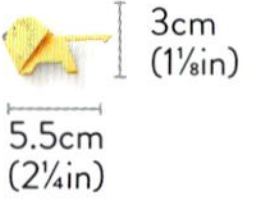

7.5cm
(3in)

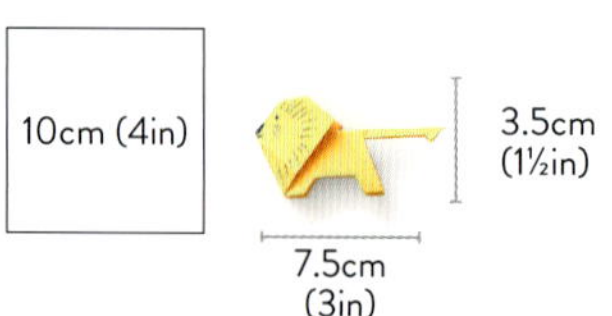

3cm
(1⅛in)

5.5cm
(2¼in)

10cm (4in)

3.5cm
(1½in)

7.5cm
(3in)

15cm (6in)

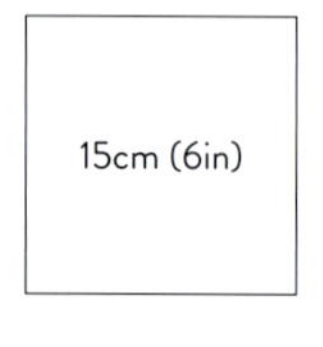

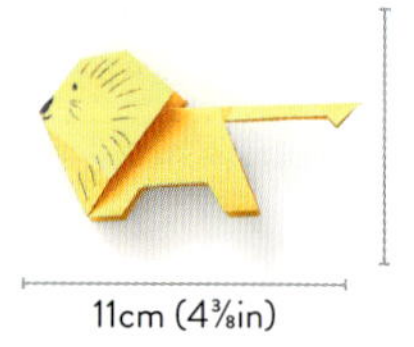

6cm
(2½in)

11cm (4⅜in)

Tip

You will need a pair of scissors and a pen or pencil so you can personalize your lion.

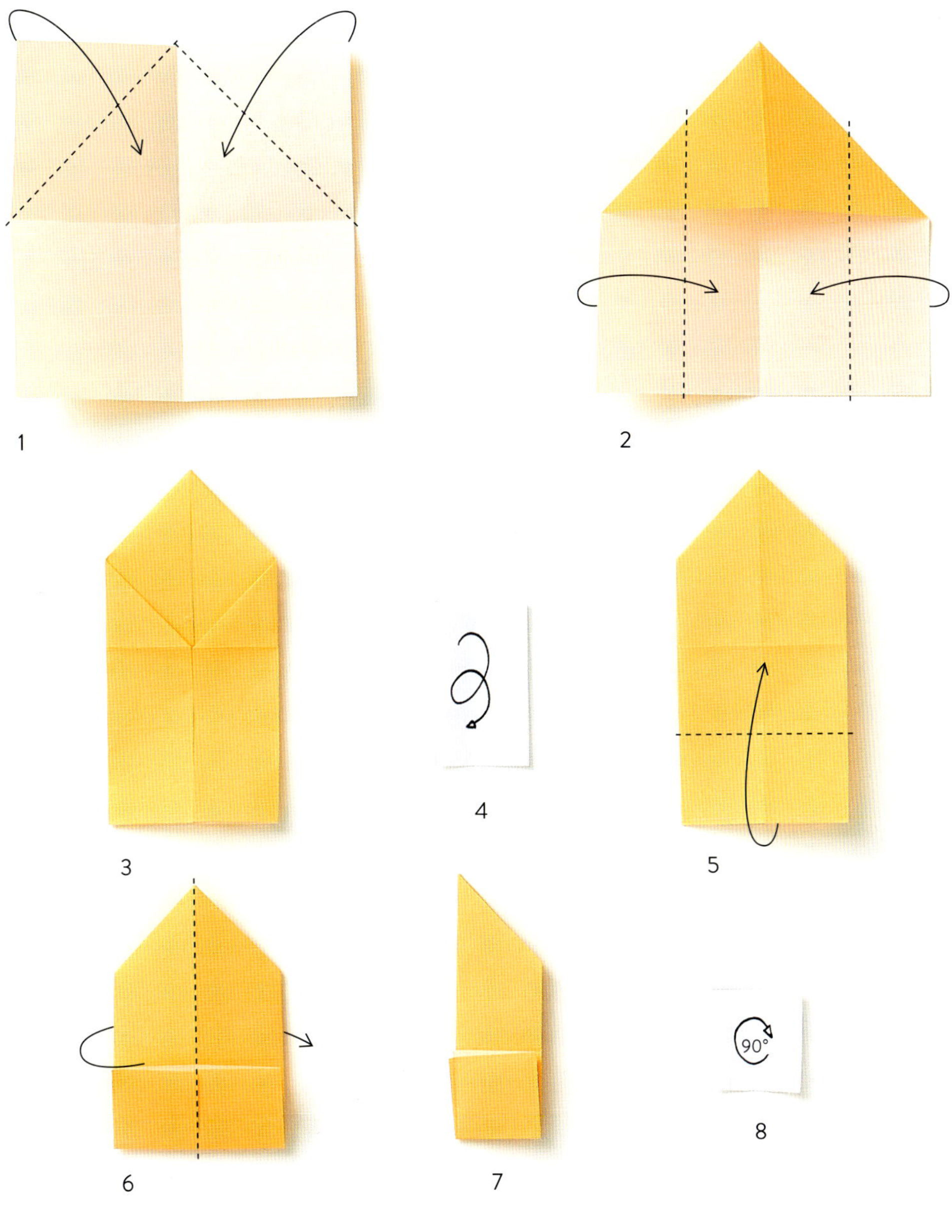

1. Place your square white side up and mark the creases of the central horizontal and vertical lines. Fold to the centre line along the dotted lines. **2. 3.** Fold along the dotted lines. You now have this shape. **4.** Flip over. **5.** Fold to the central line along the dotted line. **6. 7.** Fold in half behind along the dotted line. You now have this shape. **8.** Rotate 90° to the right.

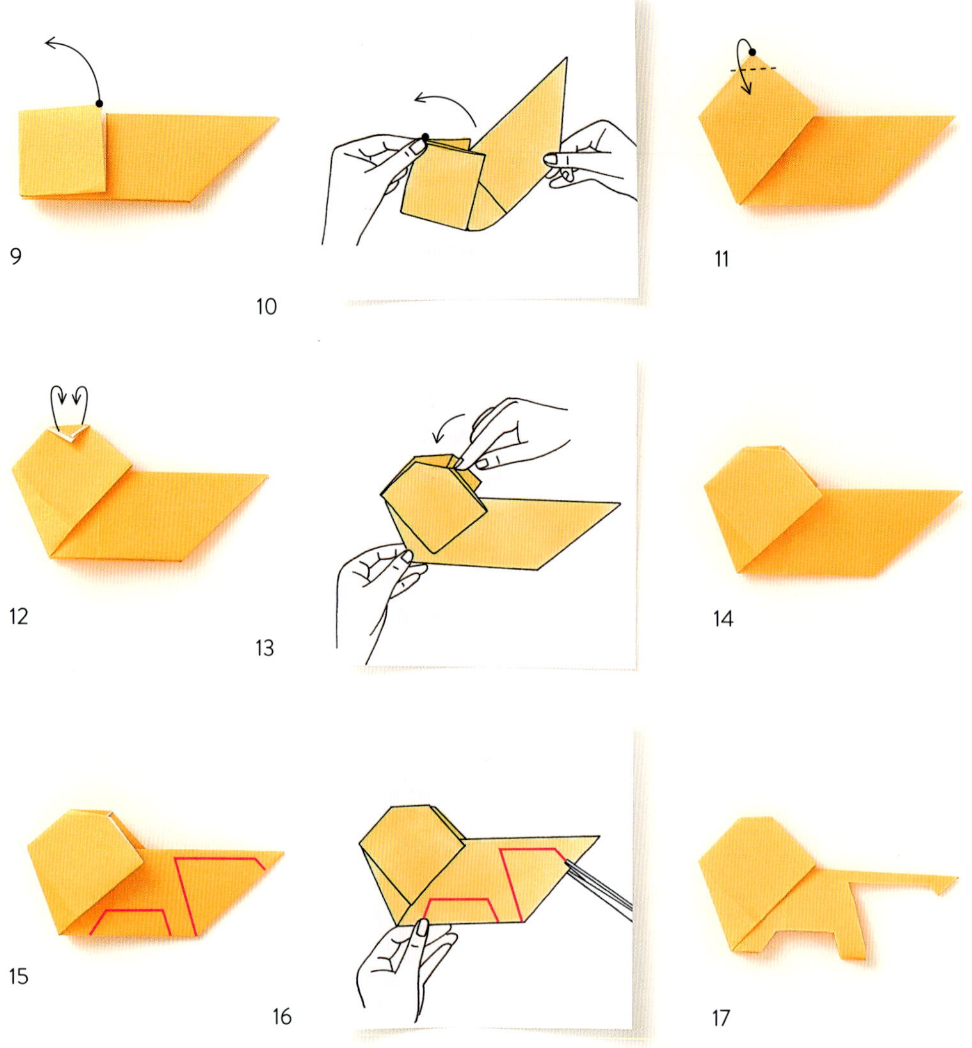

9. 10. Pinch the top of the square at the black dot, pull upwards and squash flat. **11.** Fold along the dotted line. **12. 13. 14.** Unfold and invert the fold, pushing the little triangles inside. You now have this shape. **15.** Draw the outline of the body in pencil as shown. **16.** Cut along the pencil lines. **17.** Your lion is complete. You can now personalize it.

Owl

Level ●●●○○

Size

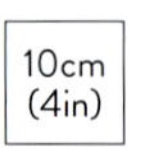
10cm
(4in)

6.5cm
(2½in)

5.5cm
(2¼in)

15cm (6in)

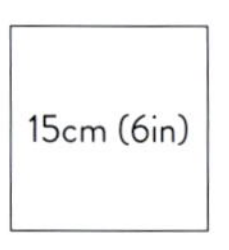
10cm
(4in)

8.5cm
(3⅜in)

20cm (8in)

13.5cm
(5½in)

11.5cm (4½in)

Tip

You will need a pen or pencil to personalize your owl.

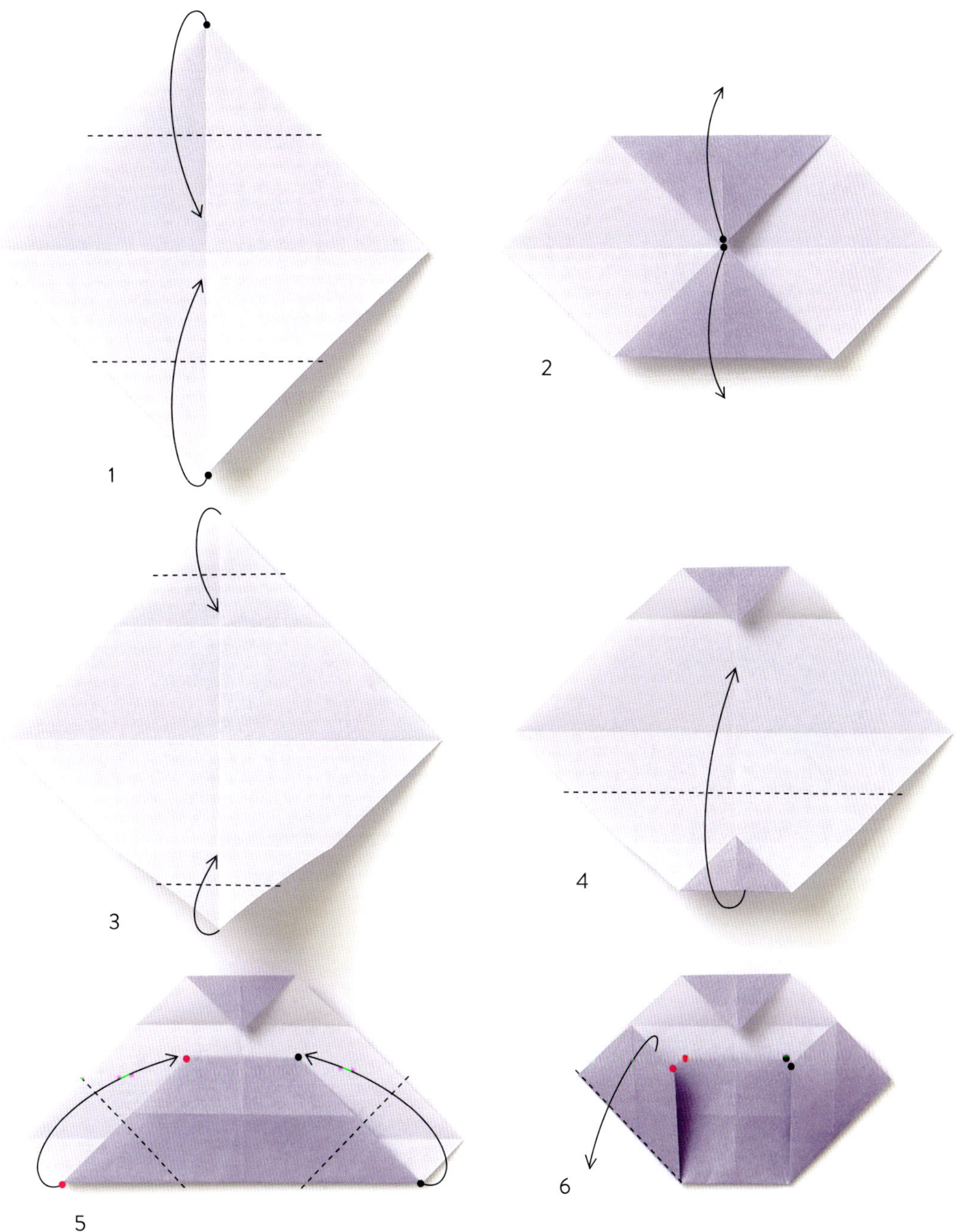

1. Place your square white side up. Mark the creases of the diagonals and rotate on to one corner. Fold the top and bottom points to the centre and mark the creases. **2.** Unfold. **3.** Fold along the dotted lines. **4.** Fold up the bottom section along the dotted line. **5.** Fold along the dotted lines, taking the black point to the black point and the red to the red. **6.** Unfold the LH fold.

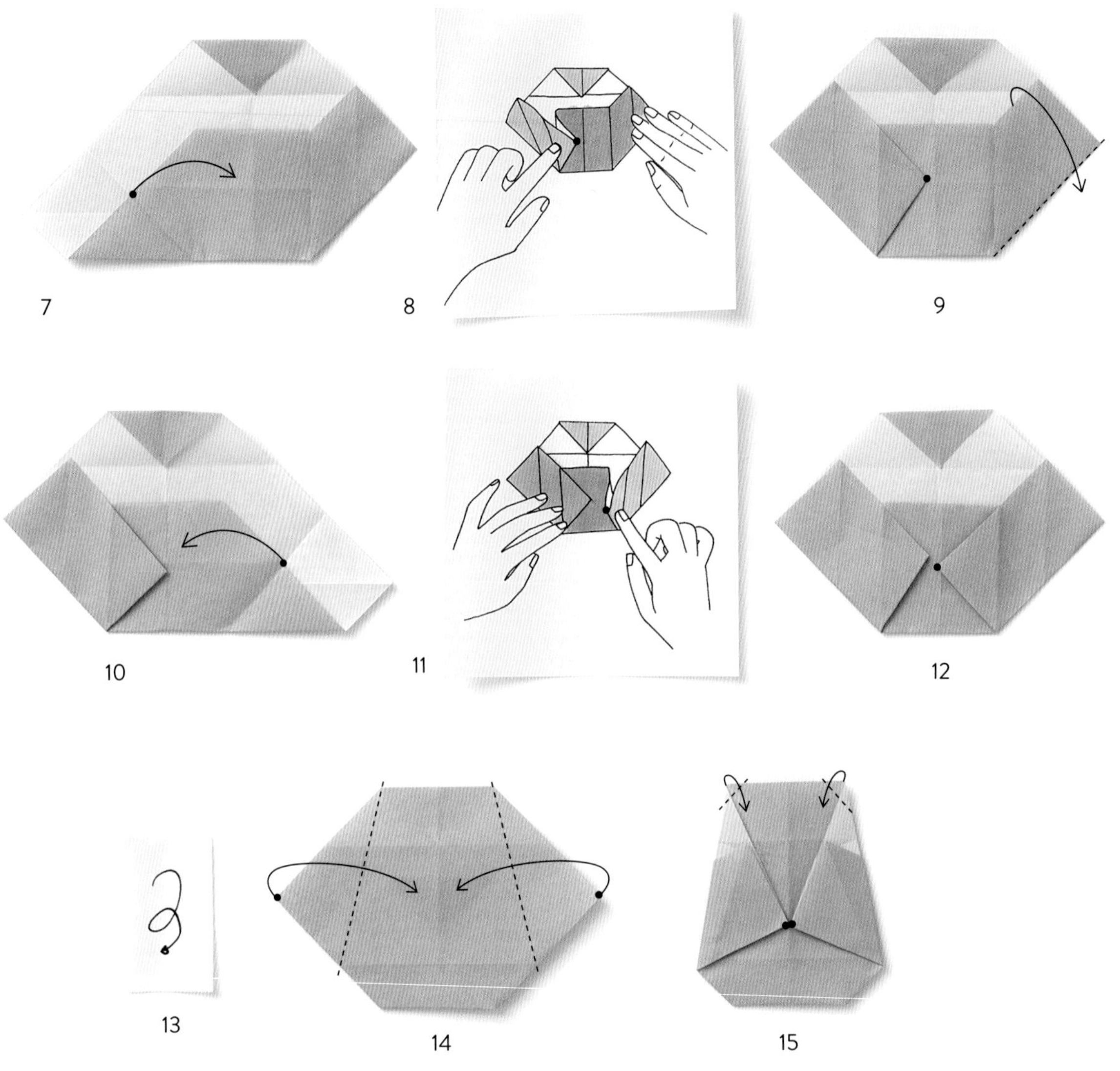

7. 8. Fold the black point to the centre. Squash flat. **9.** Unfold the RH fold. **10. 11. 12.** Fold the point with the black dot to the centre. Squash flat. **13.** Flip over. **14.** Fold the RH and LH points to the central line along the dotted lines. Squash flat. **15.** Fold along the dotted lines.

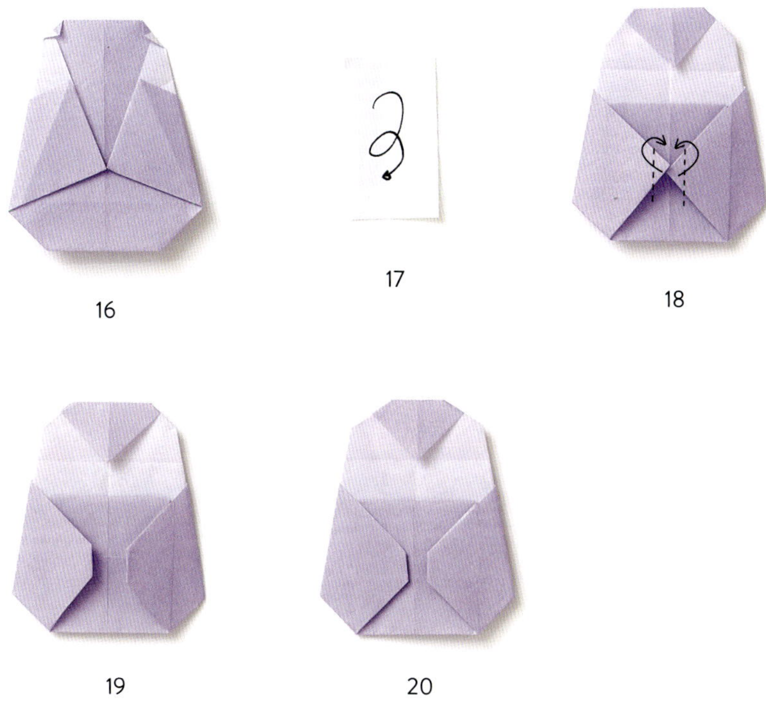

16

17

18

19

20

16. You now have this shape. **17.** Flip over. **18. 19.** Fold the two points inside along the dotted lines. You now have this shape. **20.** Your owl is complete. You can now personalize it.

Shirt

Level ●●●○○

Size

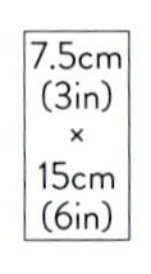

Tip

This design is made using a rectangular sheet of paper.

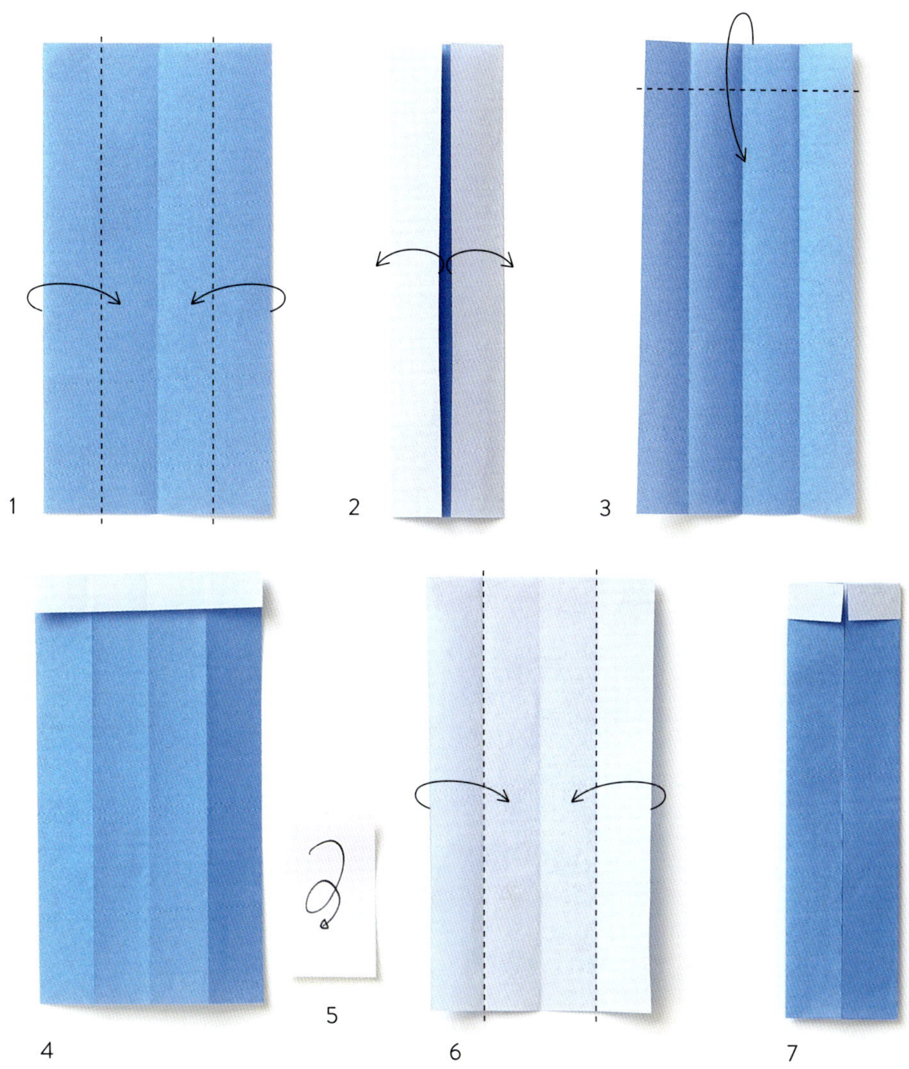

1. Place your rectangle coloured side up. Mark the central vertical line and fold along the dotted lines.
2. Unfold. **3. 4.** Fold the top along the dotted line. You now have this shape. **5.** Flip over. **6. 7.** Fold along the dotted lines. You now have this shape.

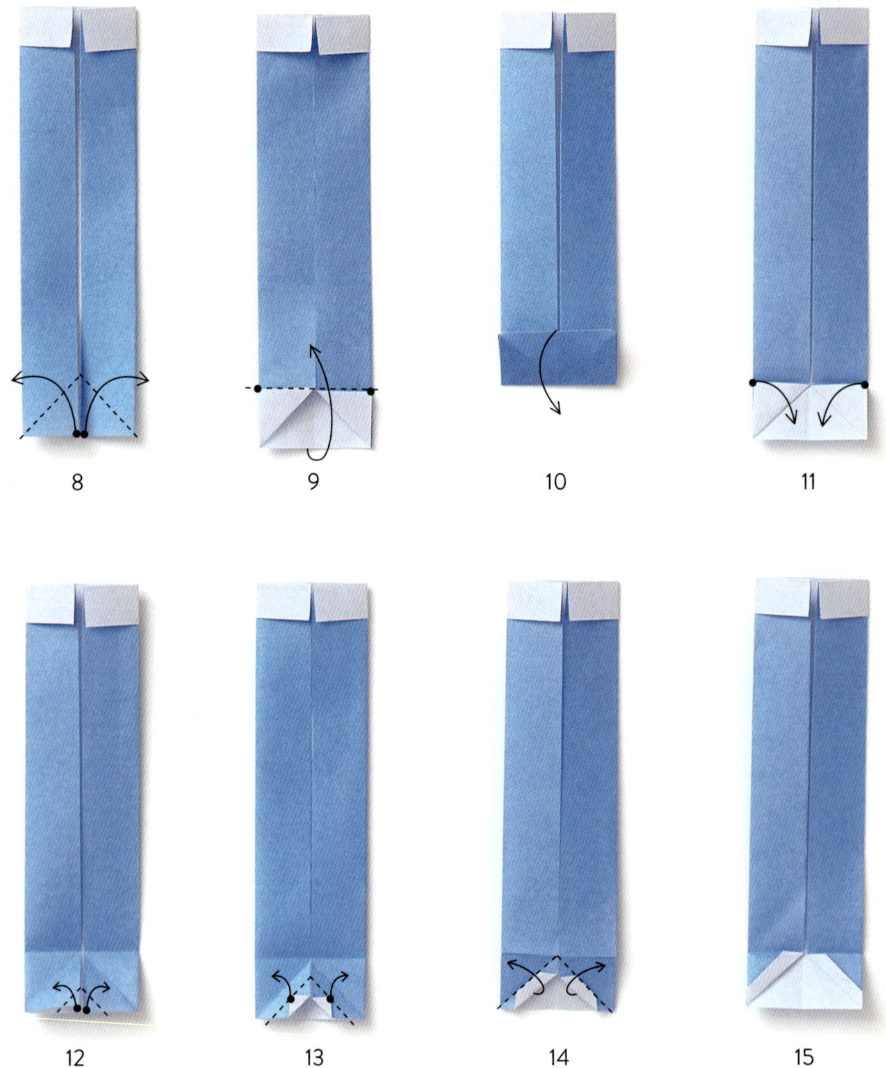

8. Fold along the dotted lines. **9.** Fold along the dotted line. **10.** Unfold. **11.** Unfold the folds made in step 8. **12.** Fold along the dotted lines. **13.** Fold along the dotted lines. **14. 15.** Fold along the dotted lines. You now have this shape.

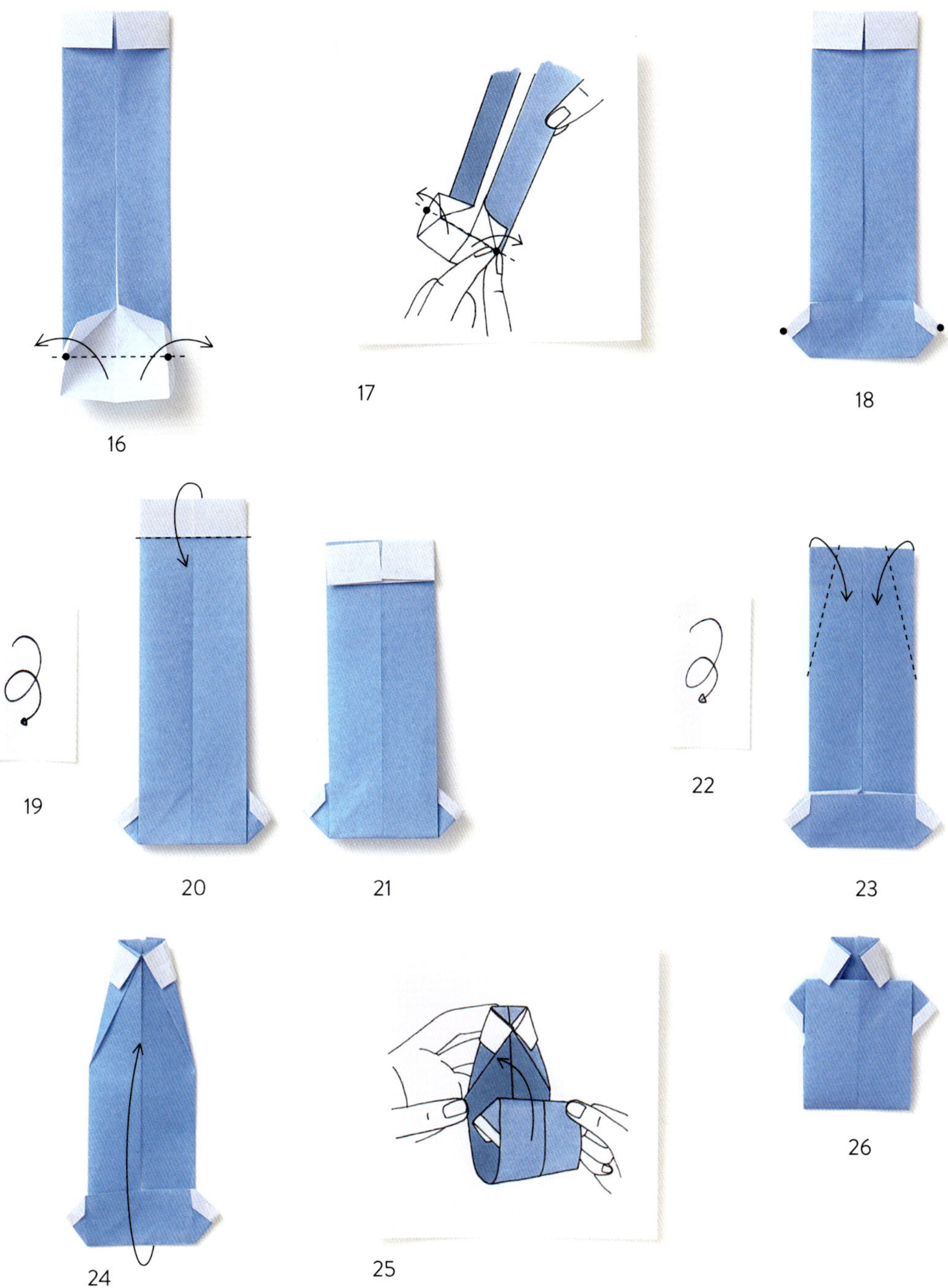

16. 17. 18. Pinch the two dots and pull the folds outwards, folding the bottom section along the dotted line. You now have this shape. **19.** Flip over. **20. 21.** Fold along the dotted line. You now have this shape. **22.** Flip over. **23.** Fold along the dotted lines. **24. 25. 26.** Fold up the bottom section, tucking it under the collar. Your shirt is complete.

Dove

Size

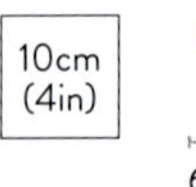
10cm (4in)

6cm (2½in)

6.5cm (2½in)

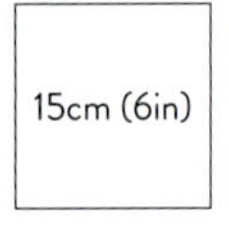
15cm (6in)

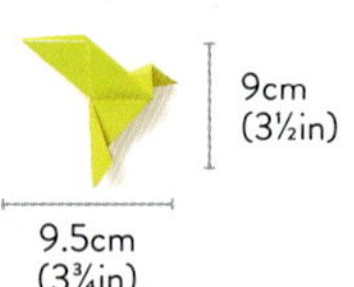
9cm (3½in)

9.5cm (3¾in)

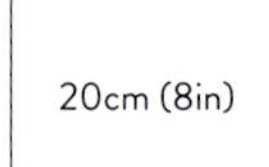
20cm (8in)

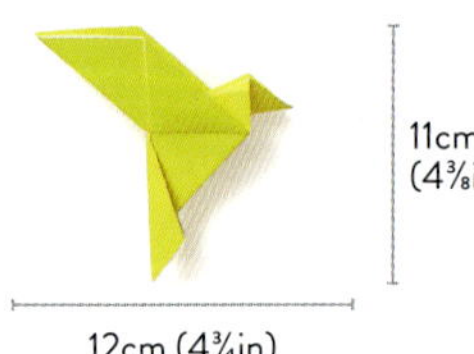
11cm (4⅜in)

12cm (4¾in)

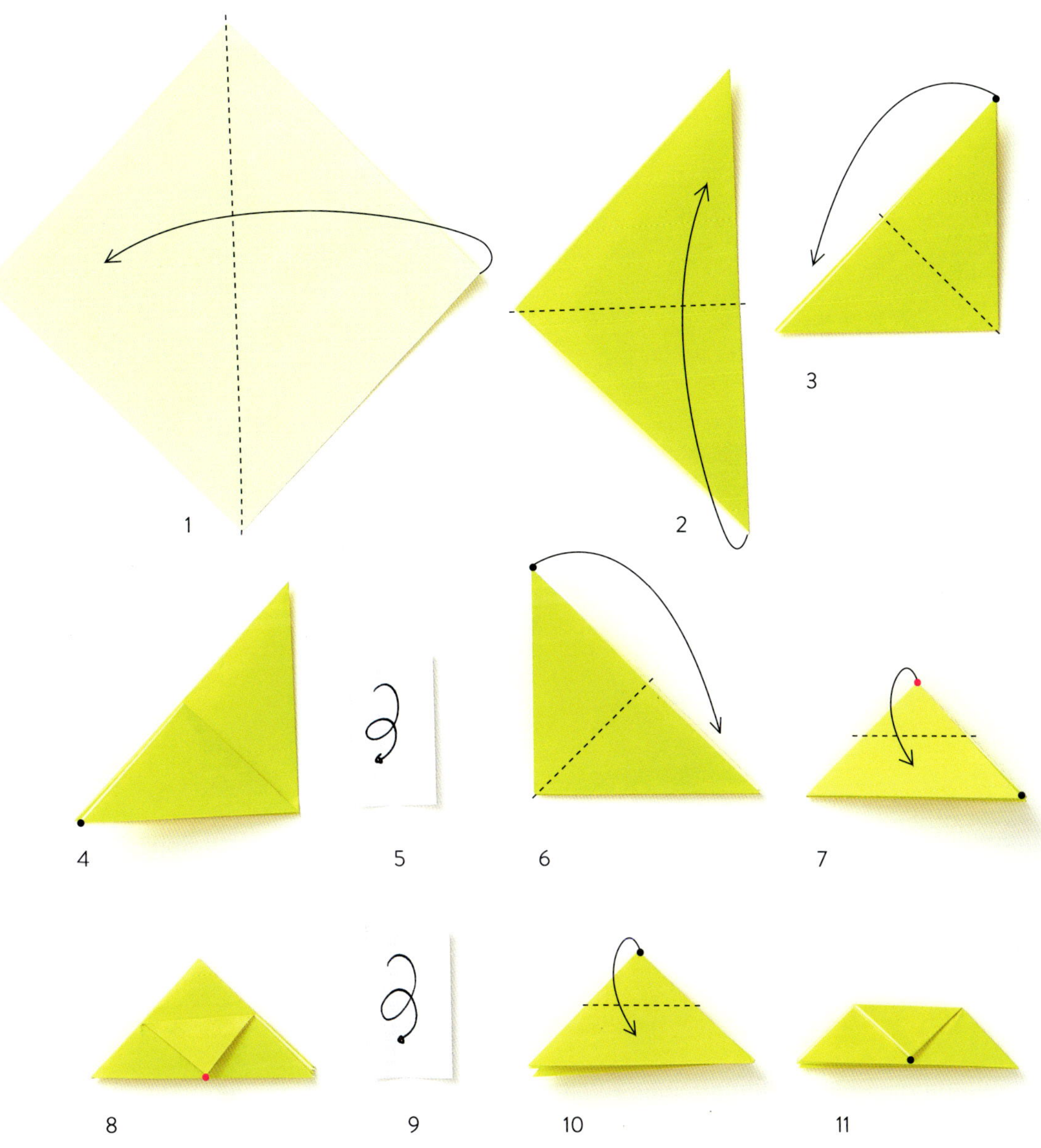

1. Place your square white side up and mark the crease of the diagonal. **2.** Rotate on to one corner and fold in half to form a triangle. **3.** Fold in half again along the dotted line. **4.** Fold the uppermost flap down to the dot. You now have this shape. **5.** Flip over. **6.** Fold in half along the dotted line. **7. 8.** Fold the uppermost flap down to the dot. You now have this shape. **9.** Flip over. **10. 11.** Fold in half along the dotted line. You now have this shape.

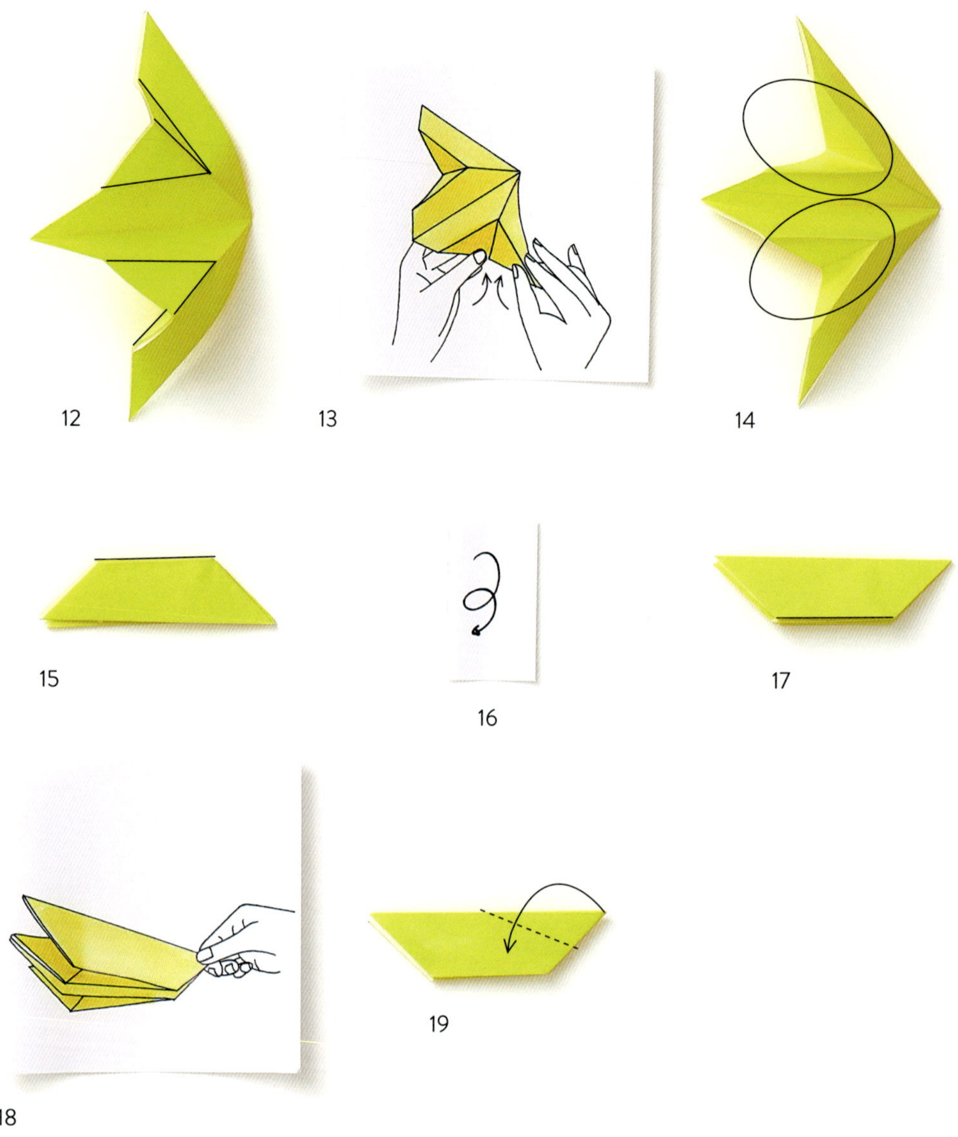

12. 13. 14. 15. Open all the folds made since step 2. Invert the folds shown. Squash flat. You now have this shape. **16. 17. 18.** Flip over and rotate (the guideline at the top should now be at the bottom). You now have this shape. **19.** Fold along the dotted line.

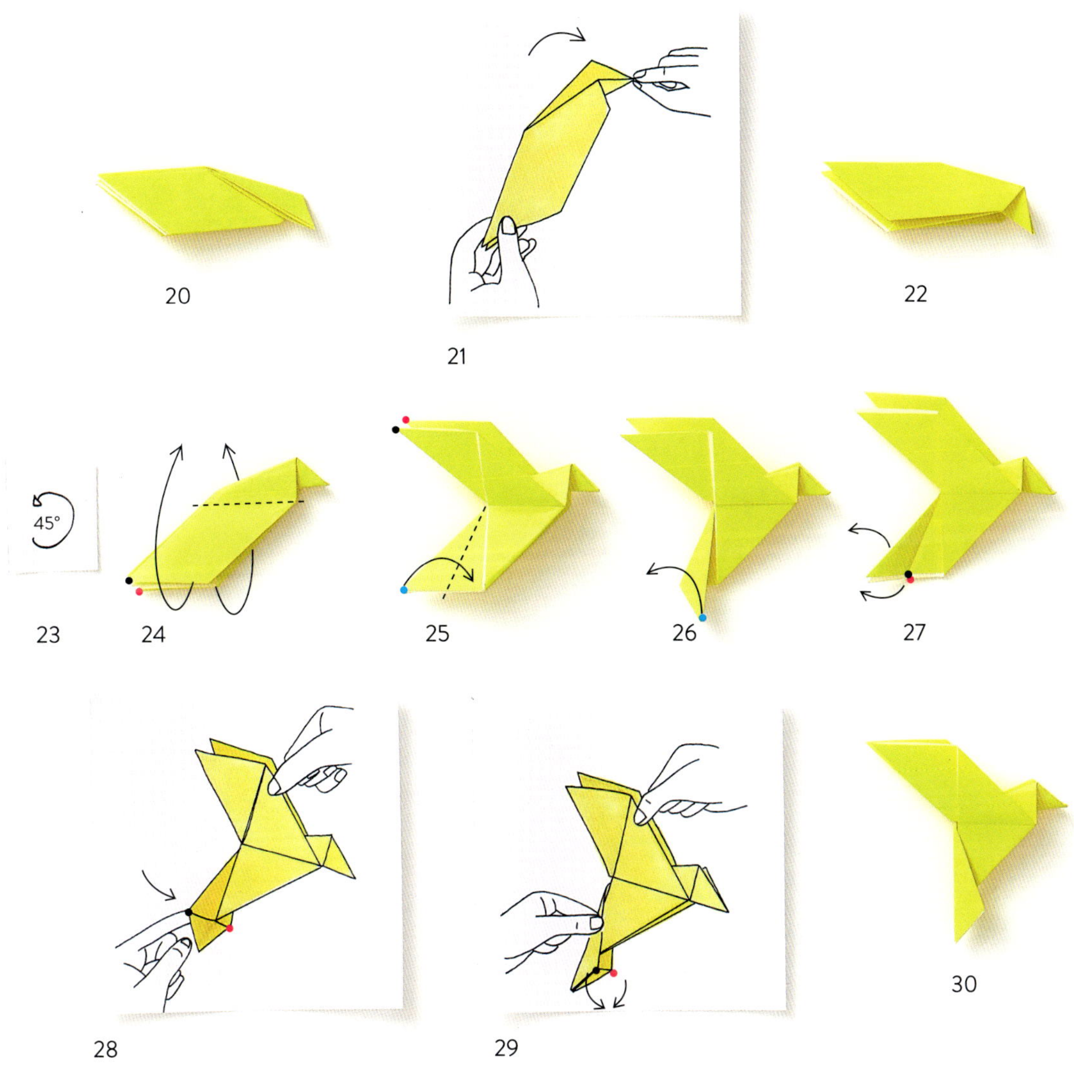

20. You now have this shape. **21. 22.** Open the fold and invert. Squash flat. You have formed the beak.
23. Rotate 45°. **24.** Fold the top layer on both sides along the dotted line. **25.** Fold along the dotted line.
26. Unfold. **27.** Open out fold. **28.** Push the central crease against the bird's body. **29.** Fold the edges of the flap inwards and squash flat, bringing the two points together. You have formed the tail. **30.** Your dove is complete.

Ceremonial kimono

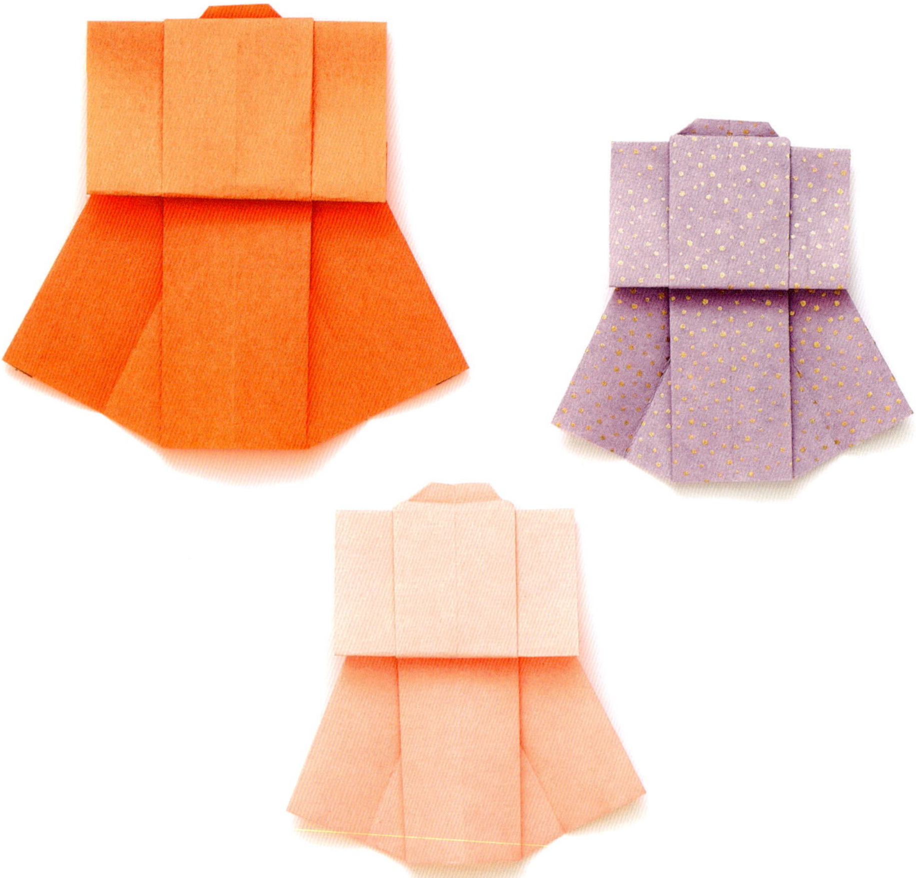

Level ●●●○○

Size

10cm
(4in) 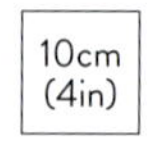 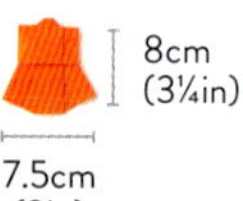 8cm
(3¼in)

7.5cm
(3in)

15cm (6in) 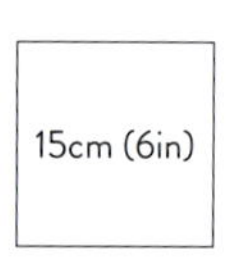 12cm
(4¾in)

11.5cm
(4½in)

20cm (8in)  15cm
(6in)

14.5cm (5¾in)

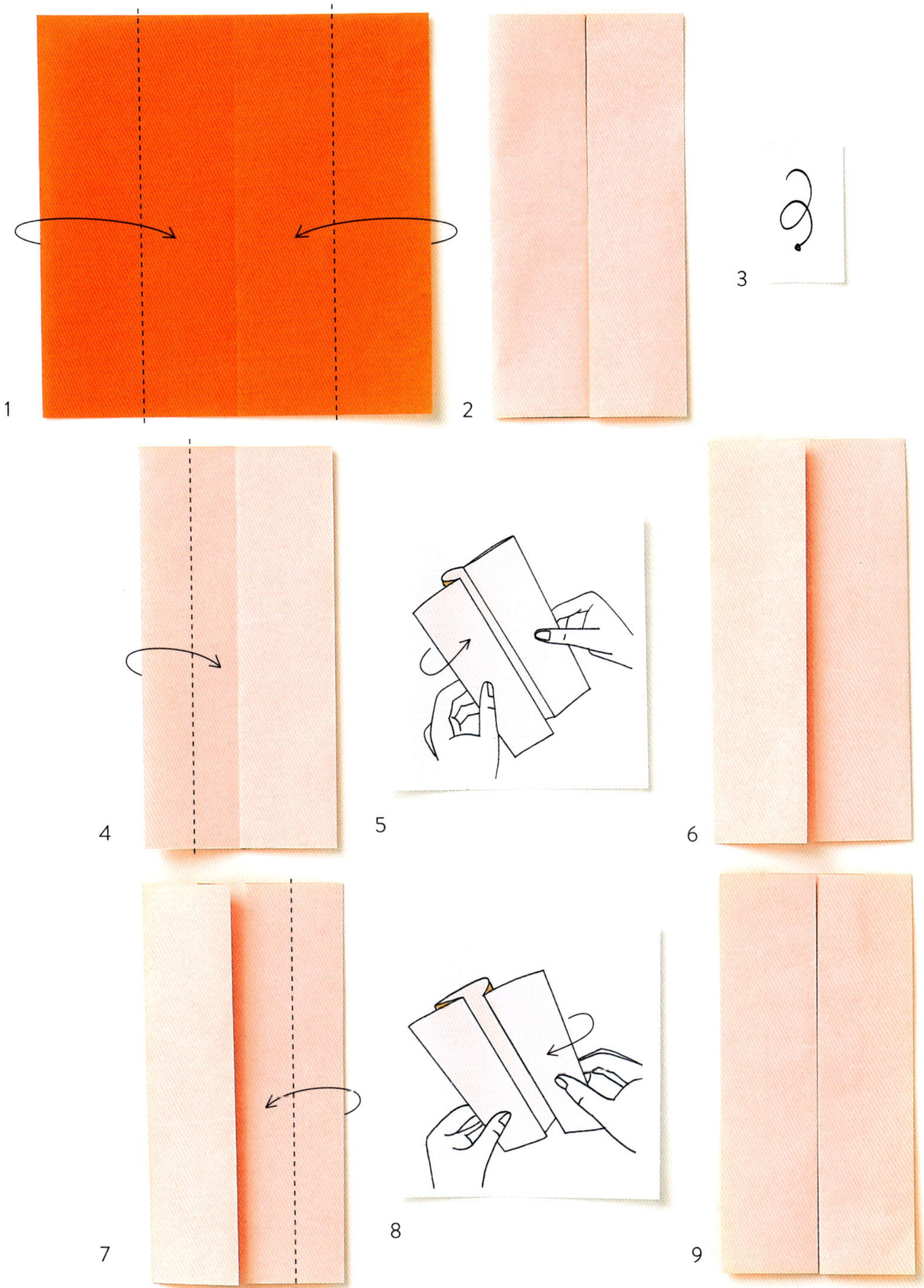

1. 2. Place your square coloured side up and mark the crease of the central vertical line. Fold along the dotted lines. You now have this shape. **3.** Flip over. **4. 5. 6.** Fold the LH side to the central line. Squash flat. You now have this shape. **7. 8. 9.** Fold the RH side to the central line. Squash flat. You now have a box pleat.

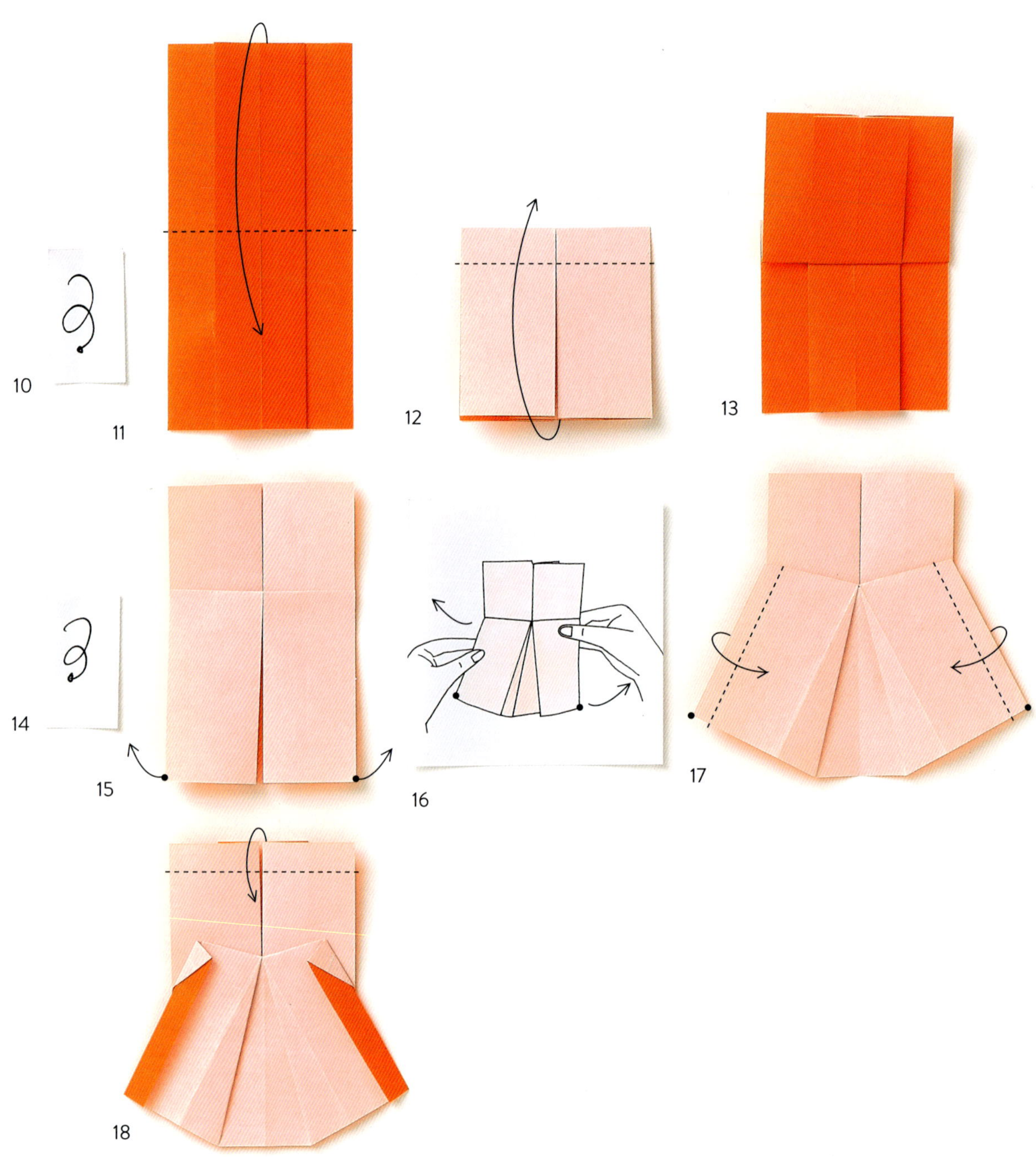

10. Flip over. **11.** Fold in half. **12. 13.** Fold upwards along the dotted line at the approximate point marked.
14. Flip over. **15. 16. 17.** Pinch the two dots and pull outwards. Squash flat. Fold along the dotted lines.
18. Fold along the dotted line.

19. 20. Pinch at the two dots and open out the two folds. Squash flat. **21.** Fold along the dotted line.
22. 23. Fold upwards along the dotted line. You now have this shape. **24.** Flip over. **25.** Your ceremonial kimono is complete.

Scallop shell

Level ●●●○○

Size

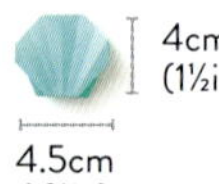

7.5cm
(3in)

4.5cm
(1¾in)

4cm
(1½in)

10cm (4in)

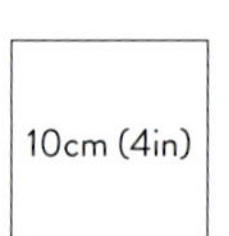
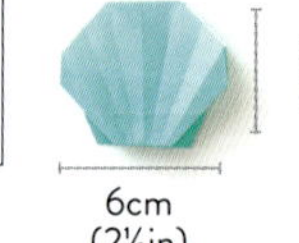

6cm
(2½in)

5cm
(2in)

15cm (6in)

9cm (3½in)

7.5cm
(3in)

Tip
You need to mark the creases very firmly in steps 15 to 17 in order to obtain attractive ridges on your shell.

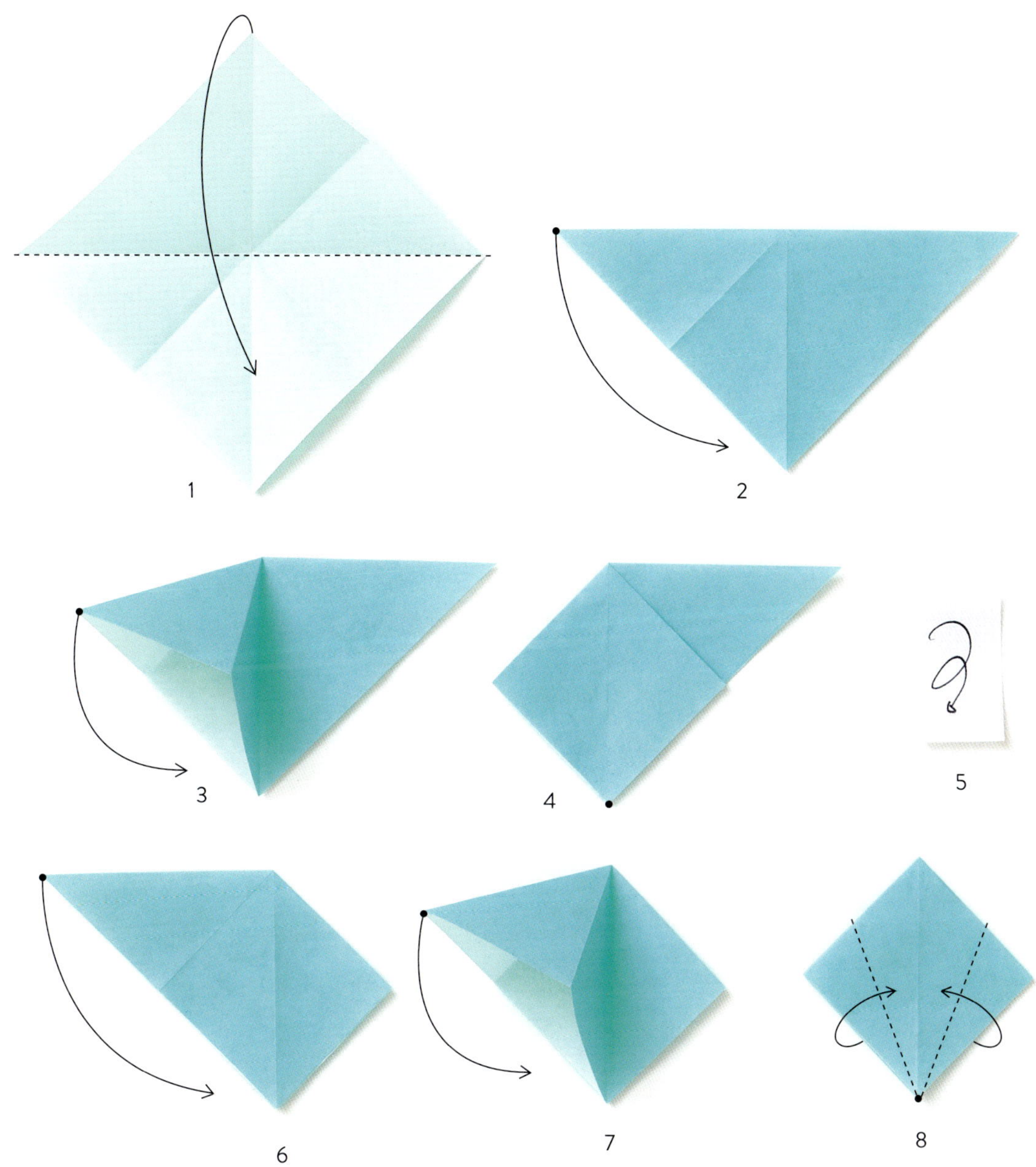

1. Place your square white side up and mark the creases of the central diagonal, horizontal and vertical lines. Rotate on to one corner and fold in half along the dotted line. **2. 3. 4.** Fold the top LH point to the bottom point, opening out the fold to form a diamond. Squash flat. **5.** Flip over. **6. 7.** Fold the top LH point to the bottom point, opening out the fold to form a diamond. Squash flat. **8.** Fold the bottom RH and LH edges of the topmost flaps up to the central line.

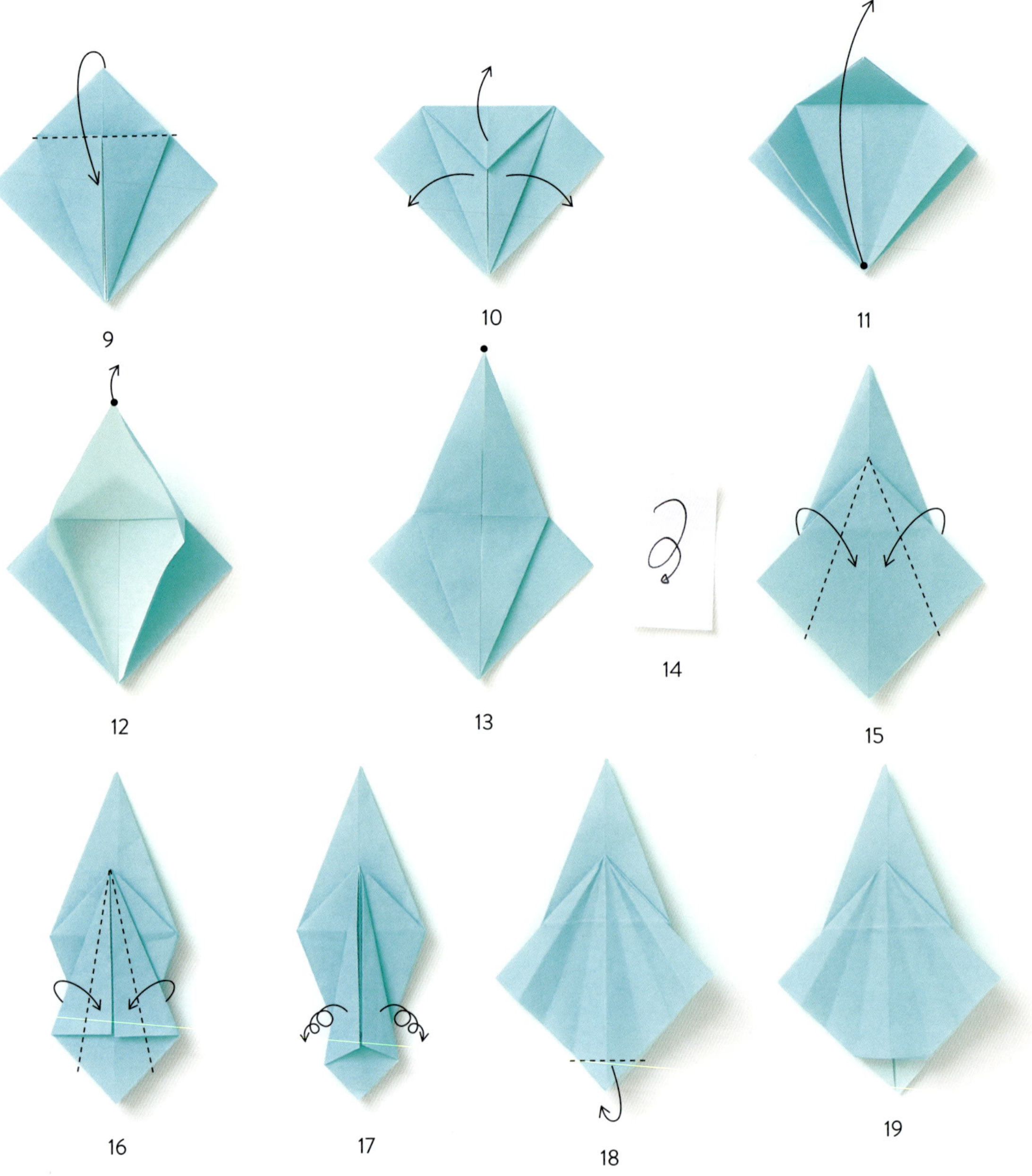

9. Fold the top point downwards along the dotted line. **10.** Unfold all the flaps. **11. 12. 13.** Pinch the bottom corner and pull it upwards gently. Squash flat. **14.** Flip over. **15.** Fold the top RH and LH edges to the central line. **16.** Fold to the central line along the dotted lines. **17.** Unfold the folds made in steps 15 and 16. **18. 19.** Fold the top layer inwards along the dotted line. You now have this shape.

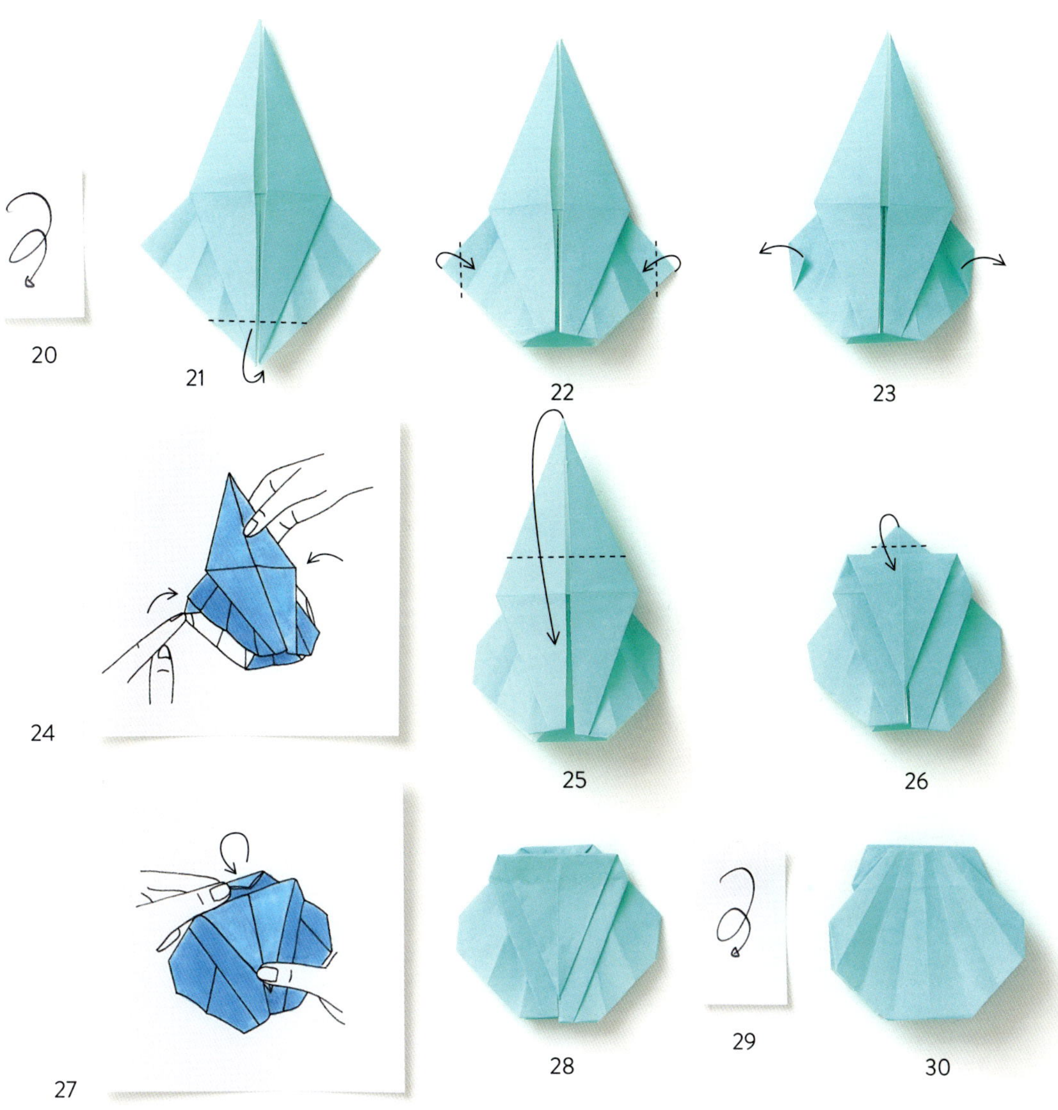

20. Flip over. **21.** Fold inwards along the dotted line. **22.** Fold along the dotted lines. **23. 24.** Unfold, invert and squash flat. **25.** Fold along the dotted line at the approximate point marked. **26. 27. 28.** Fold the point along the dotted line. Tuck the little point inside, allowing the top of the fold to extend slightly beyond the top layer. You now have this shape. **29.** Flip over. **30.** Your scallop shell is complete.

Dress

Level ●●●○○

Size

10cm
(4in)

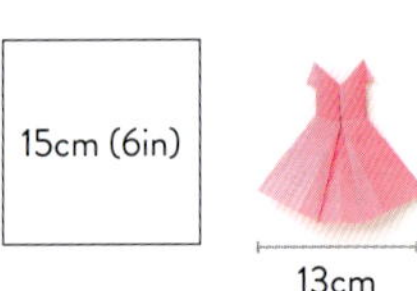
8cm
(3¼in)
8.5cm
(3⅜in)

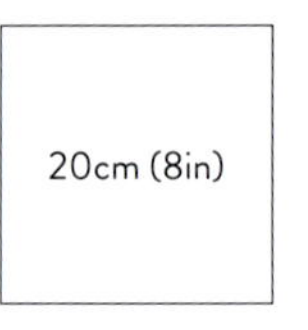
15cm (6in)
12cm
(4¾in)
13cm
(5⅛in)

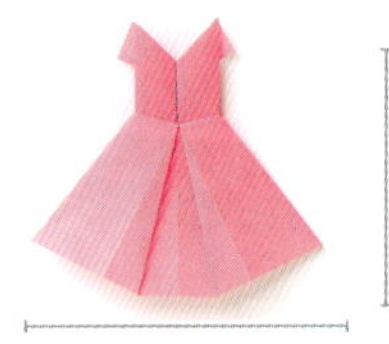
20cm (8in)
9cm
(3½in)
15cm (6in)

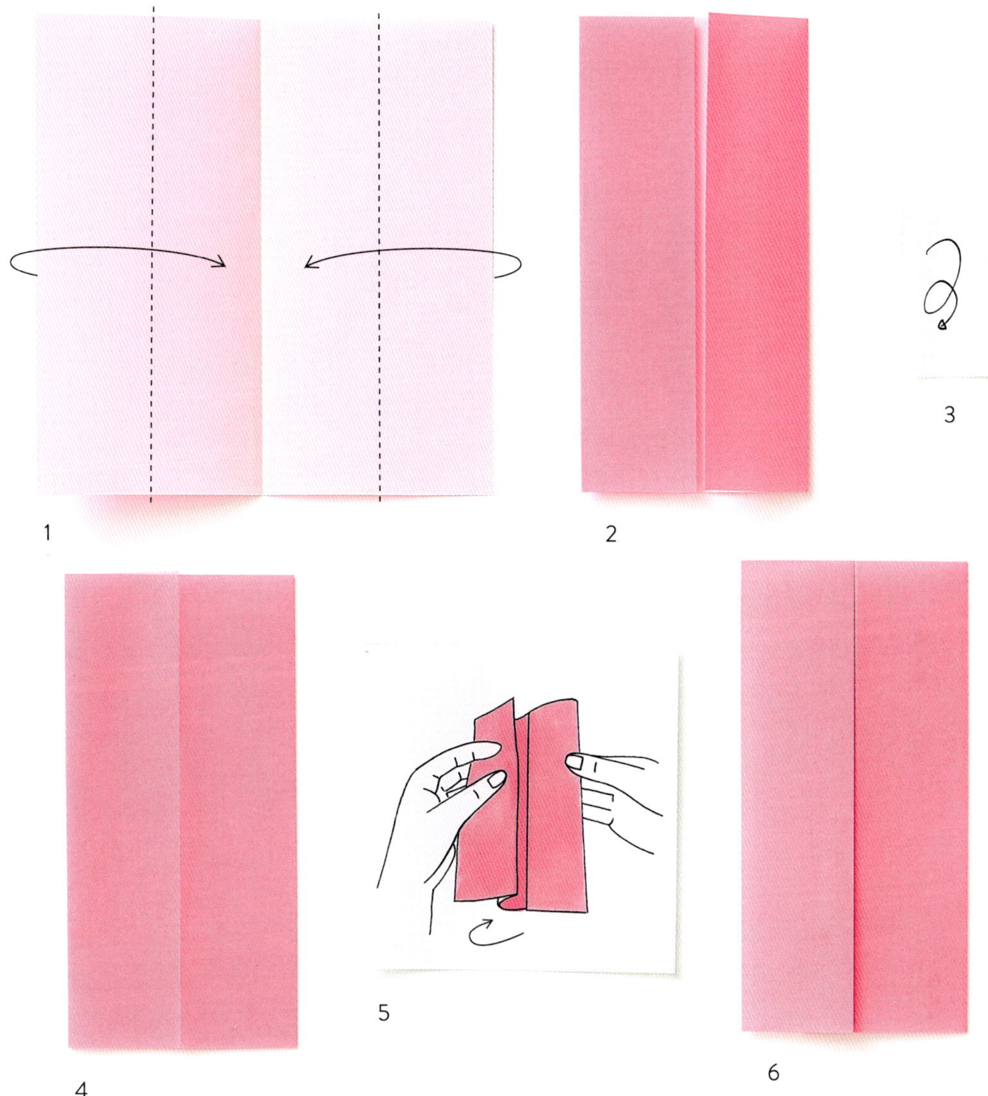

1. 2. Place your square white side up and mark the crease of the central vertical line. Fold along the dotted lines. You now have this shape. **3.** Flip over. **4. 5. 6.** Fold the LH side to the central line. Squash flat. You now have this shape.

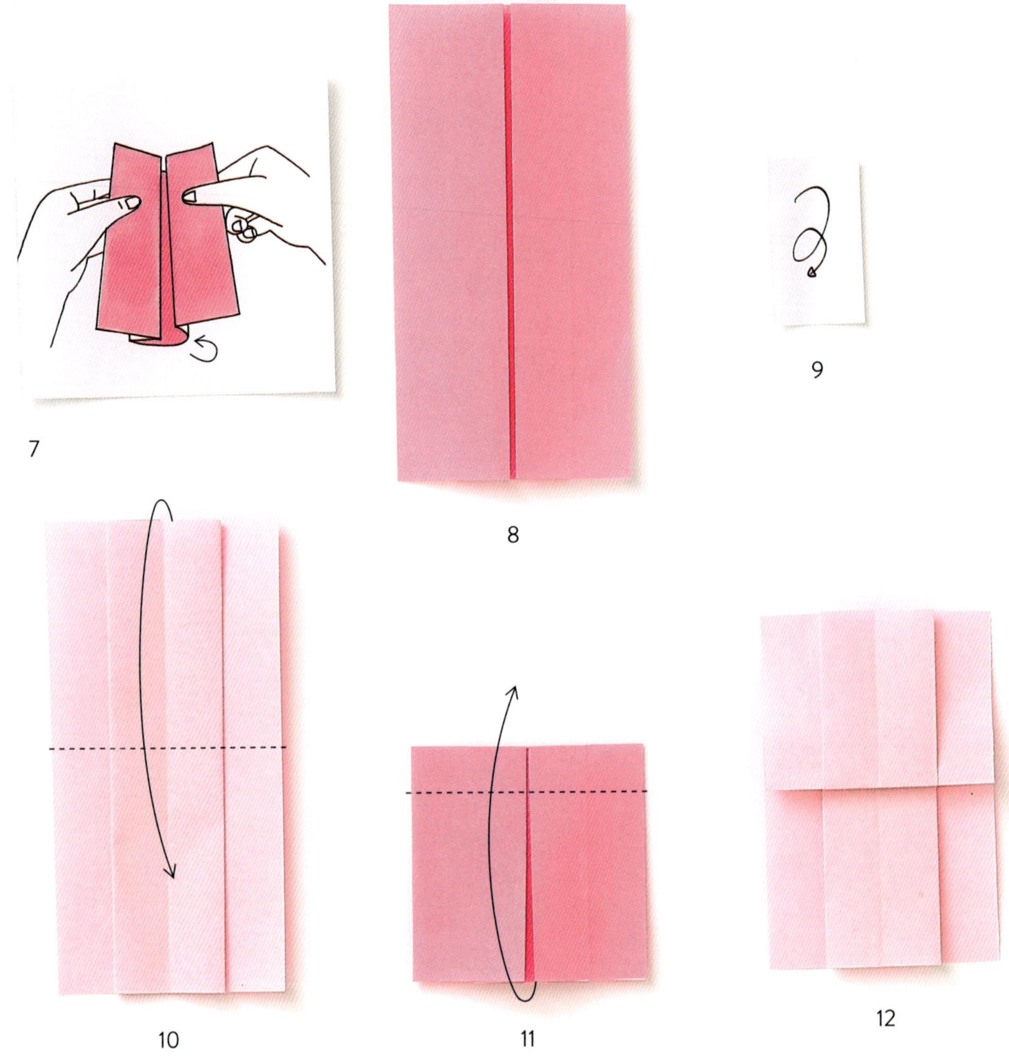

7. 8. Fold the RH side to the central line. Squash flat. You now have a box pleat. **9.** Flip over. **10.** Fold in half along the dotted line. **11. 12.** Fold the top section along the dotted line at the approximate point marked. You now have this shape.

13. Flip over. **14. 15.** Pinch the two marked dots and carefully pull them outwards to slightly open out the fold. Squash flat. **16.** Flip over. **17.** Fold the top layer along the dotted lines. **18.** Unfold. **19. 20.** Pinch the two dots on the left and right to open out the fold and bring the central point downwards. Squash flat. Fold along the dotted lines.

21

22

23

24

25

21. Fold the top and the bottom of the LH edge of the dress. Do the same with the RH edge.
22. 23. Fold out along the dotted lines. You now have this shape. **24.** Flip over. **25.** Your dress is complete.

Hydrangea

Level ●●●●○

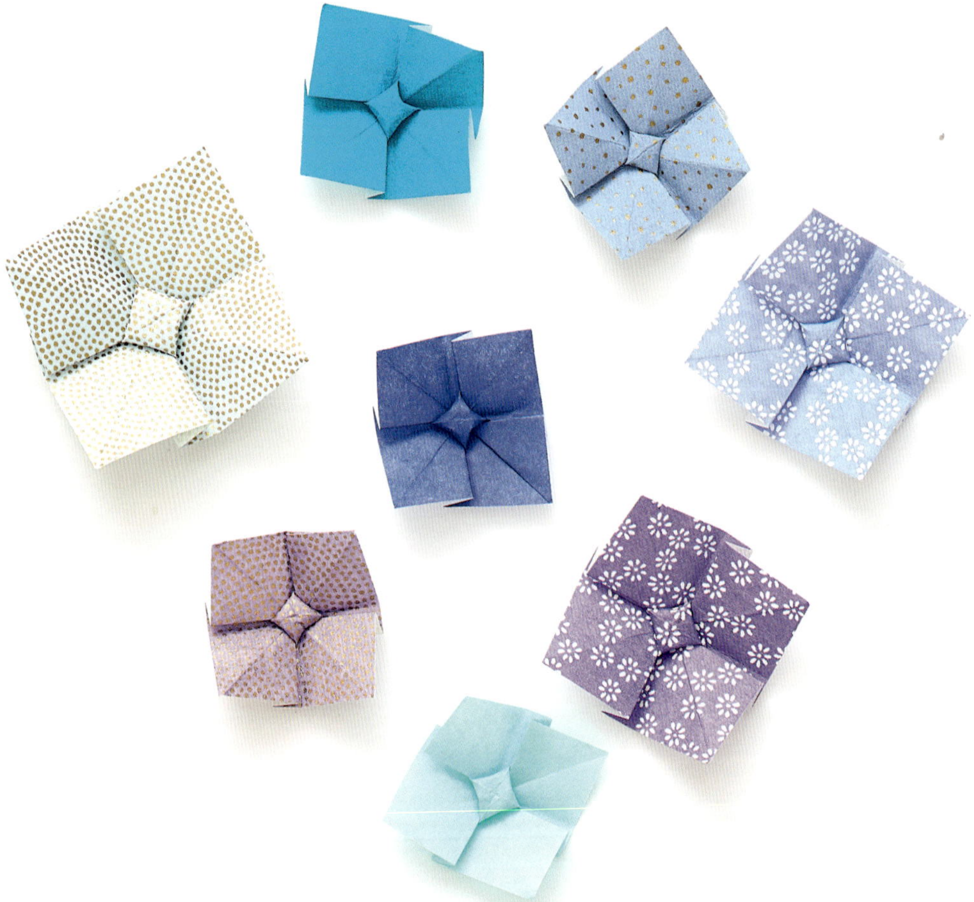

Size

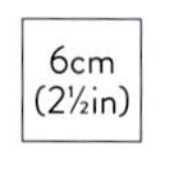

6cm (2½in)

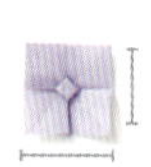

5.5cm (2¼in)

5.5cm (2¼in)

7.5cm (3in)

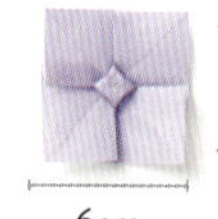

6cm (2½in)

6cm (2½in)

10cm (4in)

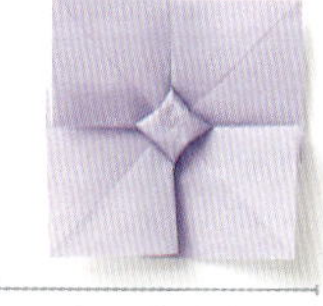

8cm (3¼in)

8cm (3¼in)

Tip

You can make several flowers to create a hydrangea head.

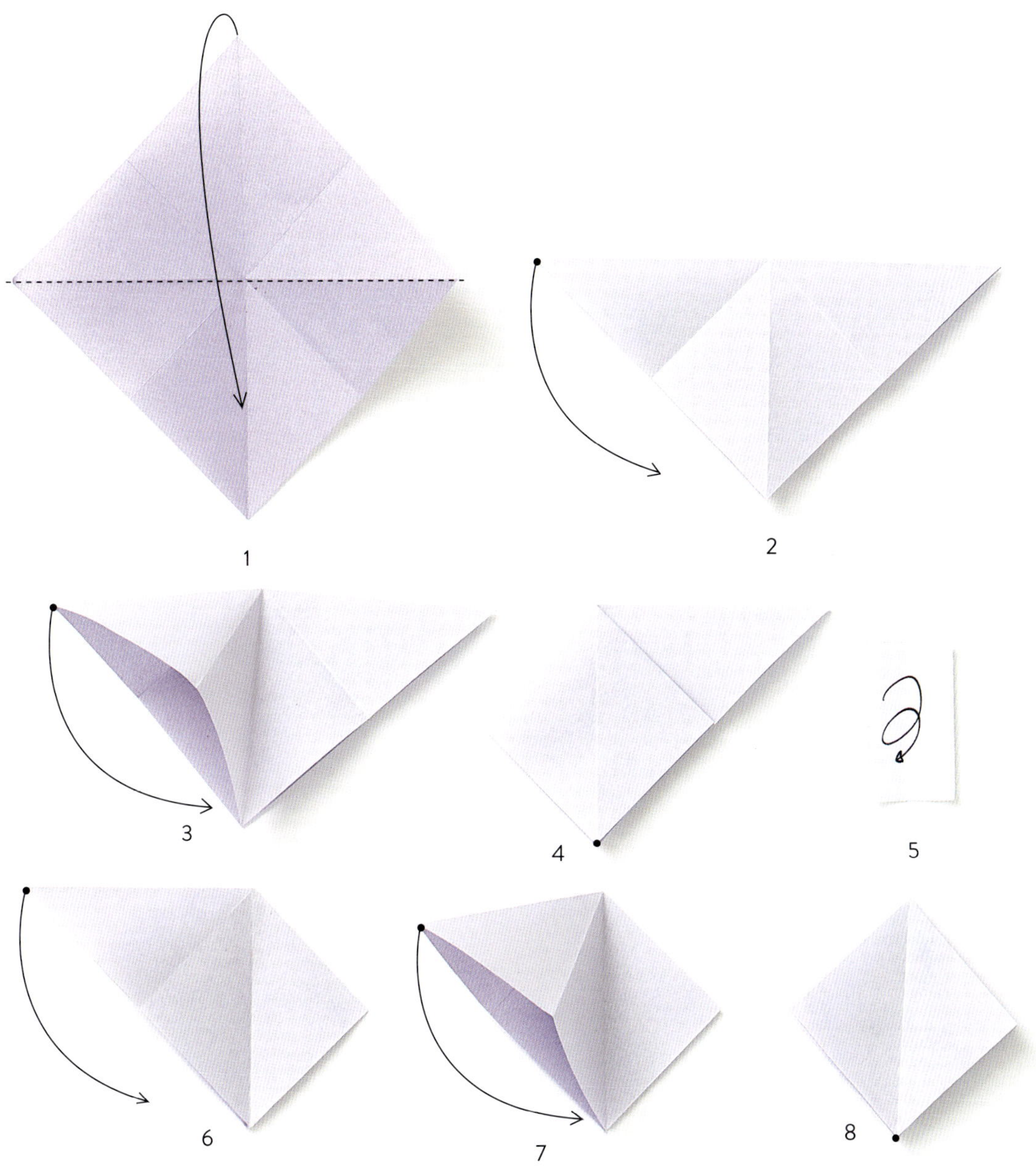

1. Place your square coloured side up. Mark the creases of the central diagonal, horizontal and vertical lines. Rotate on to one corner and fold in half to form a triangle. **2. 3. 4.** Fold the LH point to the bottom, opening out the fold to form a diamond. Squash flat. **5.** Flip over. **6. 7. 8.** Fold the LH point to the bottom, opening out the fold to form a diamond. Squash flat.

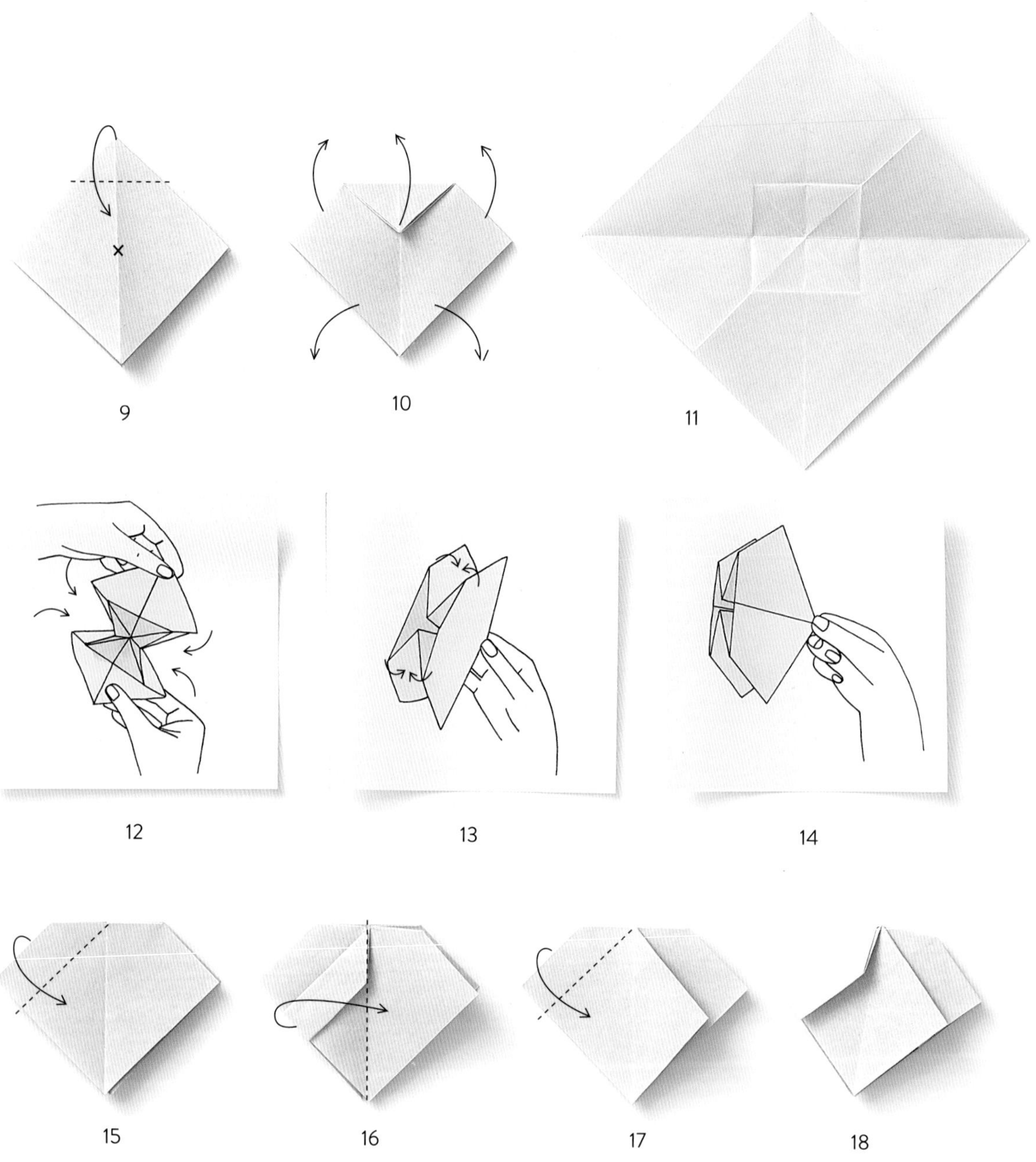

9. Fold to the central X along the dotted line. **10. 11.** Unfold all the folds and flip over. **12. 13. 14.** Invert the folds to form a small square in the centre and push inwards. Squash flat. You now have this shape. **15.** Fold the LH section of the top layer along the dotted line. **16.** Fold this flap over the RH section. **17. 18.** Fold along the dotted line. You now have this shape.

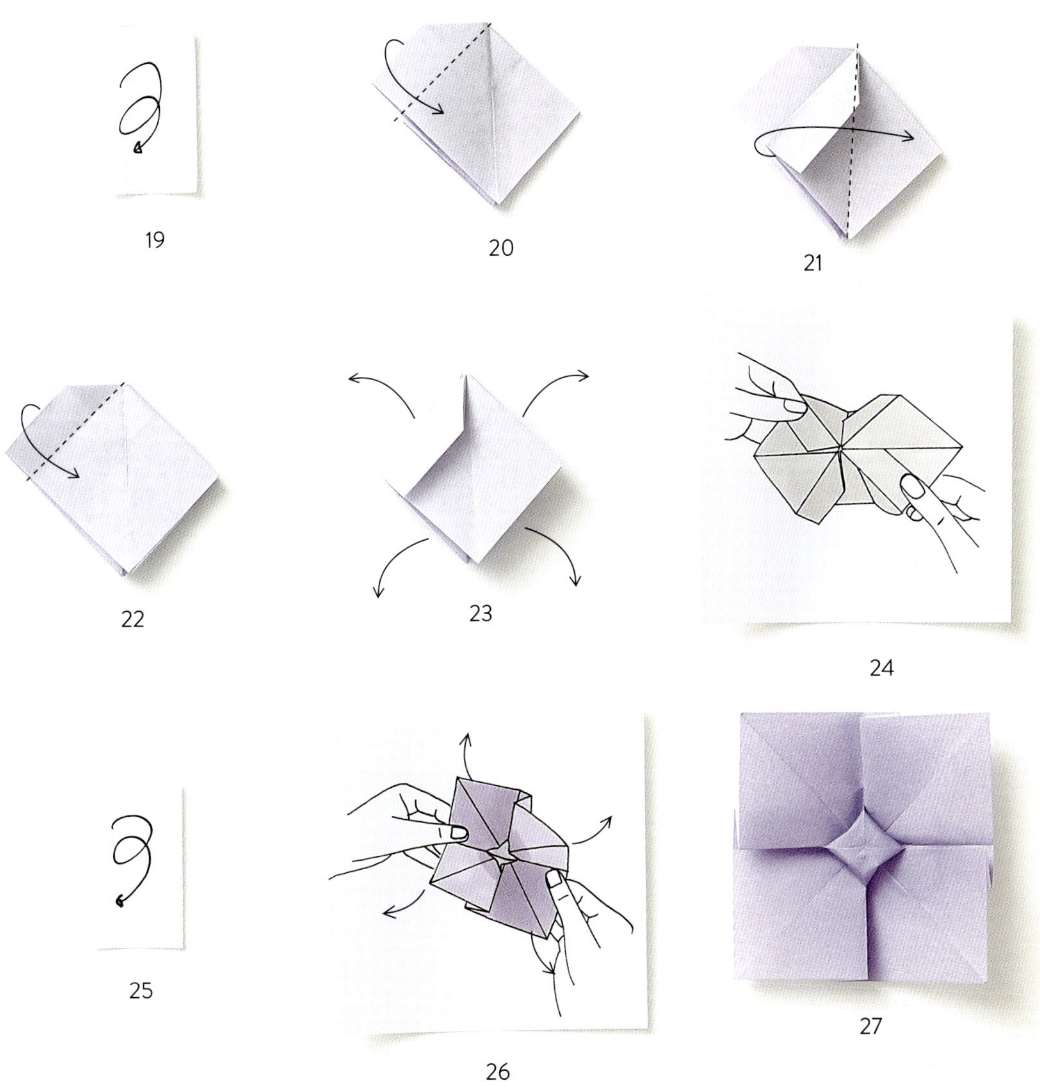

19. Flip over. **20. 21. 22. 23.** Repeat steps 15 to 18 on this side. **24.** Gently open out. **25.** Flip over.
26. 27. Pull very gently to finish opening out the flower and form its heart. Your hydrangea is complete.

Simple kimono

Level ●●●○○

Size

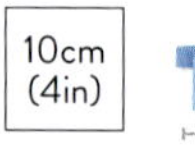 10cm (4in)

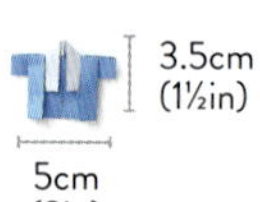 5cm (2in) — 3.5cm (1½in)

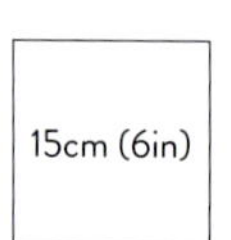 15cm (6in)

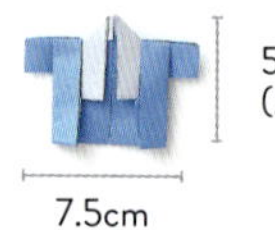 7.5cm (3in) — 5.5cm (2¼in)

 20cm (8in) — 9.5cm (3¾in) — 7cm (2¾in)

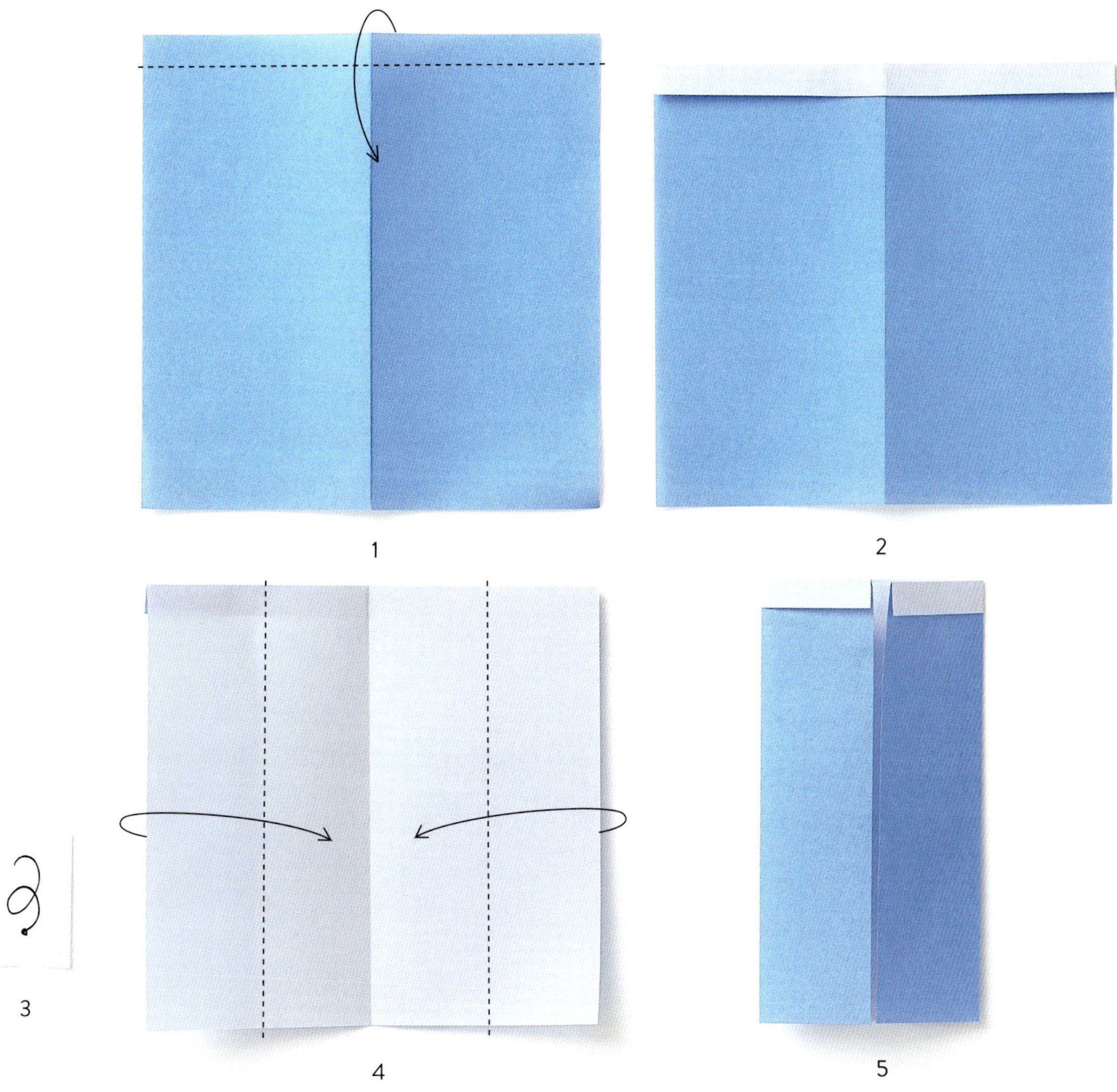

1. 2. Place your square coloured side up, mark the crease of the central vertical line. Fold along the dotted line. **3.** Flip over. **4. 5.** Fold to the central line along the dotted lines. You now have this shape.

6. Fold to the central line along the dotted lines, leaving a small gap as shown in the picture. **7. 8.** Fold the bottom section behind along the dotted line. **9. 10.** Fold the top section behind along the dotted line. **11.** Fold in the two sides, leaving the collar showing.

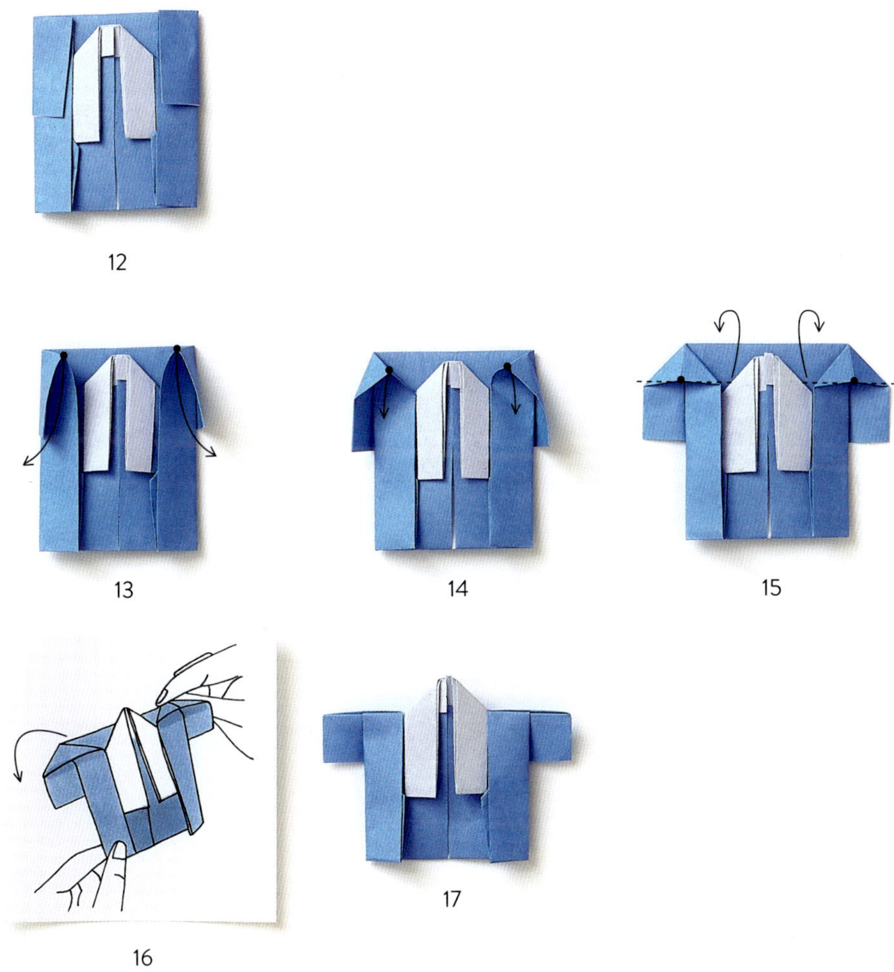

12. You now have this shape. **13. 14.** Open out the indicated folds, press on the dots and squash flat.
15. 16. Fold behind along the dotted lines. **17.** Your kimono is complete.

Frog

Level ●●●○○

Size

7.5cm (3in)	4.2cm (1⅝in)	3.5cm (1½in)
10cm (4in)	5.5cm (2¼in)	5cm (2in)
15cm (6in)	8.5cm (3⅜in)	7cm (2¾in)

Tip
You can make your frog jump by pressing down on the base of its back!

1. Place your square white side up, mark the creases of the central diagonal, horizontal and vertical lines.
Fold in half. **2. 3. 4.** Fold the LH point to the right, forming a triangle on the left. Squash flat. **5.** Flip over.
6. Take the dot on the LH side to the right.

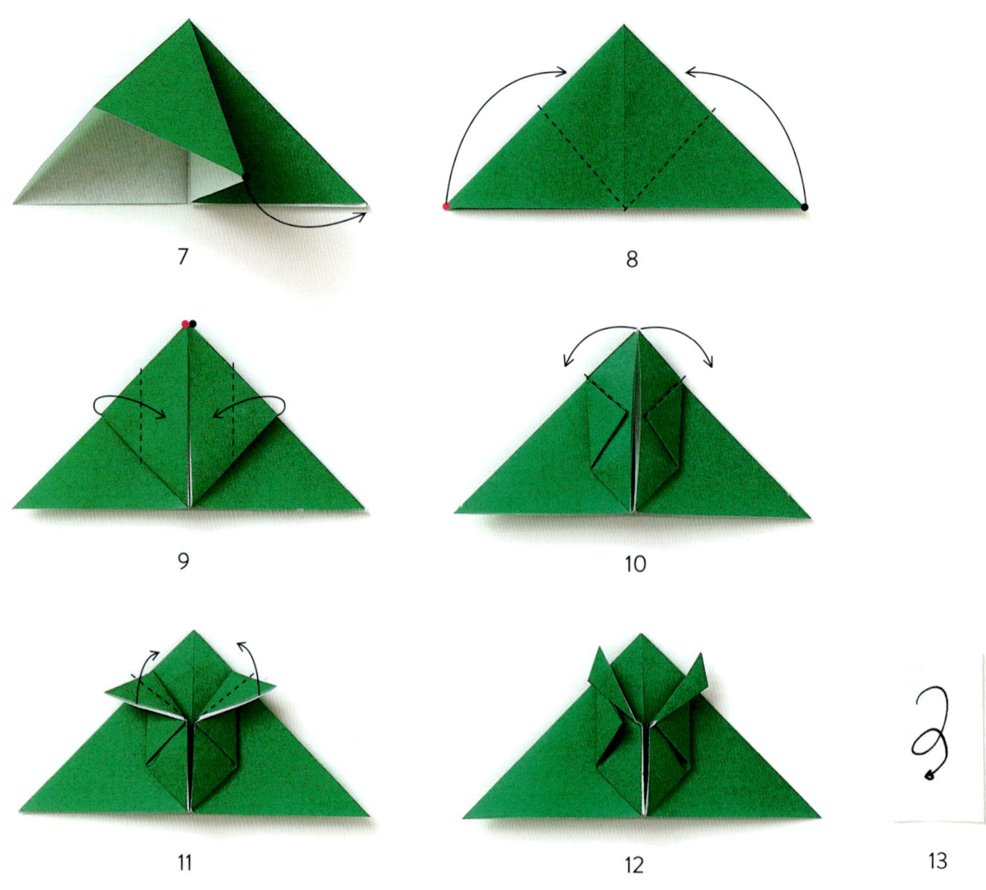

7. Continue folding the point to form a triangle. Squash flat. **8.** Fold the two bottom points of the top layer to the top, along the dotted lines. **9.** Fold along the dotted lines. **10.** Fold outwards along the dotted lines. **11. 12.** Fold upwards along the dotted lines. You now have this shape. **13.** Flip over.

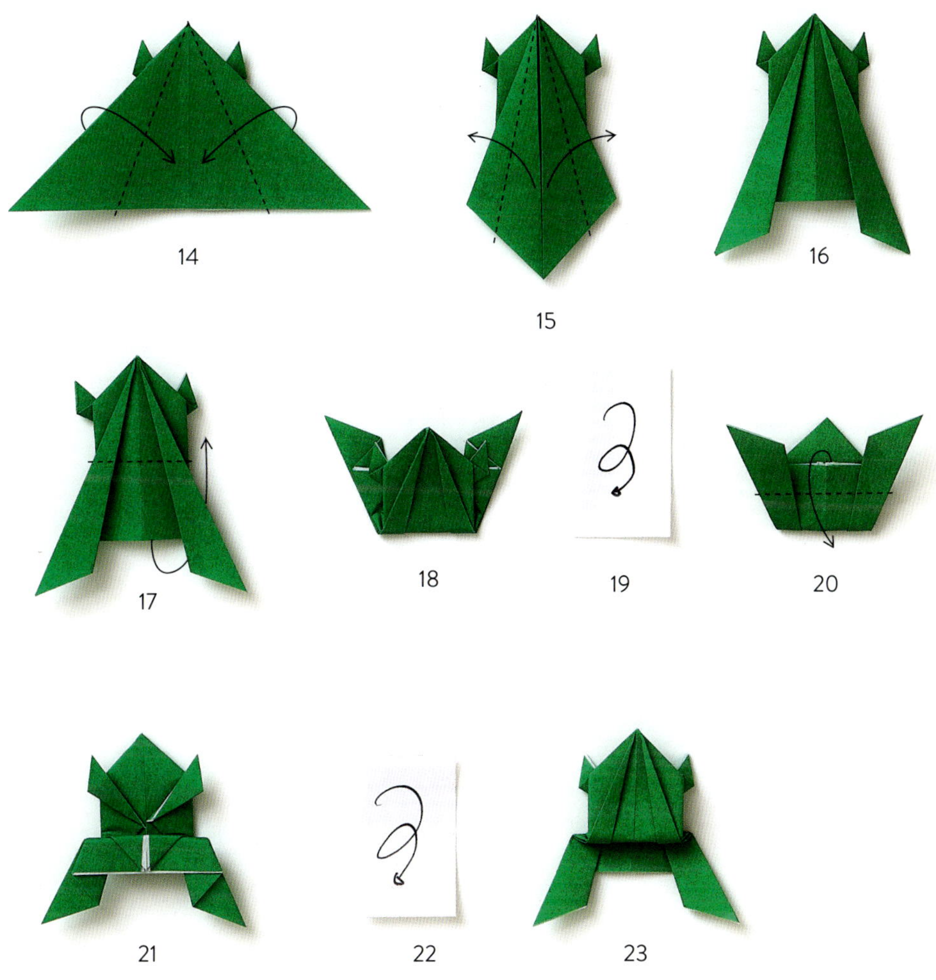

14. Fold along the dotted lines. **15. 16.** Fold outwards along the dotted lines. You now have this shape.
17. 18. Fold behind along the dotted lines **19.** Flip over. **20. 21.** Fold the top layer downwards along
the dotted line. You now have this shape. **22.** Flip over. **23.** Your frog is complete.

Snail

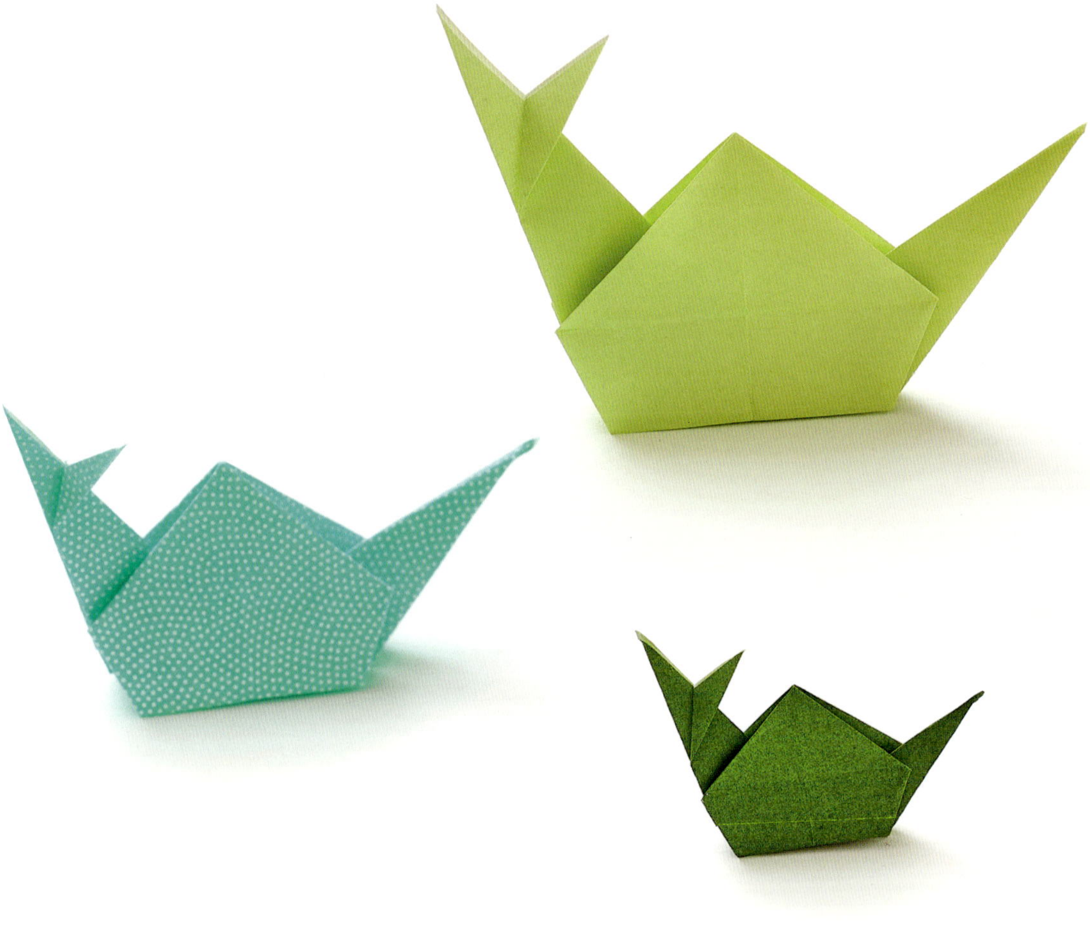

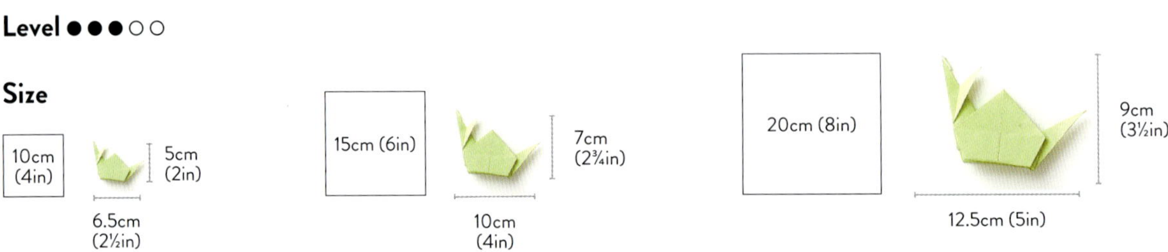

Level ●●●○○

Size

10cm (4in)

5cm (2in)

6.5cm (2½in)

15cm (6in)

7cm (2¾in)

10cm (4in)

20cm (8in)

9cm (3½in)

12.5cm (5in)

Tip

You will need a pair of scissors. This design will stand up by itself, and it can be used as a place card.

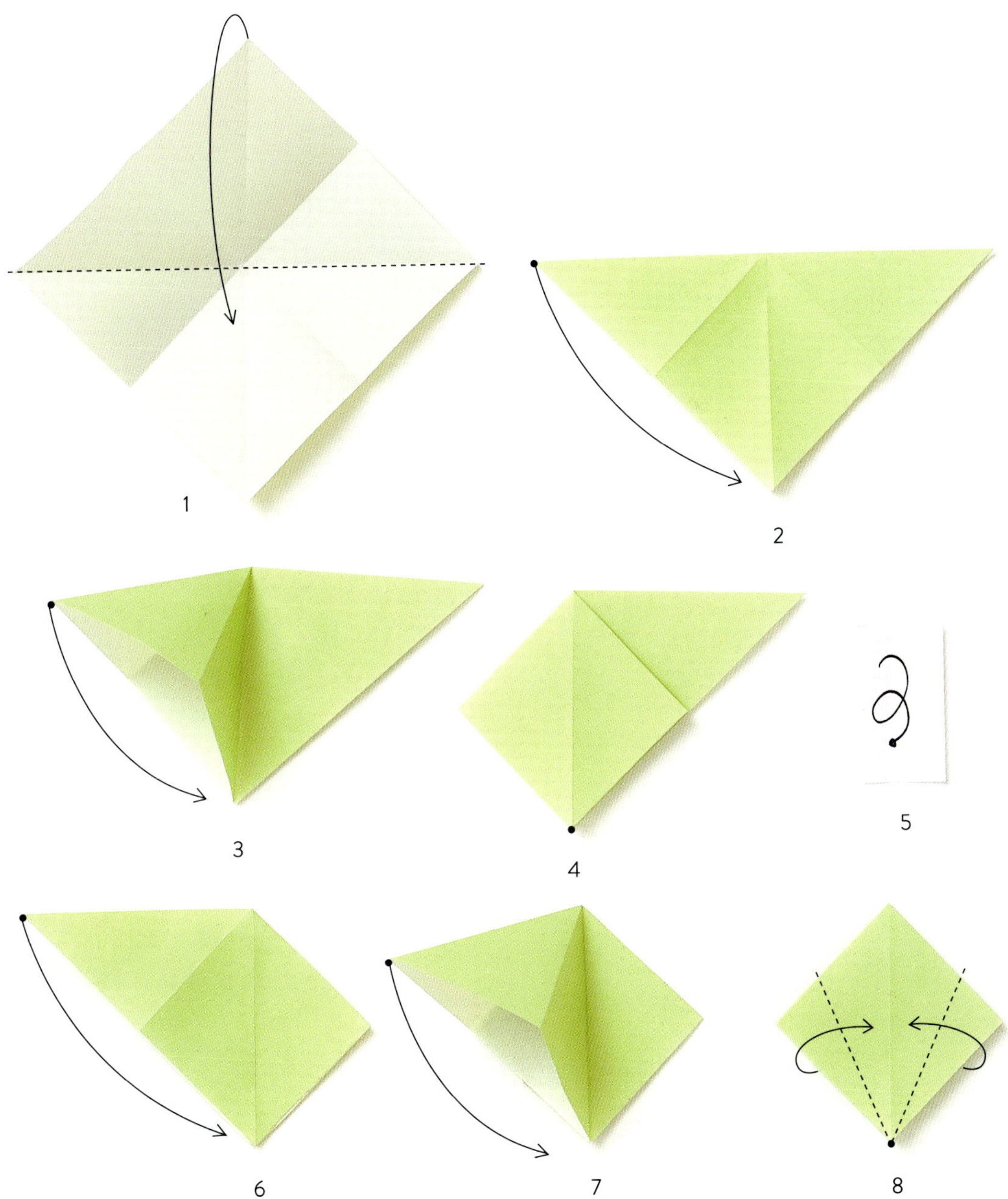

1. Place your square white side up and mark the creases of the central diagonal, horizontal and vertical lines. Rotate on to one corner and fold in half to form a triangle. **2. 3. 4.** Fold the LH point to the bottom, opening out the fold to form a diamond. Squash flat. **5.** Flip over. **6. 7.** Fold the LH point to the bottom, opening out the fold to form a diamond. Squash flat. **8.** Fold the bottom RH and LH edges of the topmost flaps up to the central line.

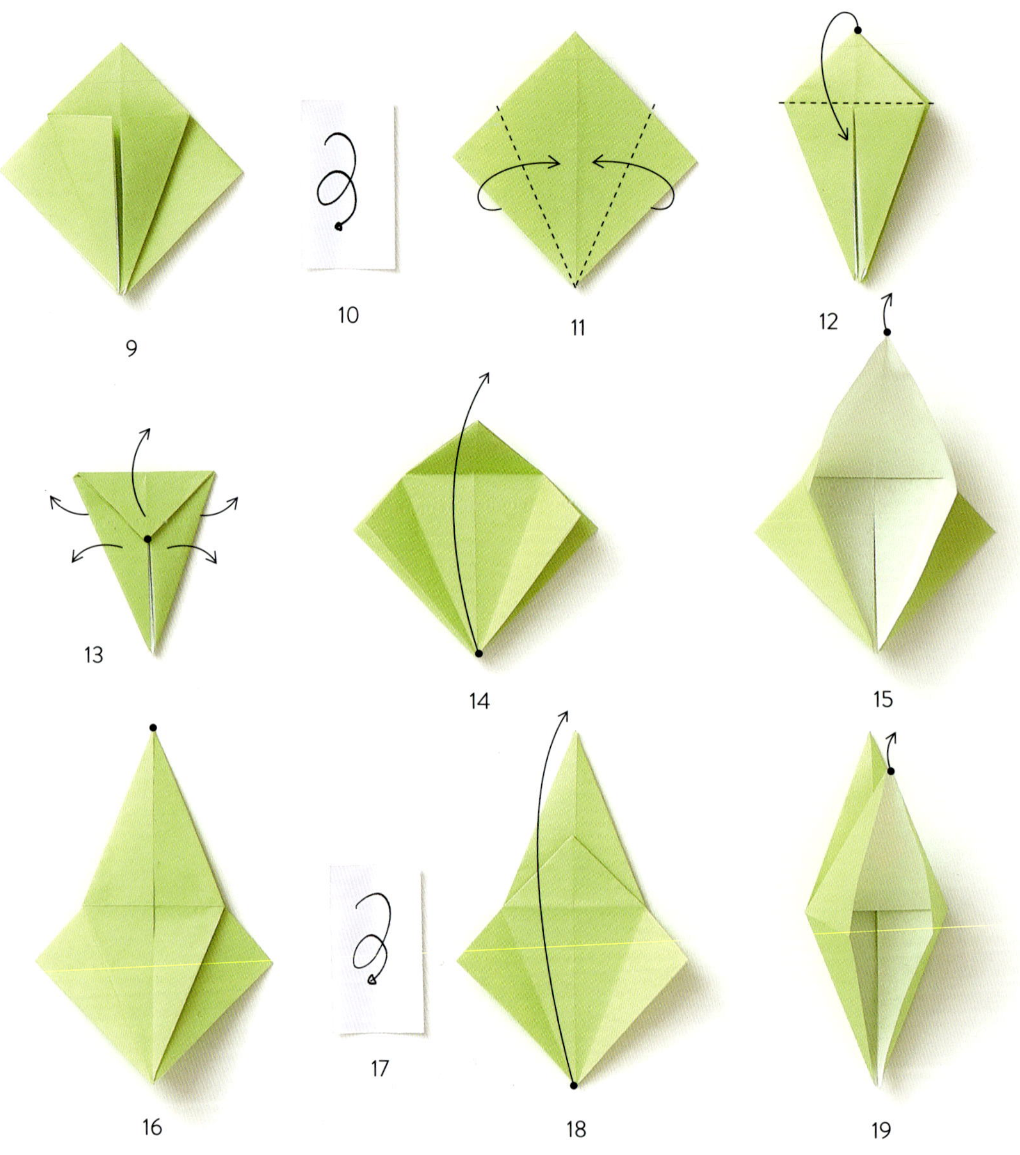

9. You now have this shape. **10.** Flip over. **11.** Fold the bottom RH and LH edges of the topmost flaps up to the central line. **12.** Fold the top point along the dotted line. **13.** Unfold all the flaps. **14. 15. 16.** Pinch the bottom corner and pull it upwards carefully. Squash flat. **17.** Flip over. **18. 19.** Pinch the bottom corner and pull it upwards carefully. Squash flat.

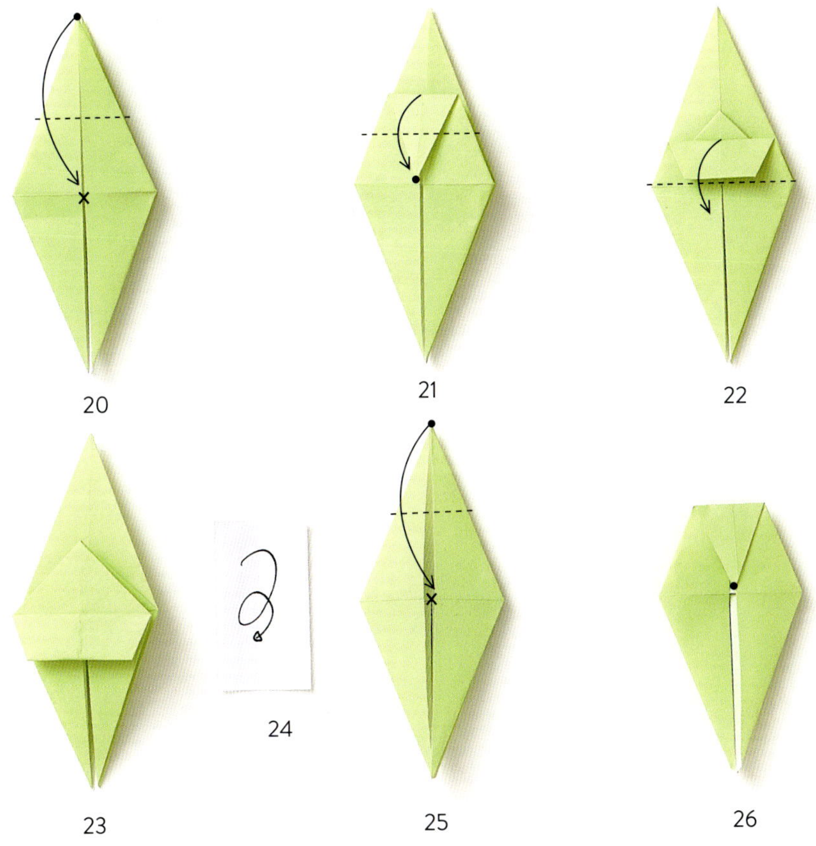

20. Fold the top layer to the central cross along the dotted line. **21.** Fold in half along the dotted line. **22.** Fold down the fold from step 21 along the dotted line. **23.** You now have this shape. **24.** Flip over. **25. 26.** Fold the top layer to the central cross along the dotted lines. You now have this shape.

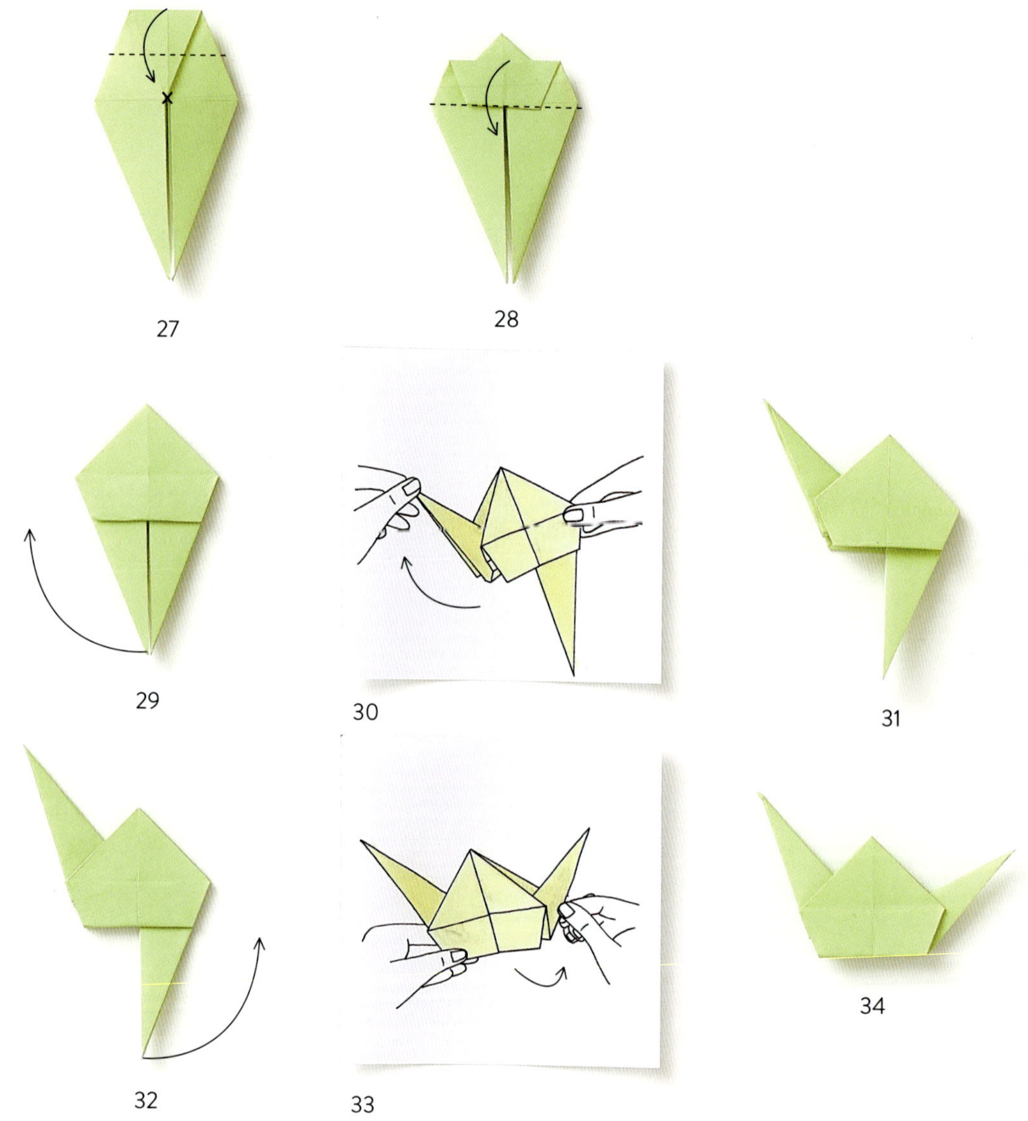

27. Fold to the central cross along the dotted line. **28.** Fold down the fold from step 27 along the dotted line.
29. 30. 31. Fold the LH point up. Open the fold and invert. Squash flat. You have formed the snail's head.
32. 33. 34. Fold the RH point up. Open the fold and invert it, pointing it at a lower angle than the head.
Squash flat. You have formed the tail.

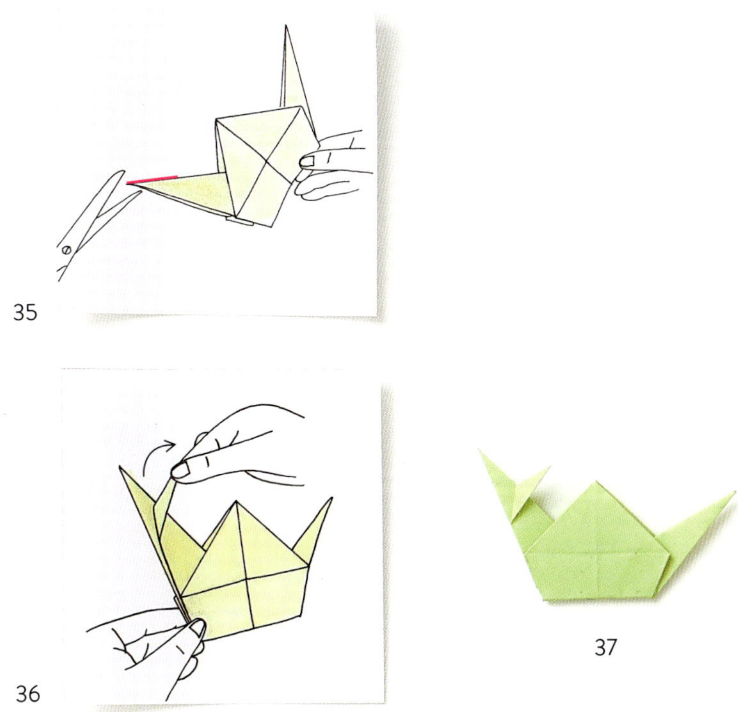

35

36

37

35. Cut the point of the head to create antennae. **36. 37.** Angle the antennae as you choose. Your snail is complete.

Cherry blossom

Level ●●●●○

Size

10cm
(4in)

8cm
(3¼in)

8cm
(3¼in)

15cm (6in)

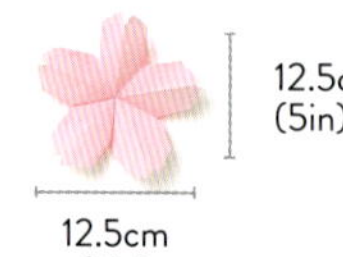

12.5cm
(5in)

12.5cm
(5in)

20cm (8in)

15.5cm
(6⅛in)

15.5cm (6⅛in)

Tip
You will need a pair of scissors.

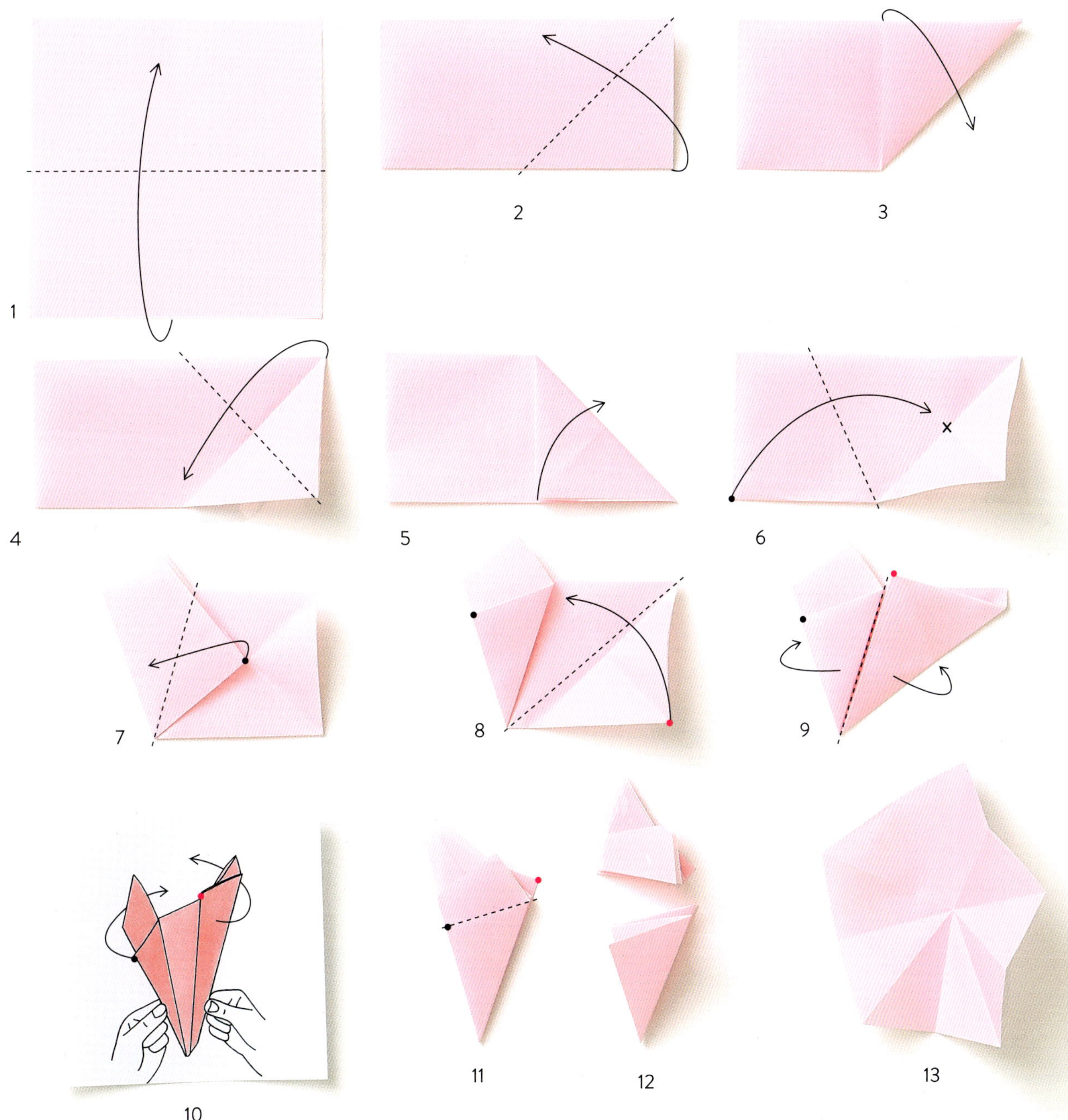

1. Place your square white side up and mark the crease of the central horizontal line. Fold in half along the dotted line. **2. 3.** Fold the RH edge along the diagonal following the dotted line. Unfold. **4. 5.** Fold the RH edge along the other diagonal. Unfold. **6.** Fold the bottom LH point to the central cross of the RH side. **7.** Fold along the dotted line. **8. 9.** Fold along the dotted line. You now have this shape. **10.** Fold the top flaps behind. **11. 12.** Cut along the dotted line. You now have this shape. **13.** Unfold.

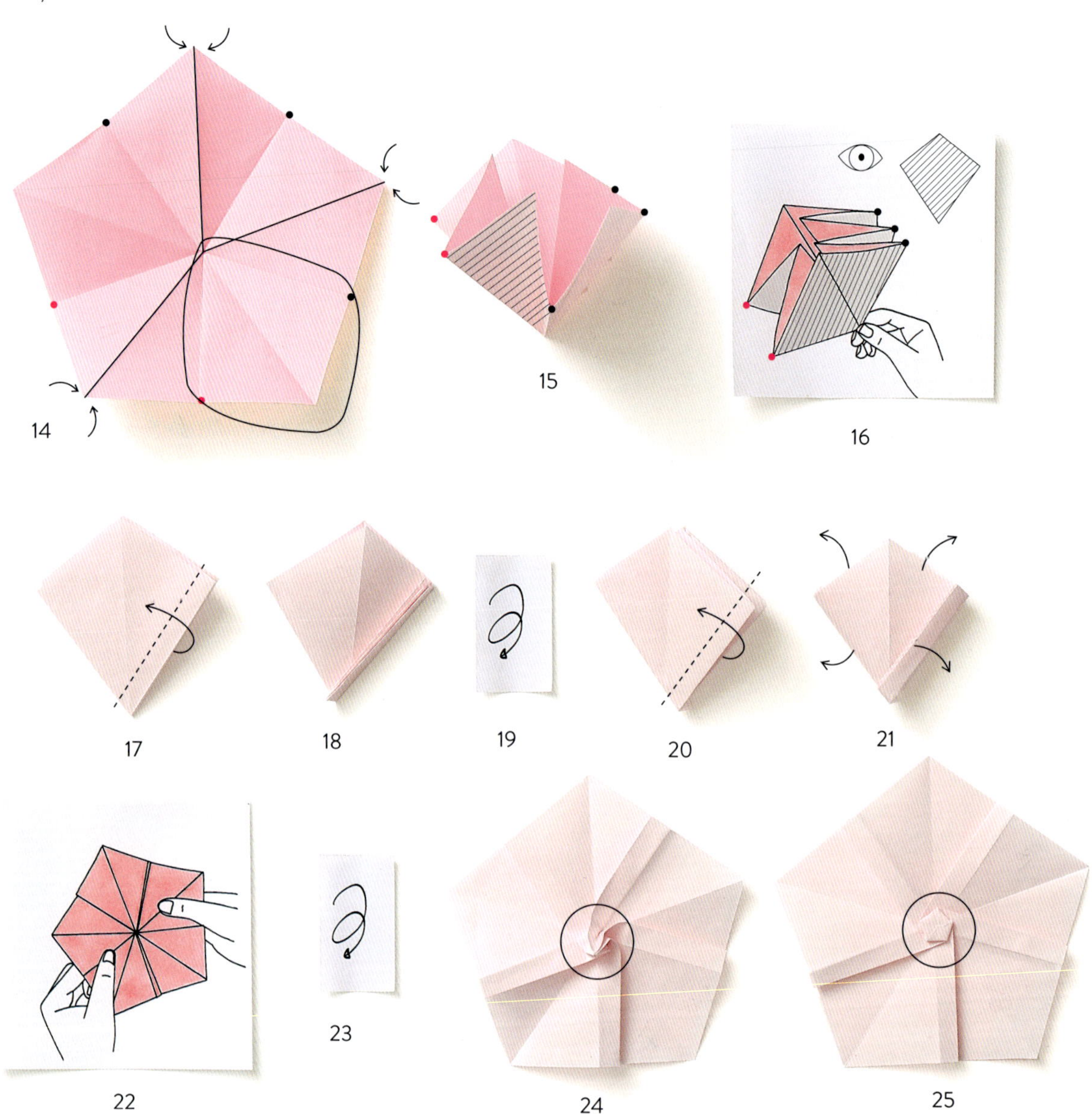

14. 15. 16. Form accordion folds by inverting the folds along the black lines to obtain a kite shape. You will have two folds in one direction and three in the other. **17. 18.** Fold all the layers on the RH edge along the dotted line. **19.** Flip over. **20.** Fold all the layers on the RH edge along the dotted line. **21. 22.** Gently open out. **23.** Flip over. **24. 25.** Flatten the centre of the flower to obtain a little star. Even if you don't achieve this step, your flower will still be very pretty!

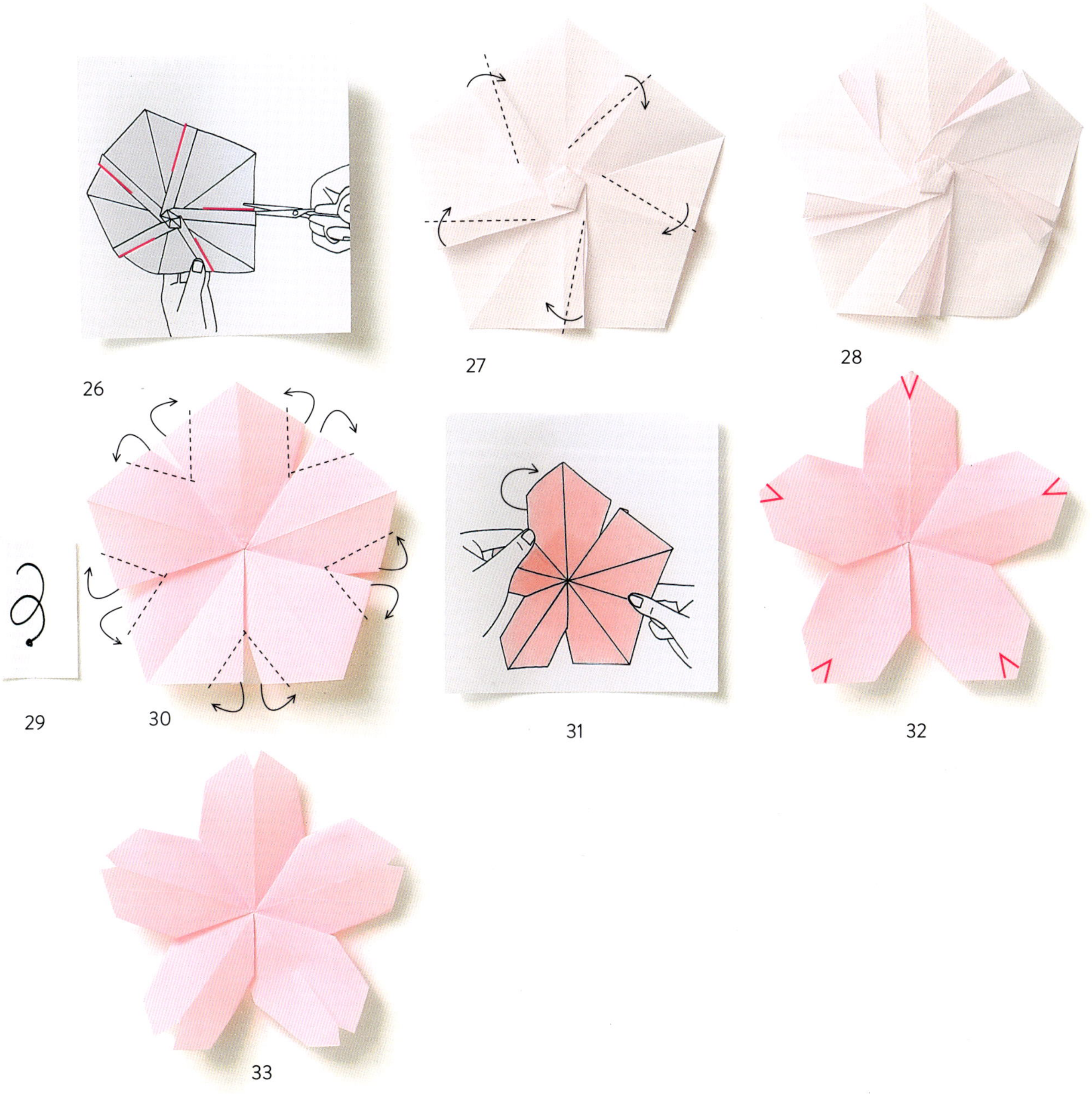

26. On the back, cut the inside of the five folds. **27. 28.** Fold along the dotted lines. You now have this shape. **29.** Flip over. **30. 31.** Fold behind along the dotted lines. **32.** Cut little triangles in each petal as shown. **33.** Your cherry blossom is complete.

Mouse

Level ●●●○○

Size

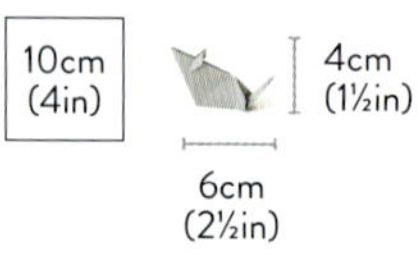
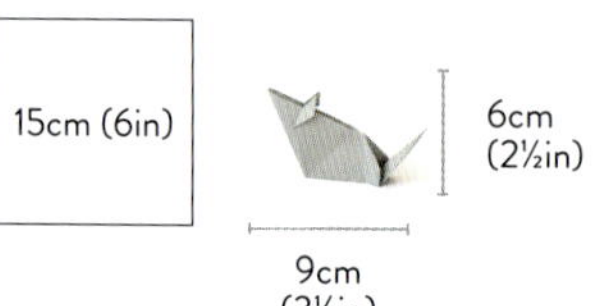
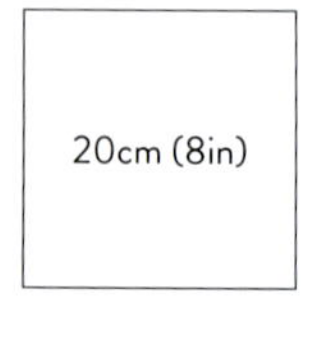
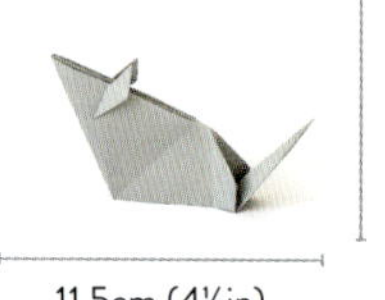

Tip

This design will stand up by itself.

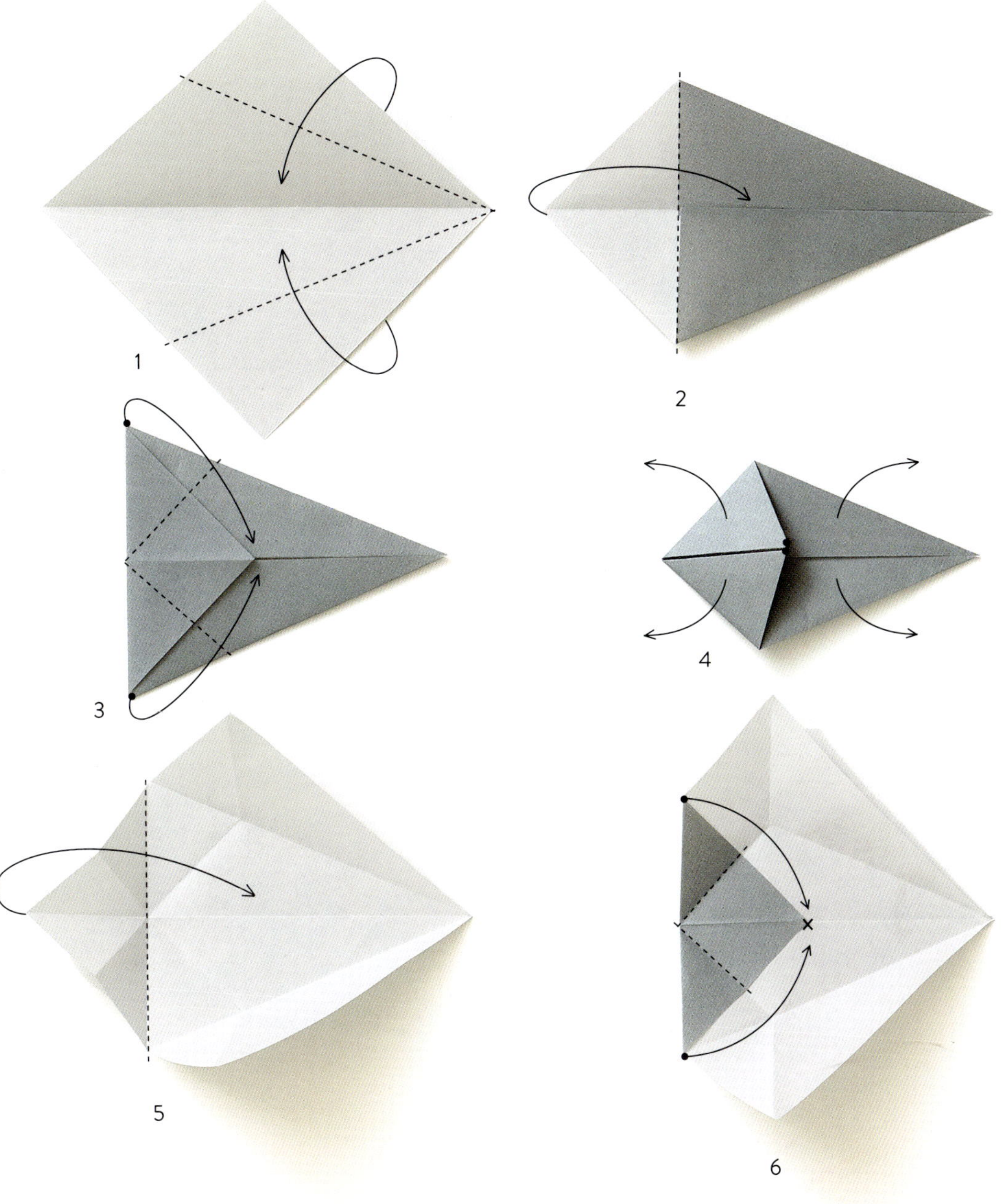

1. Place your square white side up and mark the crease of the diagonal line. Rotate on to one corner. Fold the edges to the central line. Squash flat. **2.** Fold the point to the right along the dotted line. **3.** Fold to the central line along the dotted lines. **4.** Open out all the folds. **5.** Fold along the dotted line. **6.** Pinch at the black dots and fold them towards the central cross.

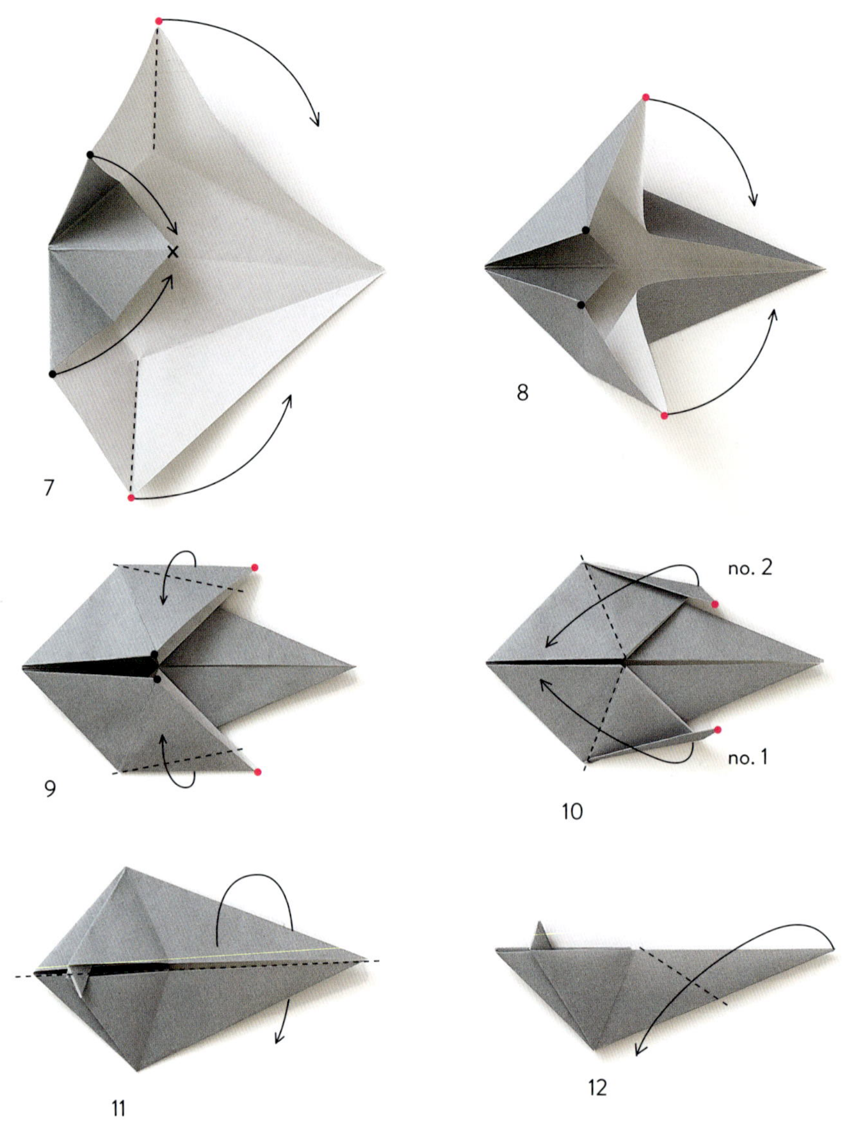

7. 8. Following on from step 6, bring the two red dots over the top as shown. **9.** Fold along the dotted lines. **10.** Fold dot no. 1 along the dotted line, then dot no. 2. **11.** Fold the top half behind. Squash flat. **12.** Fold along the dotted line.

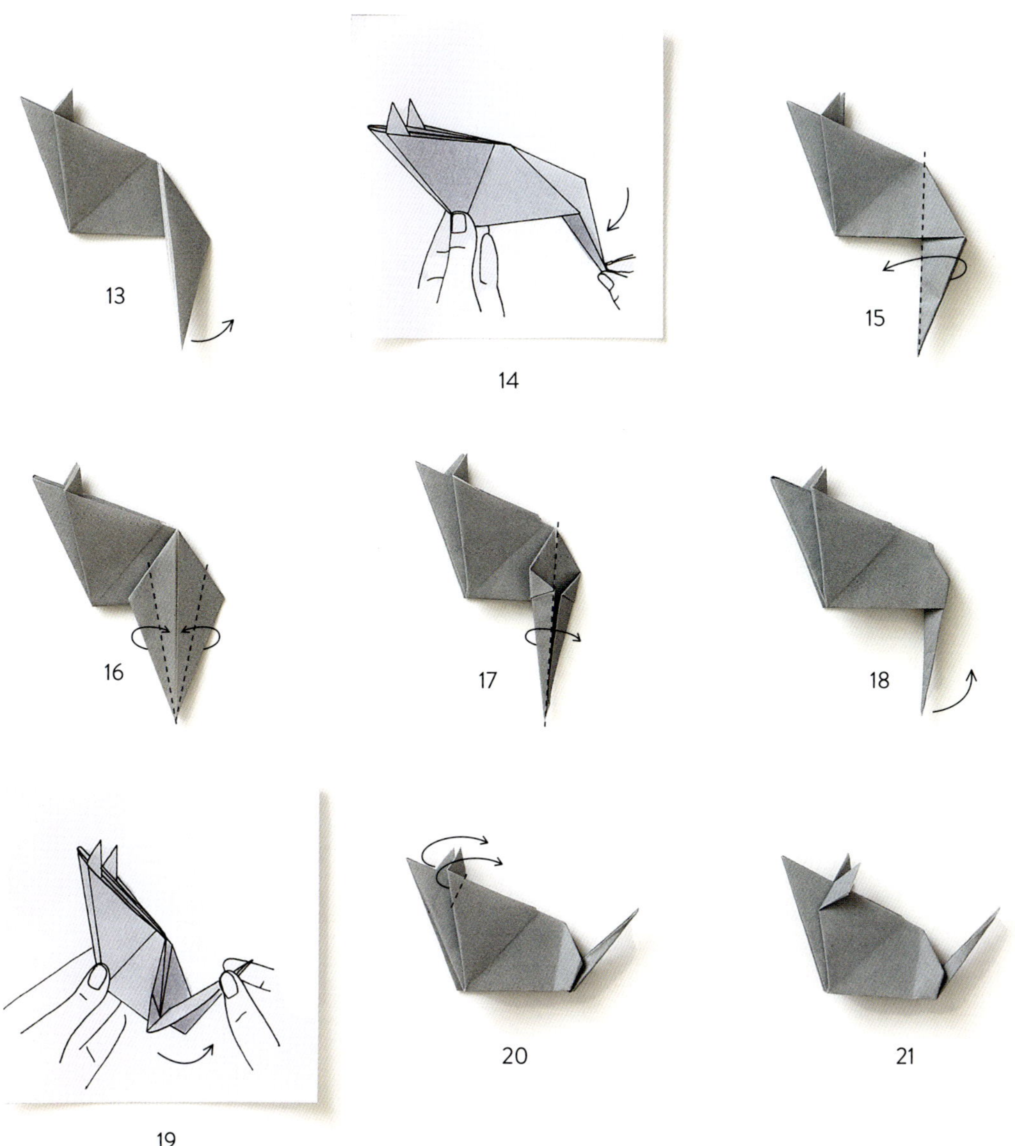

13. 14. Open out the fold, invert and squash flat. **15.** Open the uppermost flap to the left. **16.** Fold to the central line along the dotted lines. **17.** Fold in half. **18. 19.** Open the fold and invert, pulling the point upwards. Squash flat. **20.** Fold outwards along the dotted lines. You have formed the ears. **21.** Your mouse is complete.

Rabbit

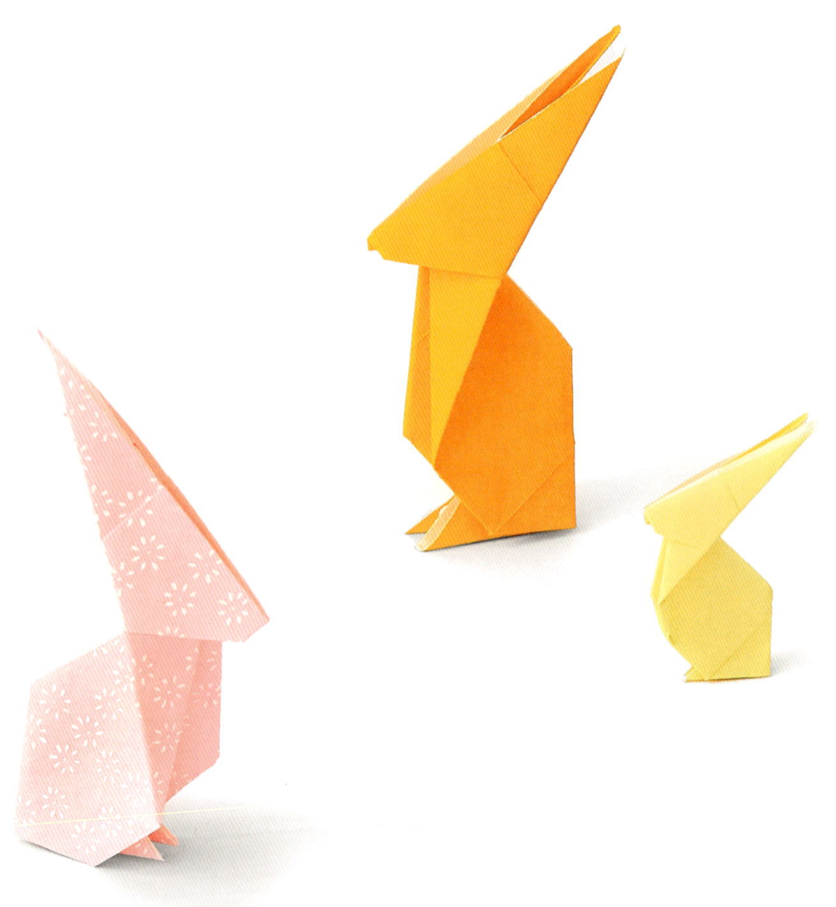

Level ●●●○○

Size

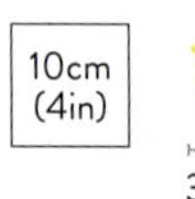
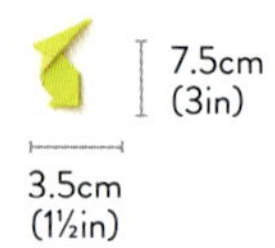
7.5cm (3in)

3.5cm (1½in)

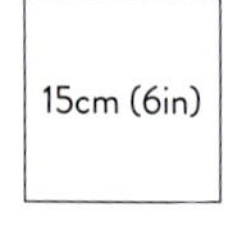
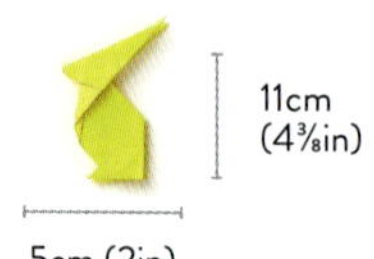
11cm (4⅜in)

5cm (2in)

20cm (8in)

14cm (5½in)

6.5cm (2½in)

Tip

This design will stand up by itself.

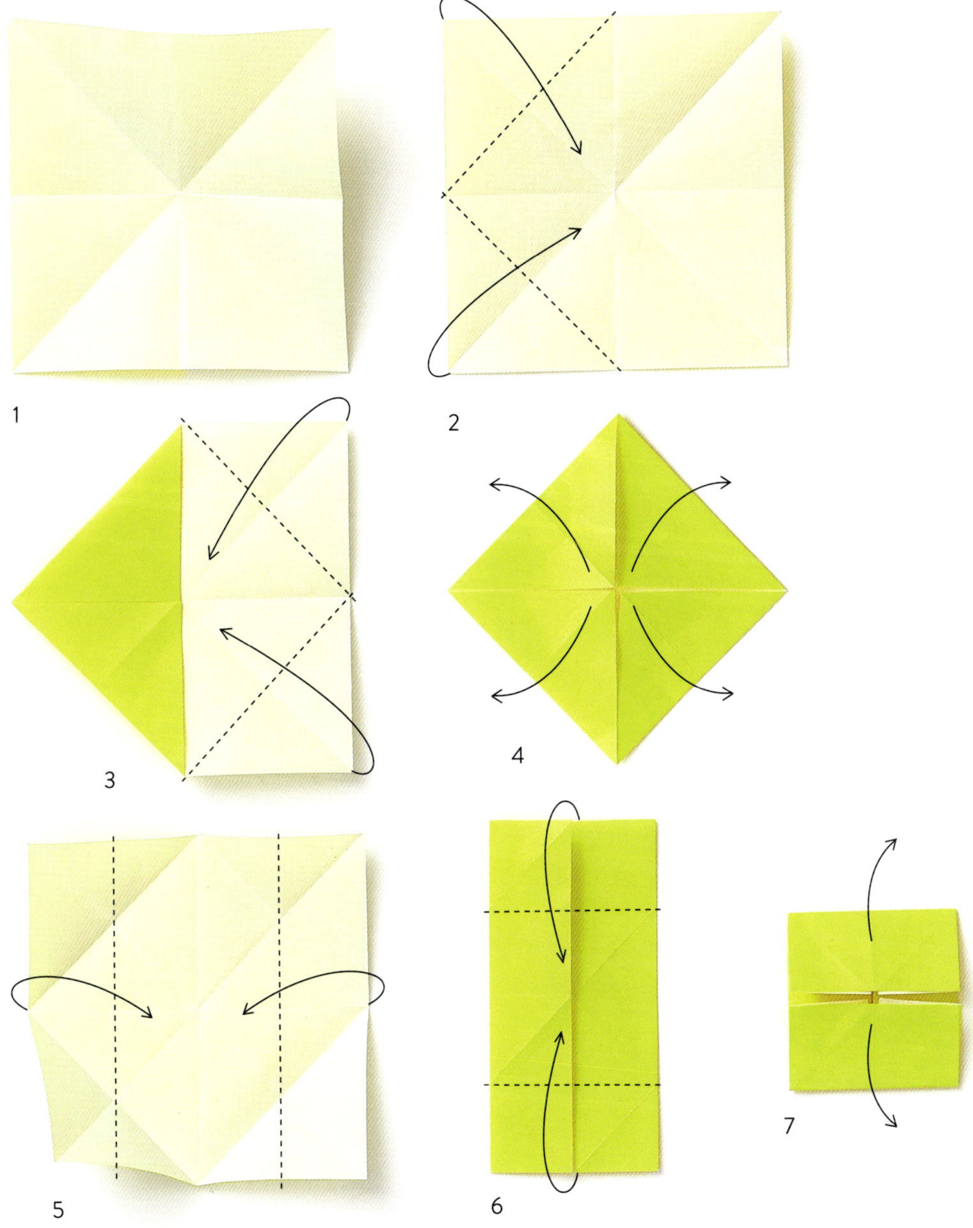

1. Place your square white side up, mark the creases of the central diagonal, horizontal and vertical lines.
2. Fold along the dotted lines. **3.** Fold along the dotted lines. **4.** Unfold. **5.** Fold to the central line along the dotted lines. **6.** Fold to the central line along the dotted lines. **7.** Unfold these last two folds.

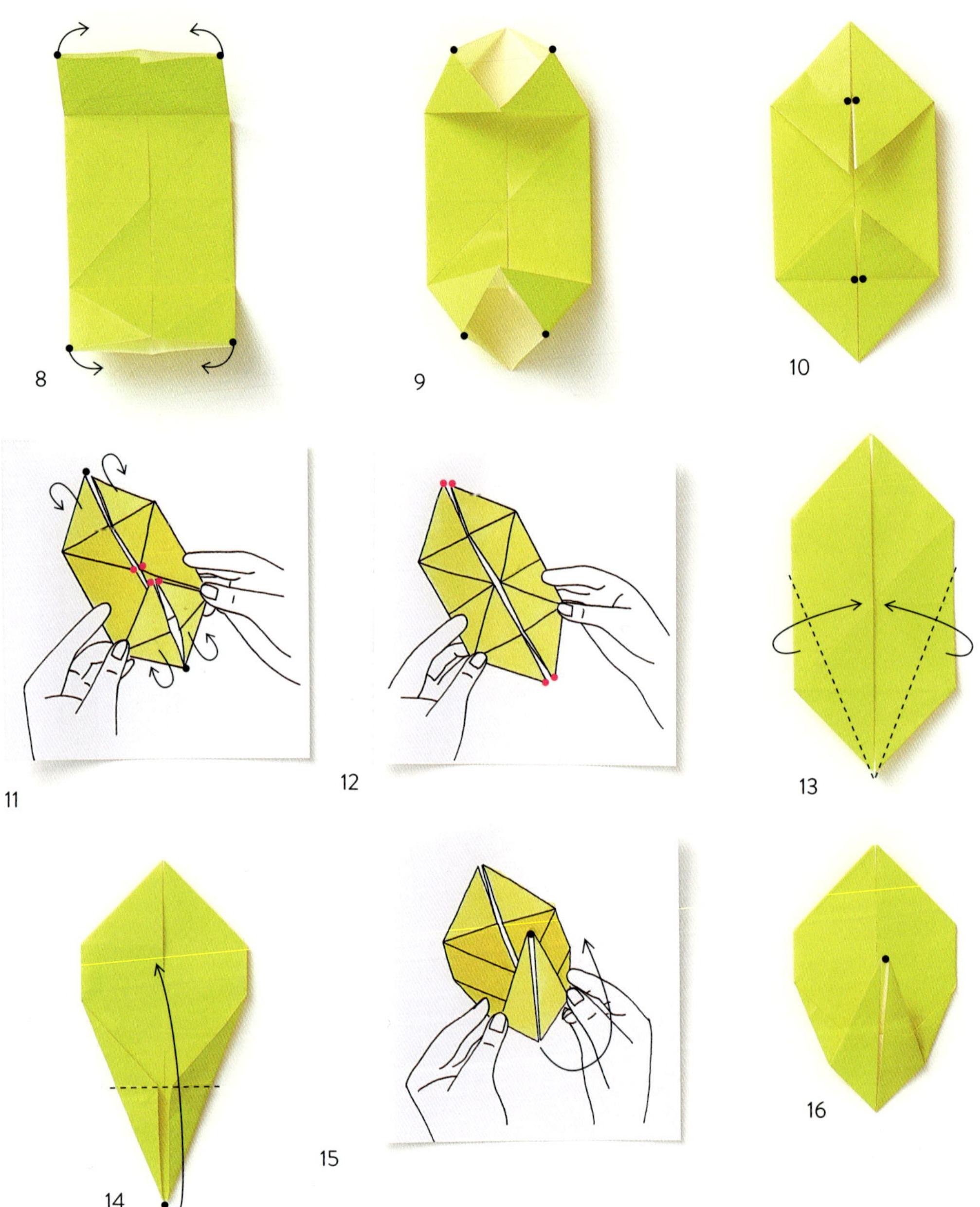

8. 9. 10. Open out, bring the two top dots together and squash flat. Do the same with the bottom two dots. You now have this shape. **11. 12.** Swing the black dots to the back so the red dots are at the top and bottom. **13.** Fold to the central line along the dotted lines. **14. 15. 16.** Fold upwards along the dotted line. You now have this shape.

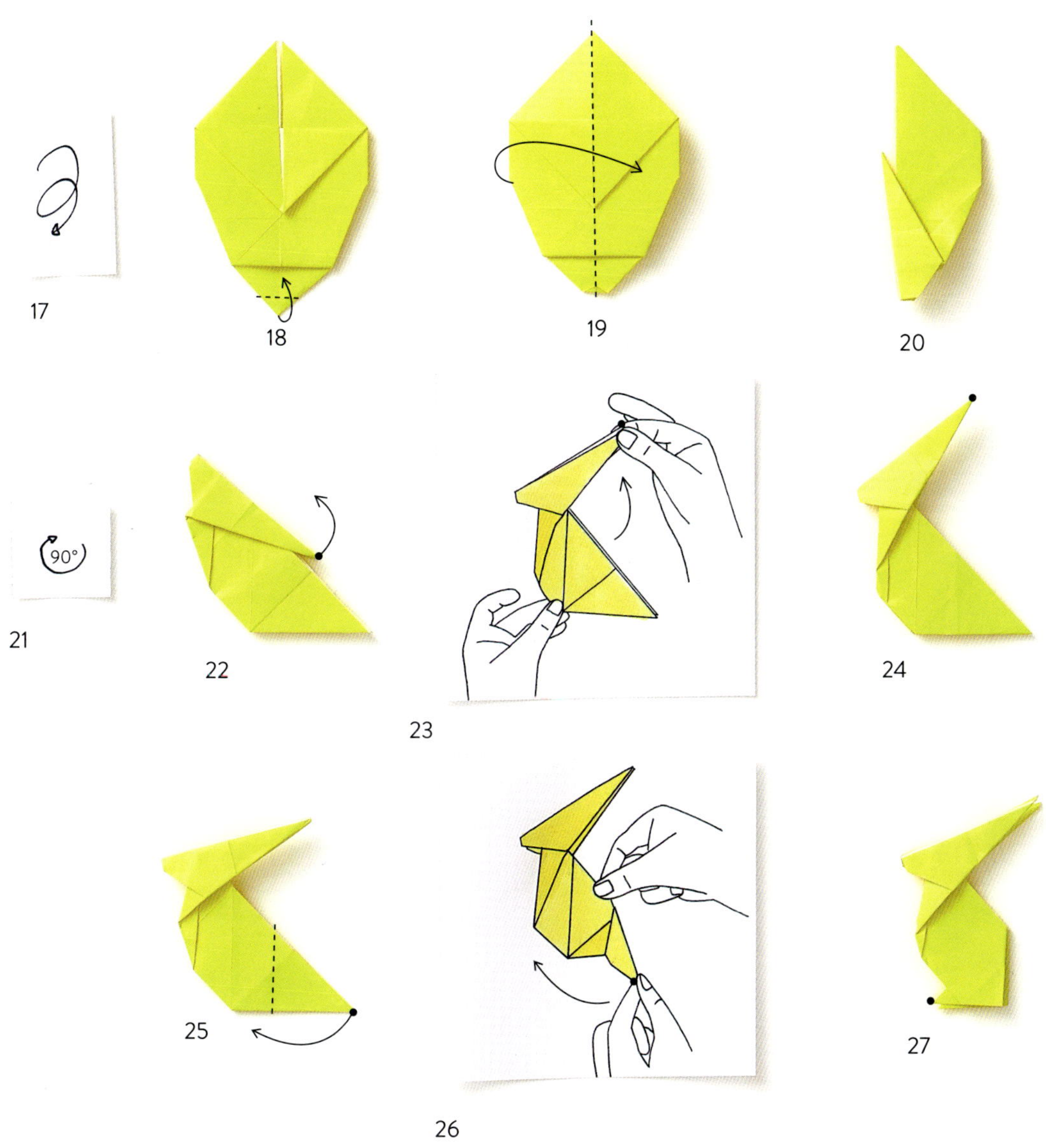

17. Flip over. **18.** Fold along the dotted line. **19. 20.** Fold in half to the right. You now have this shape.
21. Rotate clockwise 90°. **22. 23. 24.** Pinch the two dots, pull upwards and squash flat.
25. 26. 27. Fold along the dotted line. Unfold, and fold the two points inside. You have formed the rabbit's legs. Your rabbit is complete.

Ginkgo leaf

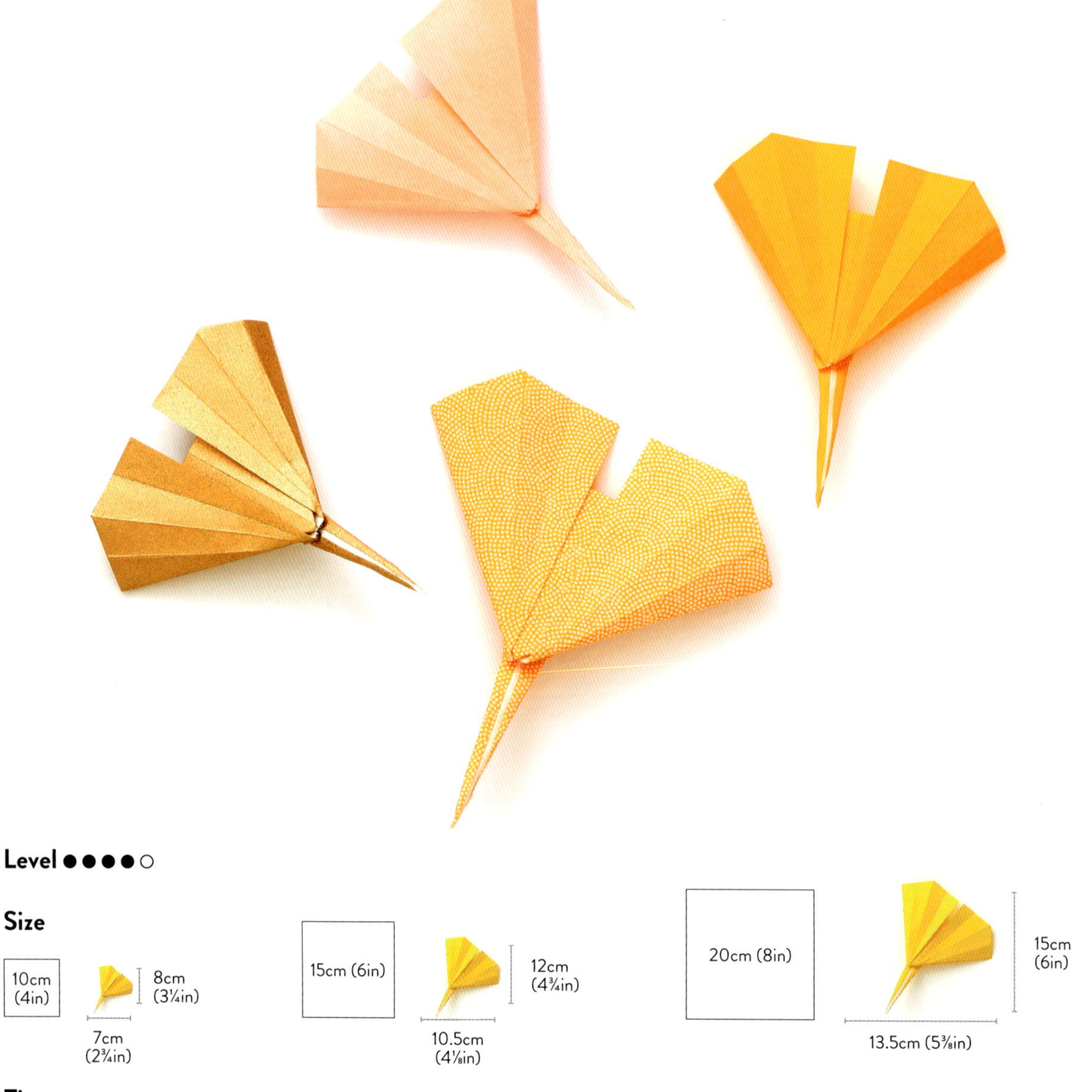

Level ●●●●○

Size

10cm (4in) — 8cm (3¼in) / 7cm (2¾in)

15cm (6in) — 12cm (4¾in) / 10.5cm (4⅛in)

20cm (8in) — 15cm (6in) / 13.5cm (5⅜in)

Tip

You need to mark the creases very firmly in steps 6 to 9 to form attractive veins.

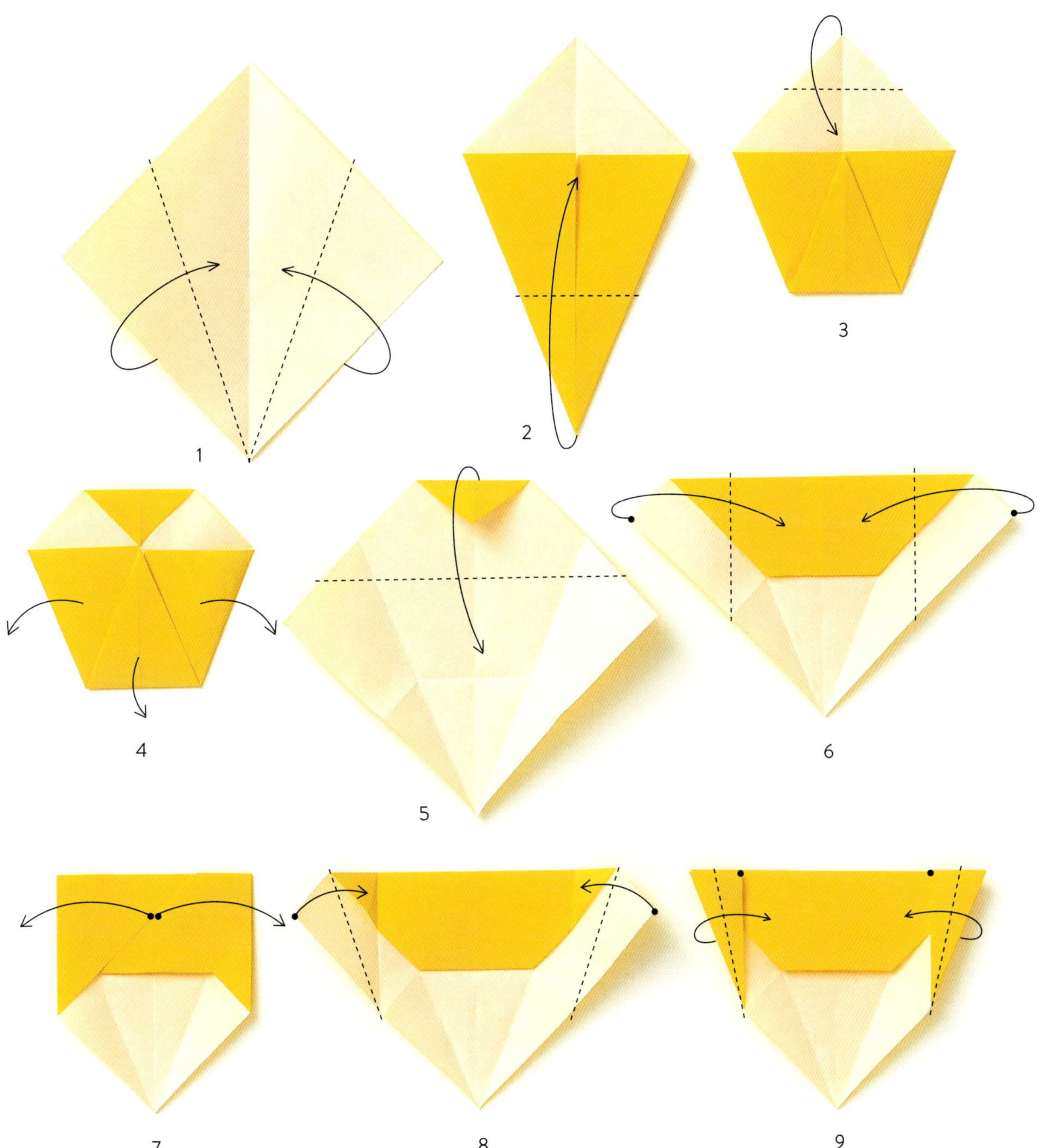

1. Place your square white side up and mark the crease of the diagonal line. Rotate on to one corner. Fold to the central line along the dotted lines. **2.** Fold the bottom point along the dotted line. **3.** Fold the top point along the dotted line. **4.** Unfold the bottom and side folds. **5.** Fold the top section along the dotted line. **6.** Fold along the dotted lines. **7.** Unfold the last folds. **8.** Fold along the dotted lines. **9.** Fold along the dotted lines.

Ginkgo leaf

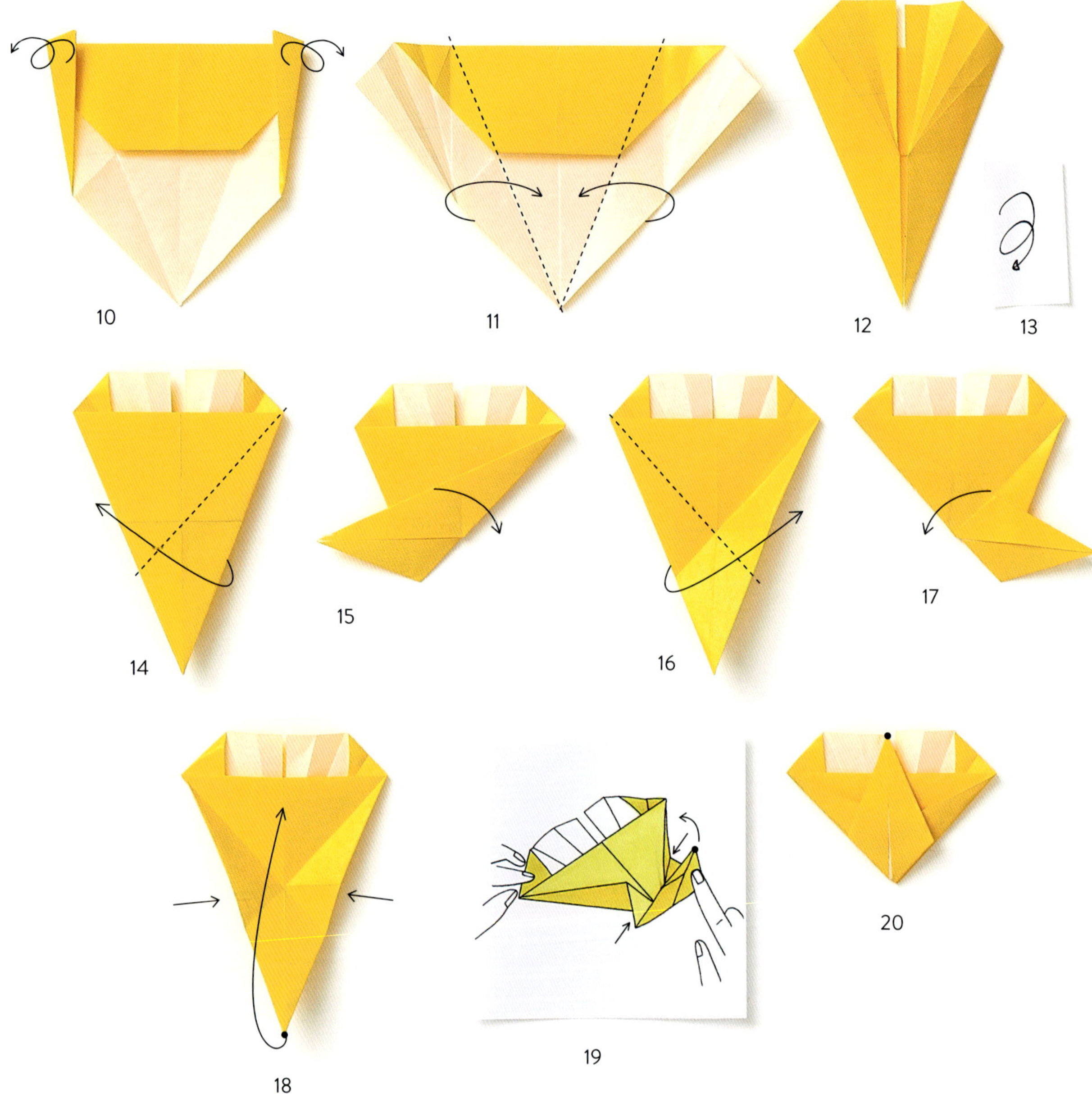

10. Unfold the last two folds on both sides. **11. 12.** Fold to the central line along the dotted lines. You now have this shape. **13.** Flip over. **14. 15.** Fold to the left along the dotted line that passes through the central point. Unfold. **16. 17.** Fold to the right along the dotted line that passes through the central point. Open out the fold. **18. 19. 20.** Fold the bottom point upwards while pushing in both sides at the same time, as shown in the drawing. Squash flat.

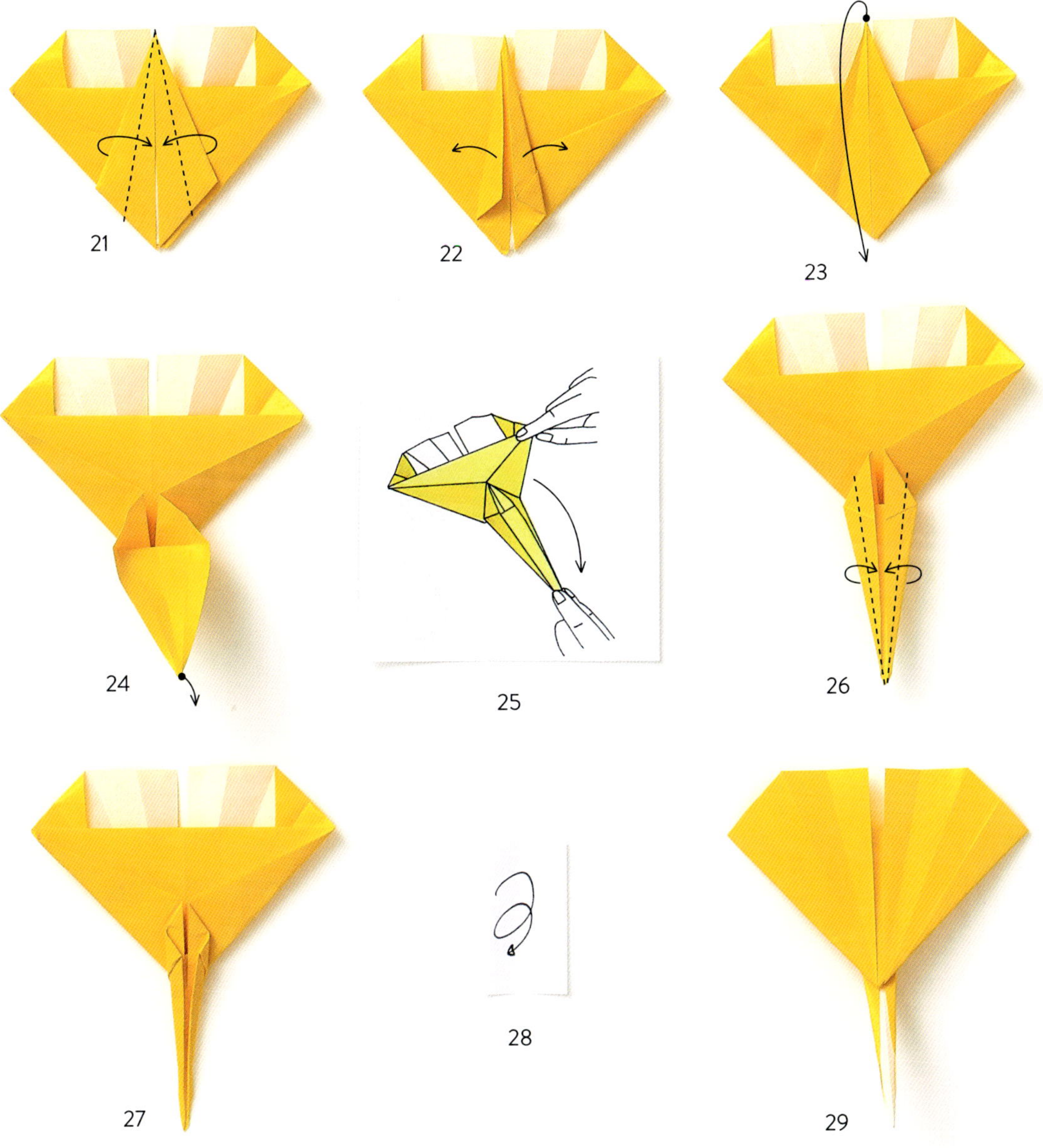

21. 22. Fold both edges to the central line along the dotted lines. Unfold these two folds. **23. 24. 25.** Pull the point gently downwards, inverting the folds. Squash flat. **26. 27.** Fold to the central line along the dotted lines. Squash flat. **28.** Flip over. **29.** Your ginkgo leaf is complete.

Morning glory

Level ●●●●○

Size

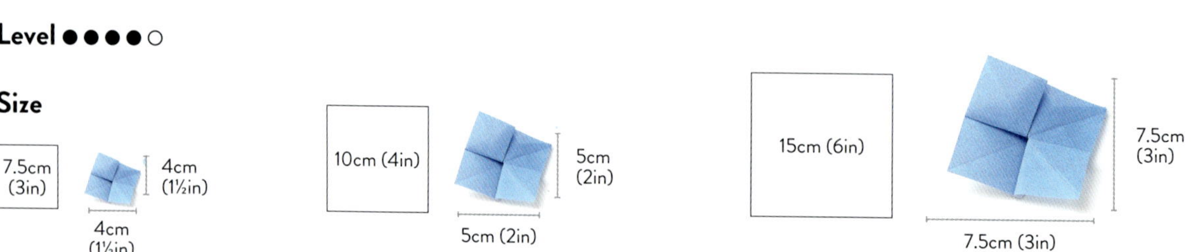

Tip

You can make this flower two- or three-dimensional!

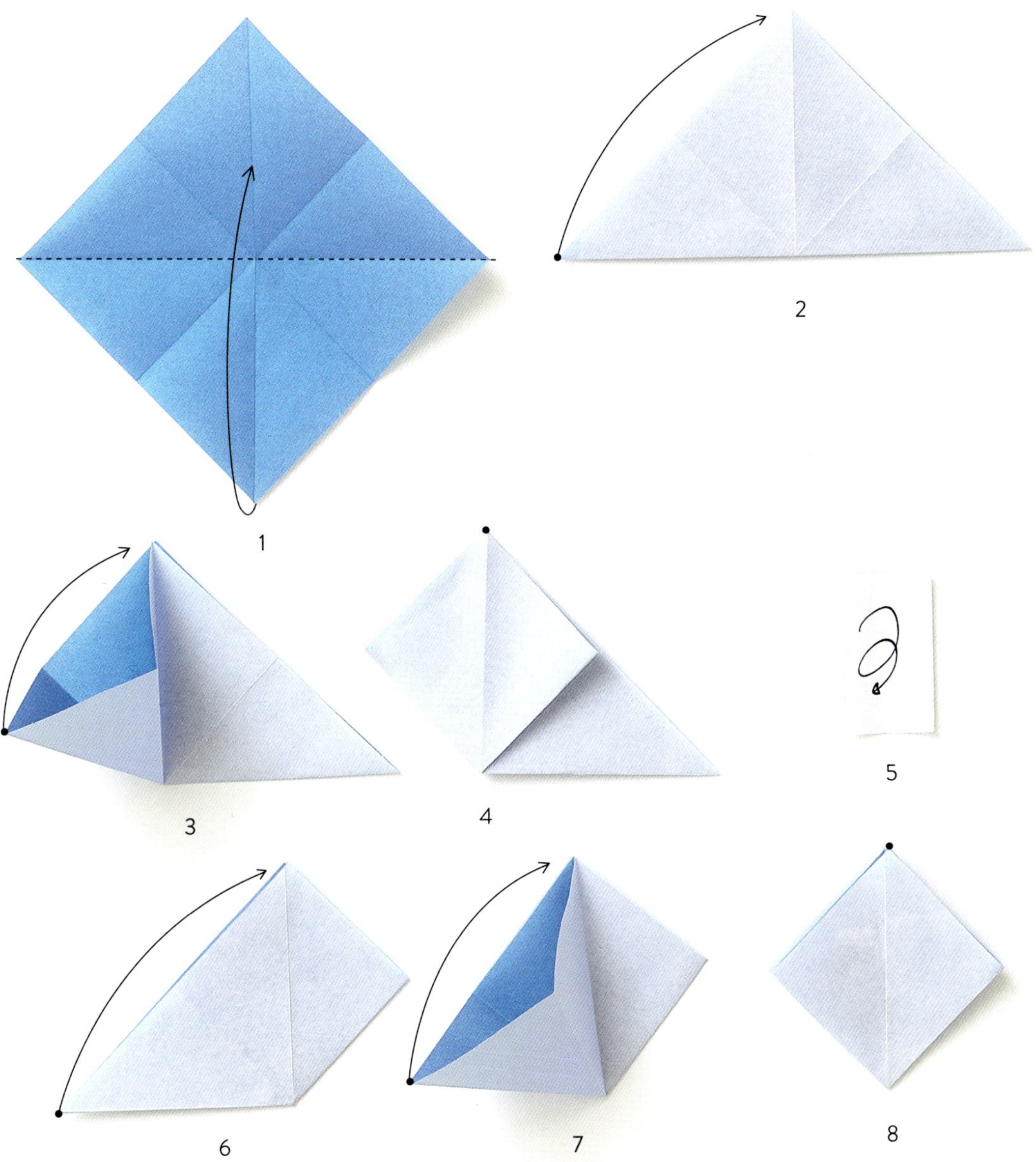

1. Place your square coloured side up. Mark the creases of the central diagonal, horizontal and vertical lines. Rotate on to one corner and fold in half to form a triangle. **2. 3. 4.** Fold the LH point to the top, opening out the fold to form a diamond. Squash flat. **5.** Flip over. **6. 7. 8.** Fold the LH point to the top, opening out the fold to form a diamond. Squash flat.

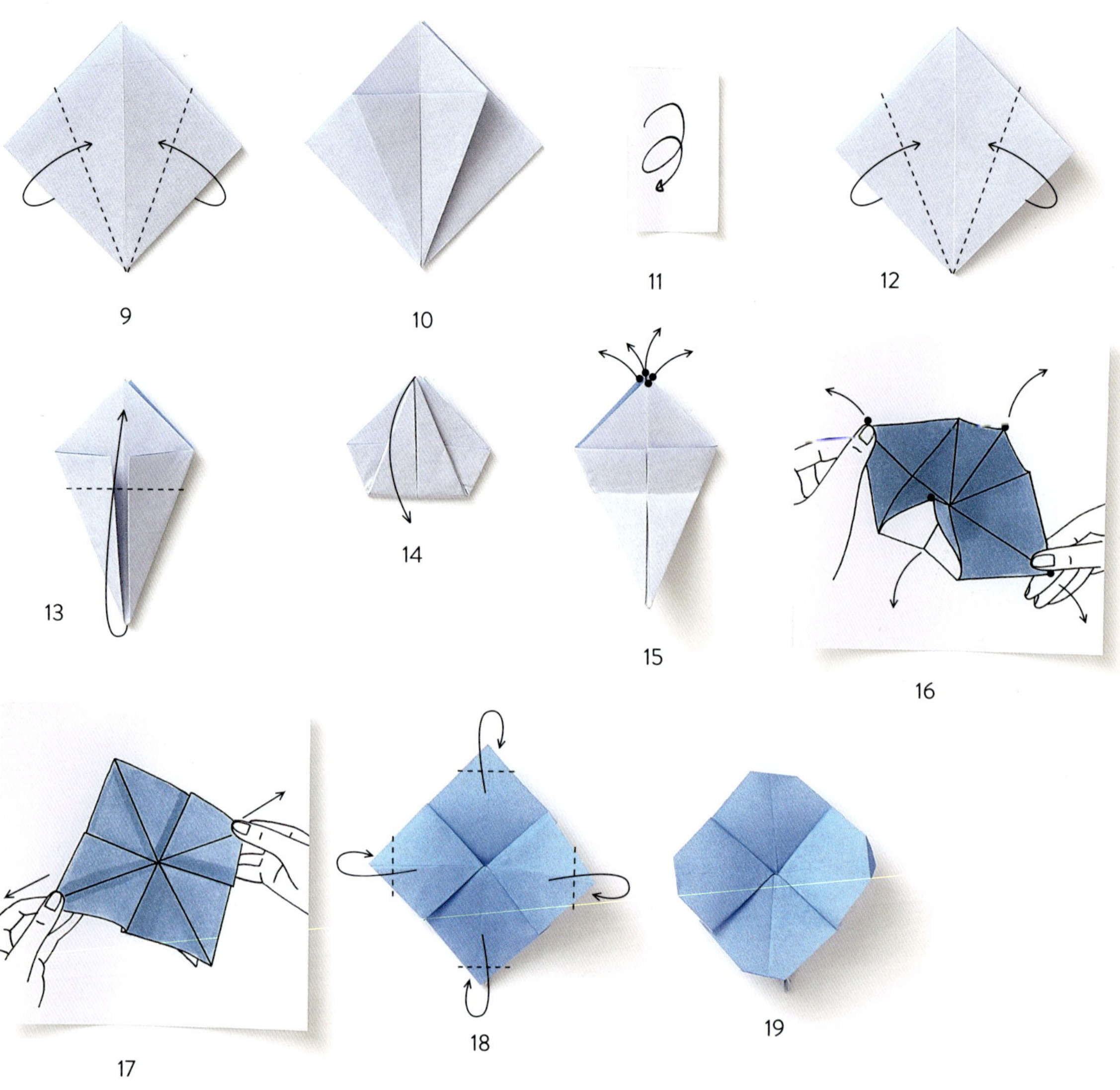

9. 10. Fold the RH and LH points of the top layer to the central line along the dotted lines. You now have this shape. **11.** Flip over. **12.** Fold the RH and LH points of the top layer to the central line along the dotted lines. **13.** Fold in half along the dotted line. **14.** Unfold. **15. 16.** Pinching the point with your fingers, open out all the top folds, pulling the four points outwards. **17.** Pull gently on the RH and LH points and flatten out. **18. 19.** Fold the four points behind along the dotted lines. Your morning glory is complete.

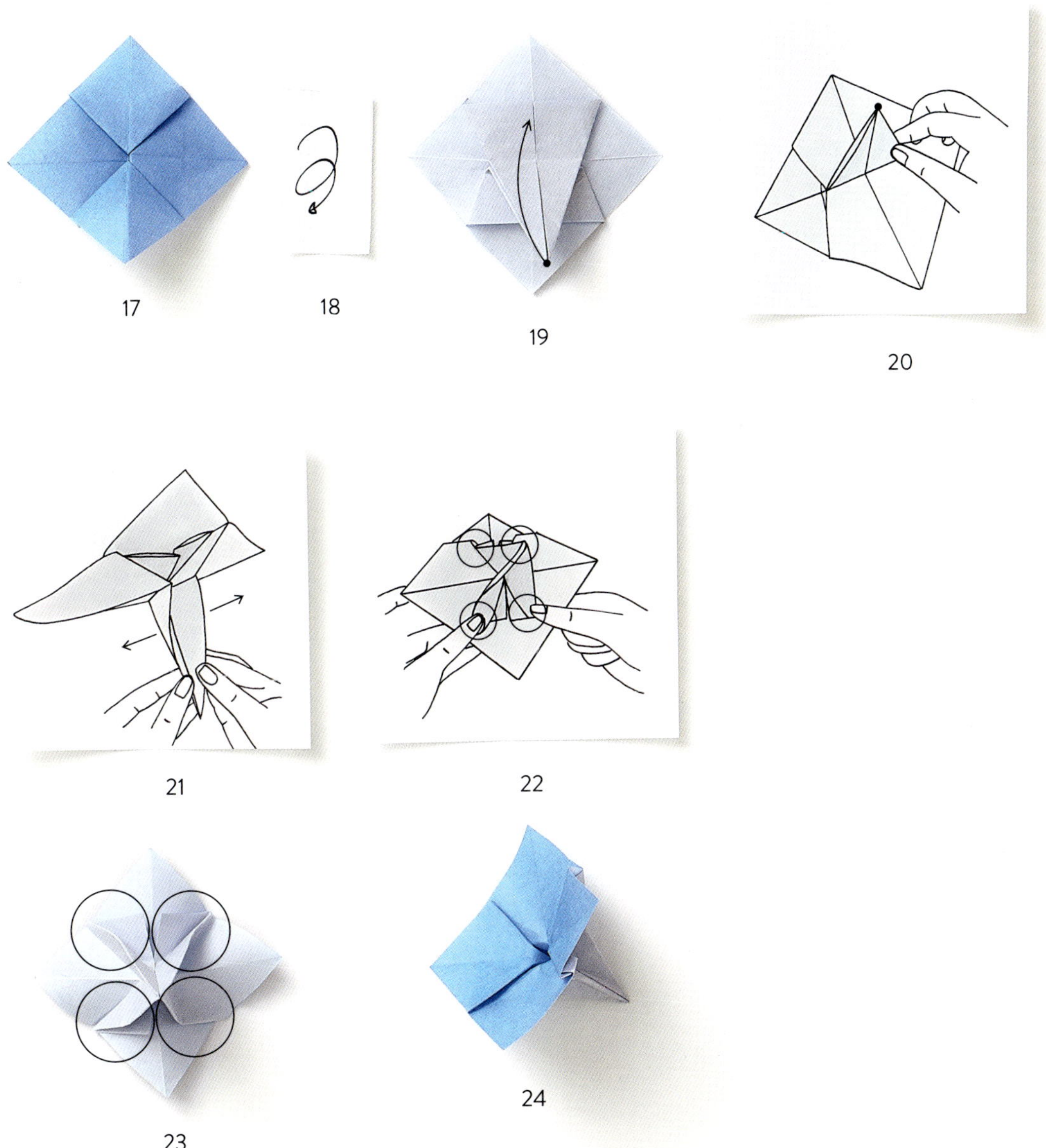

Variation: Follow the steps opposite up to and including step 17. **18.** Flip over. **19. 20.** Lift the bottom point to position it horizontally. You now have this shape. **21.** Pinch the base of the flower between your fingers and pull the folds apart to give it volume. **22. 23.** Lay the flower flat and press on the base with your fingers to structure it nicely. You now have this shape. **24.** Your three-dimensional morning glory is complete.

Campanula

Level ●●●●○

Size

7.5cm (3in)		4cm (1½in)
	2.5cm (2in)	

10cm (4in)		5cm (2in)
	3cm (1⅛in)	

15cm (6in)		7.5cm (3in)
	4.5cm (1¾in)	

Tip

You can apply a dab of glue at steps 23 and 26 to make it easier to open out the base of the flower. You can also attach this flower to a stem and make a bouquet.

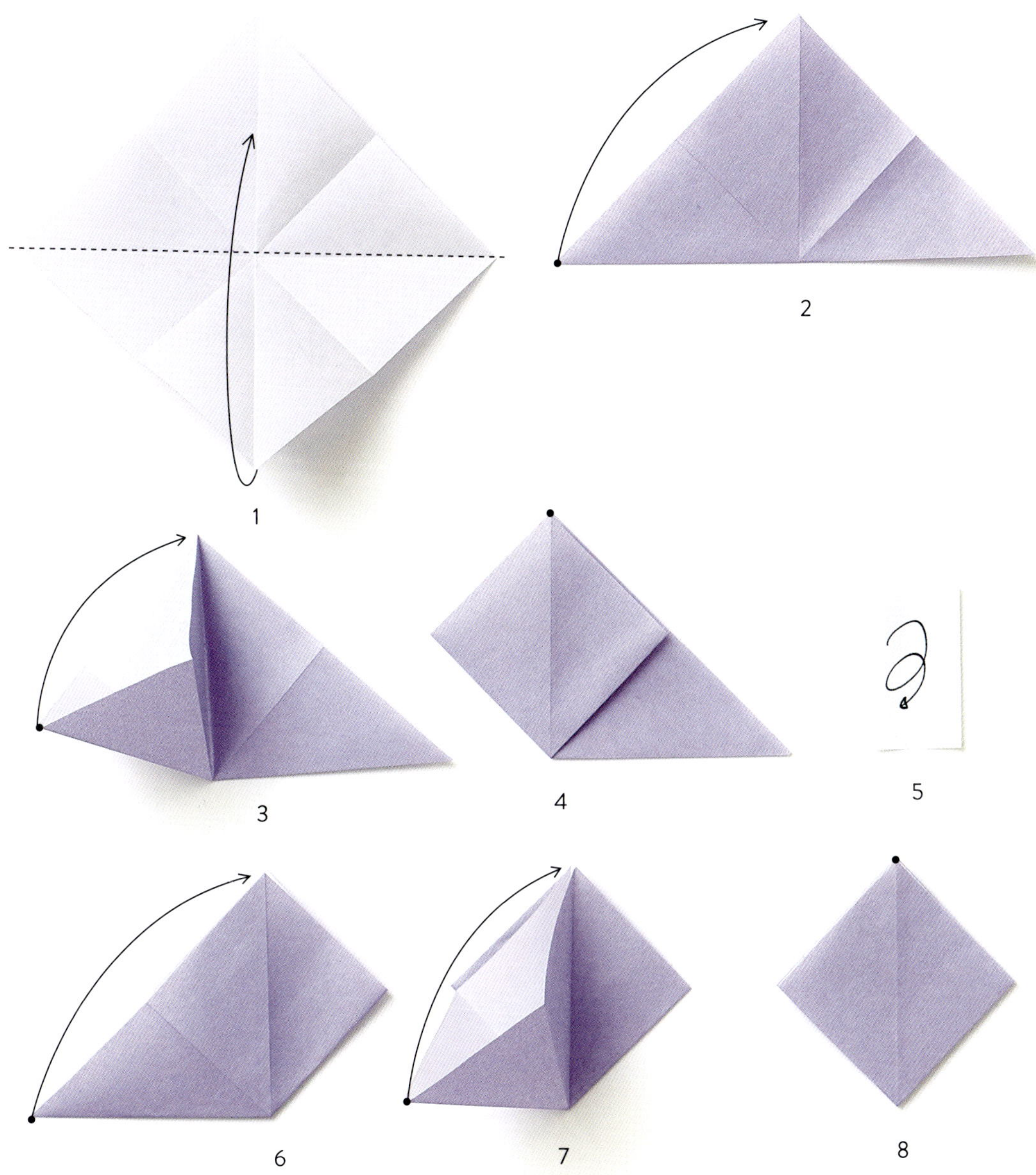

1. Place your square white side up, mark the creases of the central diagonal, horizontal and vertical lines. Rotate on to one corner and fold in half to form a triangle. **2. 3. 4.** Fold the LH point to the top, opening out the fold to form a diamond. Squash flat. **5.** Flip over. **6. 7. 8.** Fold the LH point to the top, opening out the fold to form a diamond. Squash flat.

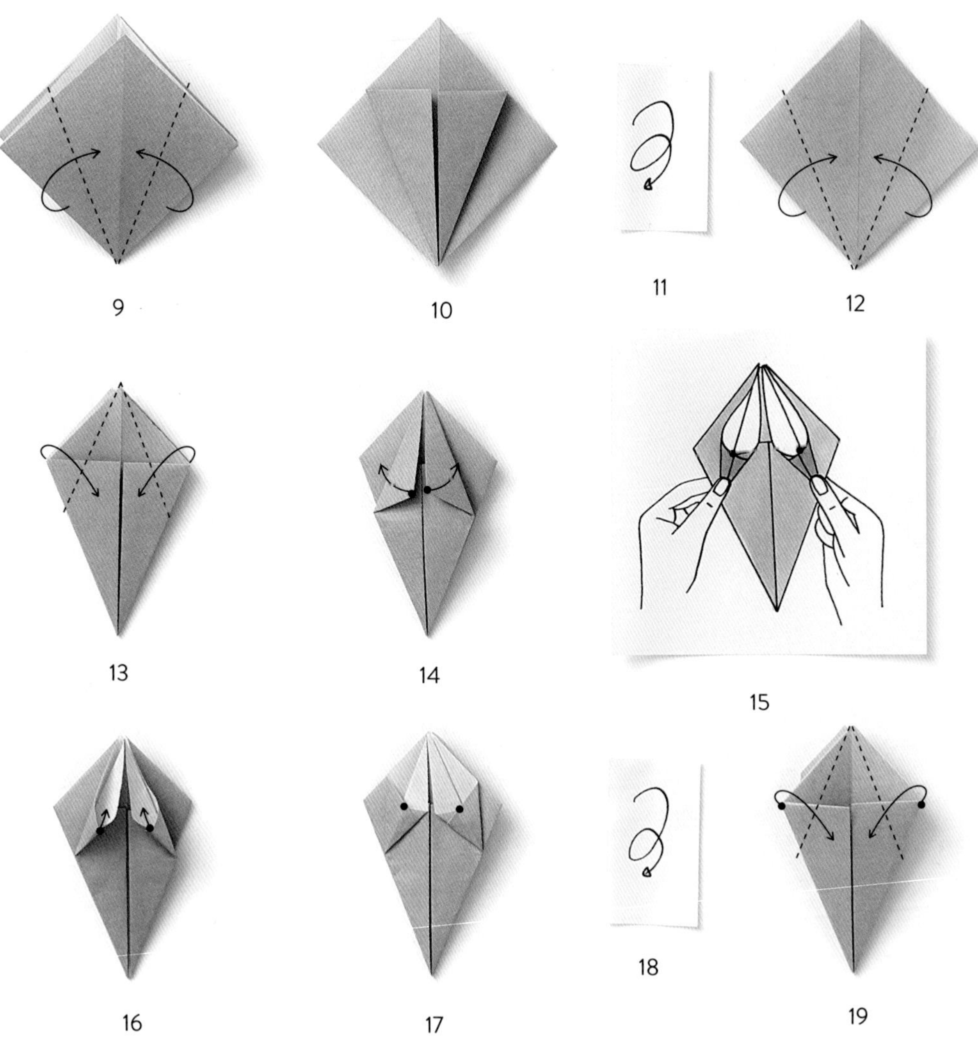

9. 10. Fold the RH and LH points to the central line along the dotted lines. **11.** Flip over. **12.** Fold to the central line along the dotted lines. **13.** Fold along the dotted lines. **14. 15. 16. 17.** Pinch at the dots and open out the two folds, exposing the white side of the paper. Squash flat. **18.** Flip over. **19.** Fold along the dotted lines.

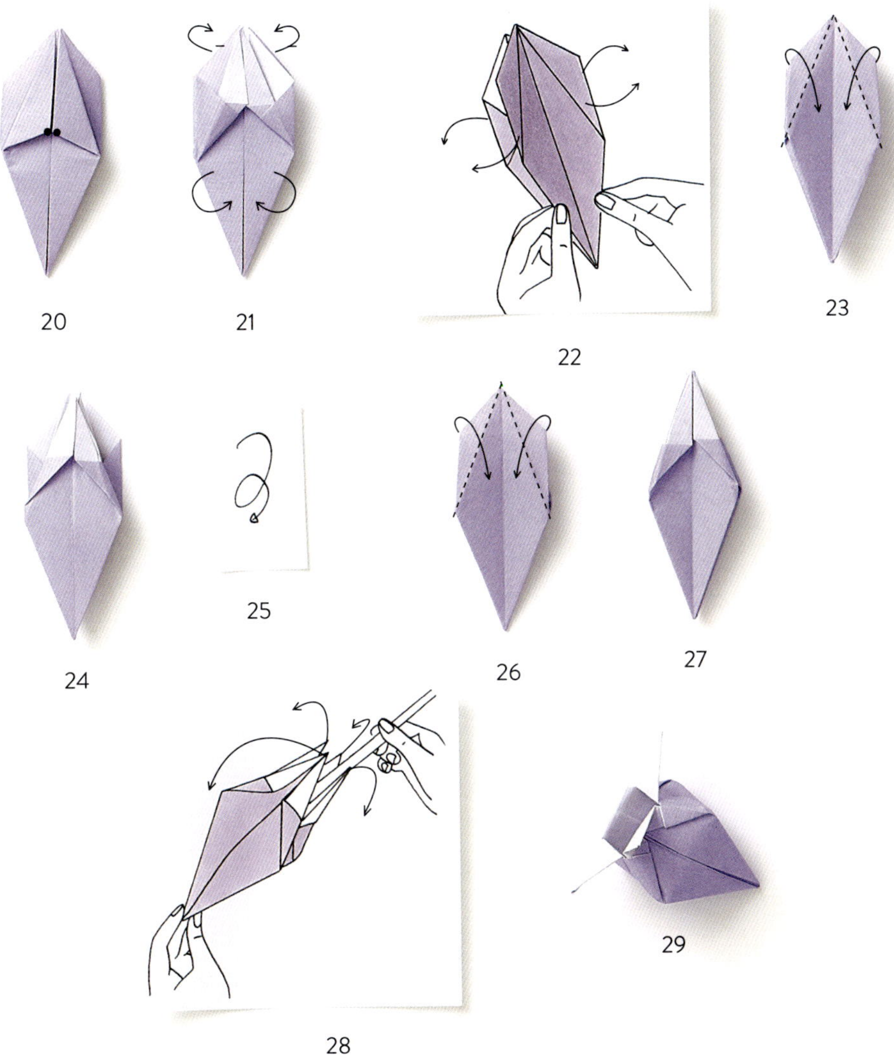

20. Pinch at the dots and open the two folds, exposing the white side of the paper as in steps 15 to 17. Squash flat. **21. 22.** Holding the flower between your fingers, fold the two front flaps and the two back flaps against each other. **23. 24.** Fold along the dotted lines and squash flat. You now have this shape. **25.** Flip over. **26. 27.** Fold along the dotted lines and squash flat. You now have this shape. **28.** Poke a long, thin stick such as a chopstick into your flower to 'inflate' it. Open out and curve the little petals. **29.** Your campanula is complete.

Cockerel

Level ● ● ● ● ○

Size

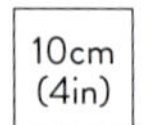
10cm
(4in)

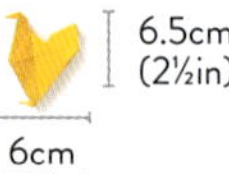

6.5cm
(2½in)

6cm
(2½in)

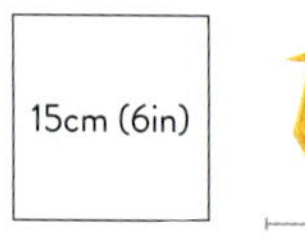
15cm (6in)

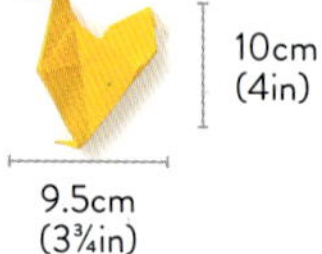
10cm
(4in)

9.5cm
(3¾in)

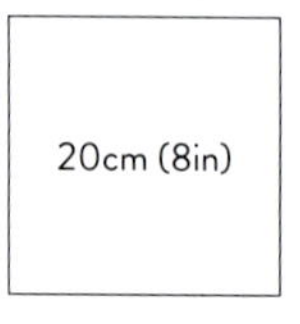
20cm (8in)

12.5cm
(5in)

12cm (4¾in)

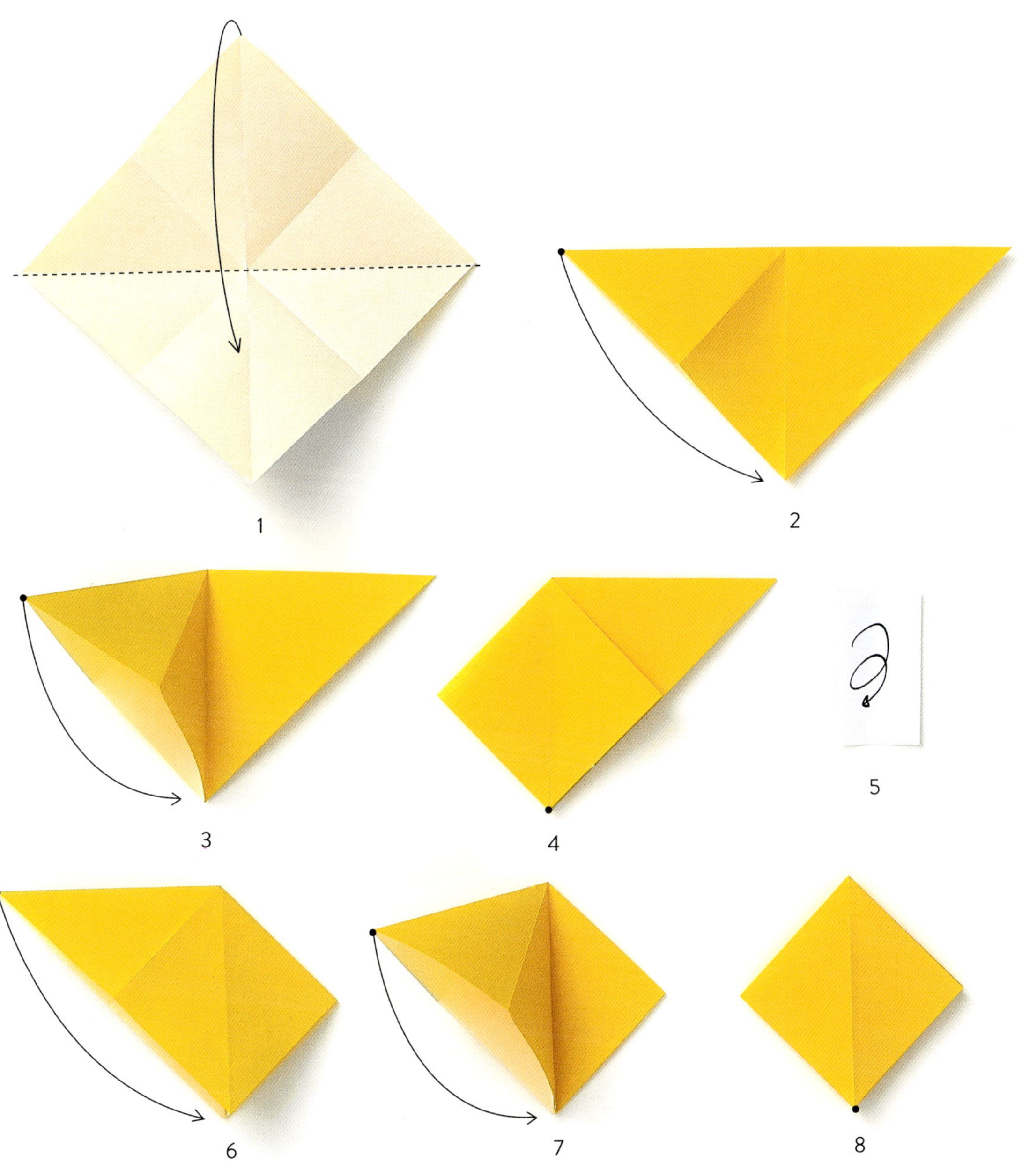

1. Place your square white side up, mark the creases of the central diagonal, horizontal and vertical lines. Rotate on to one corner and fold in half to form a triangle. **2. 3. 4.** Fold the LH point to the bottom, opening out the fold to form a diamond. Squash flat. **5.** Flip over. **6. 7. 8.** Fold the LH point to the top, opening out the fold to form a diamond. Squash flat.

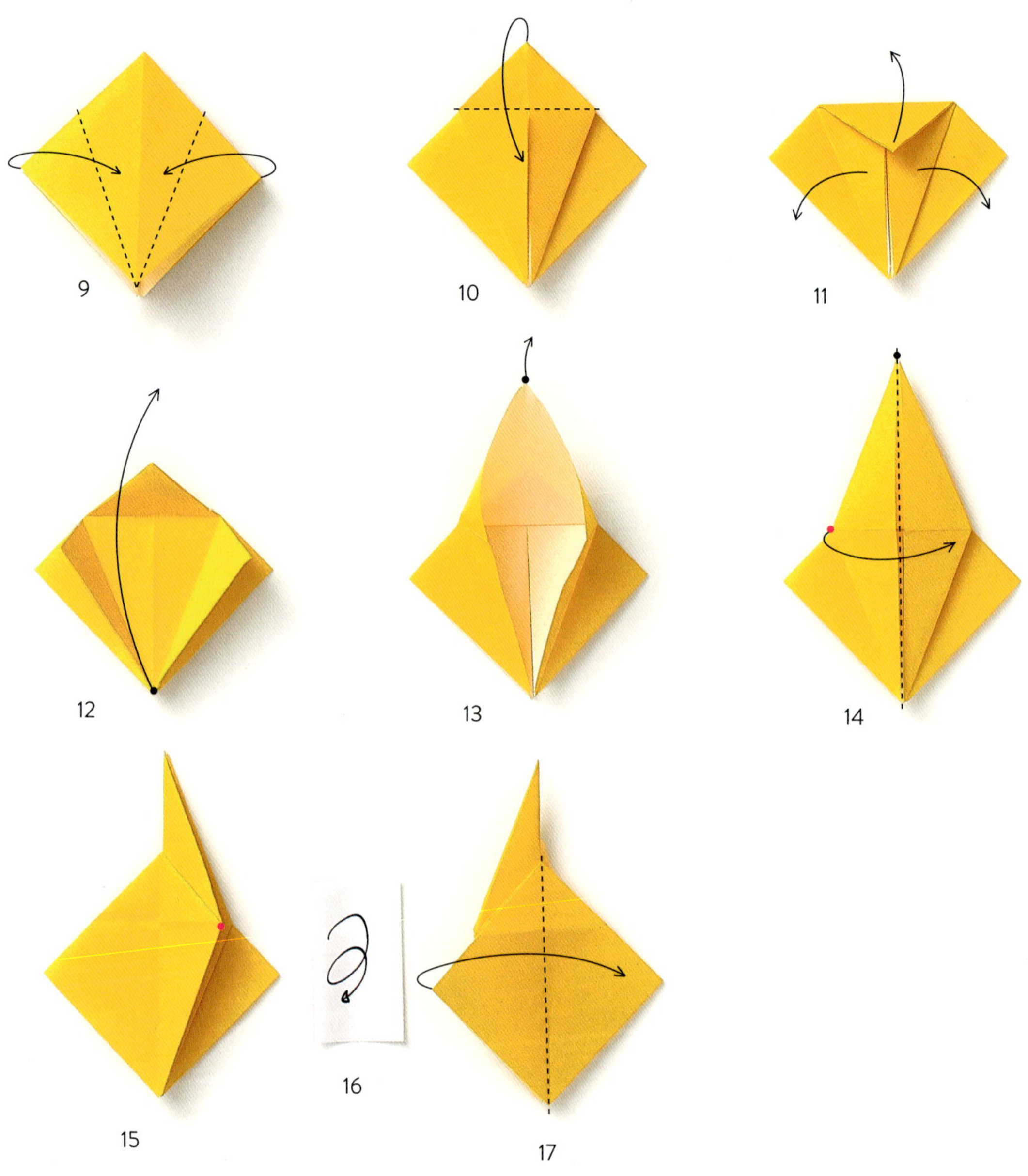

9. Fold the flaps on the top layer along the dotted lines. **10.** Fold the top point along the dotted line.
11. Unfold all the flaps. **12. 13.** Pinch the bottom point and pull it upwards carefully. Squash flat.
14. 15. Fold the LH section of the top layer to the right along the dotted line. You now have this shape.
16. Flip over. **17.** Fold the LH section of the top layer to the right along the dotted line.

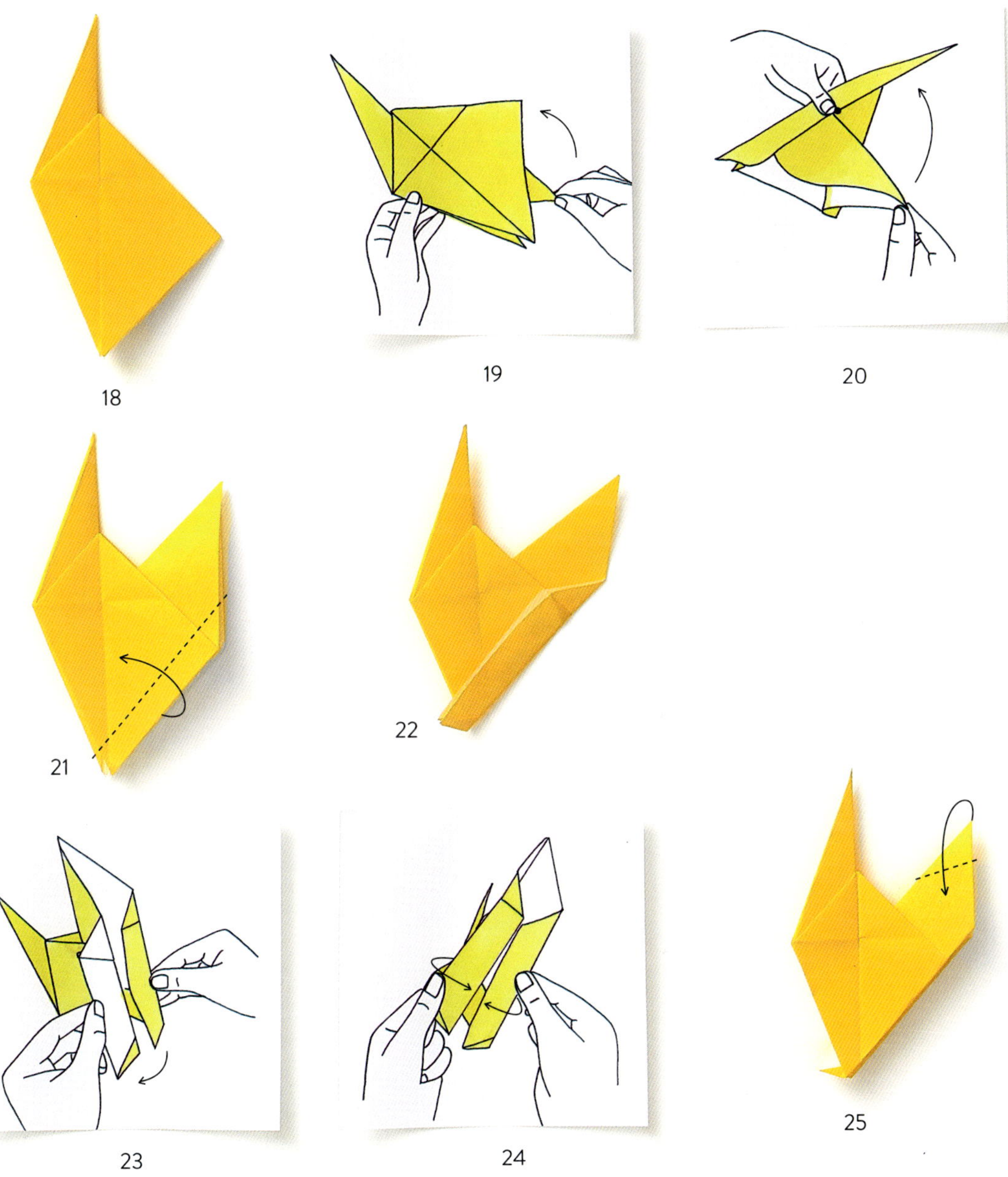

18. 19. 20. Pinch the point hidden inside and gently pull it upwards, not going beyond the angle of the black dot. Squash flat. **21. 22.** Fold along the dotted line. You now have this shape. **23. 24.** Open out this fold and invert the LH fold inwards. Squash flat. **25.** Fold along the dotted line.

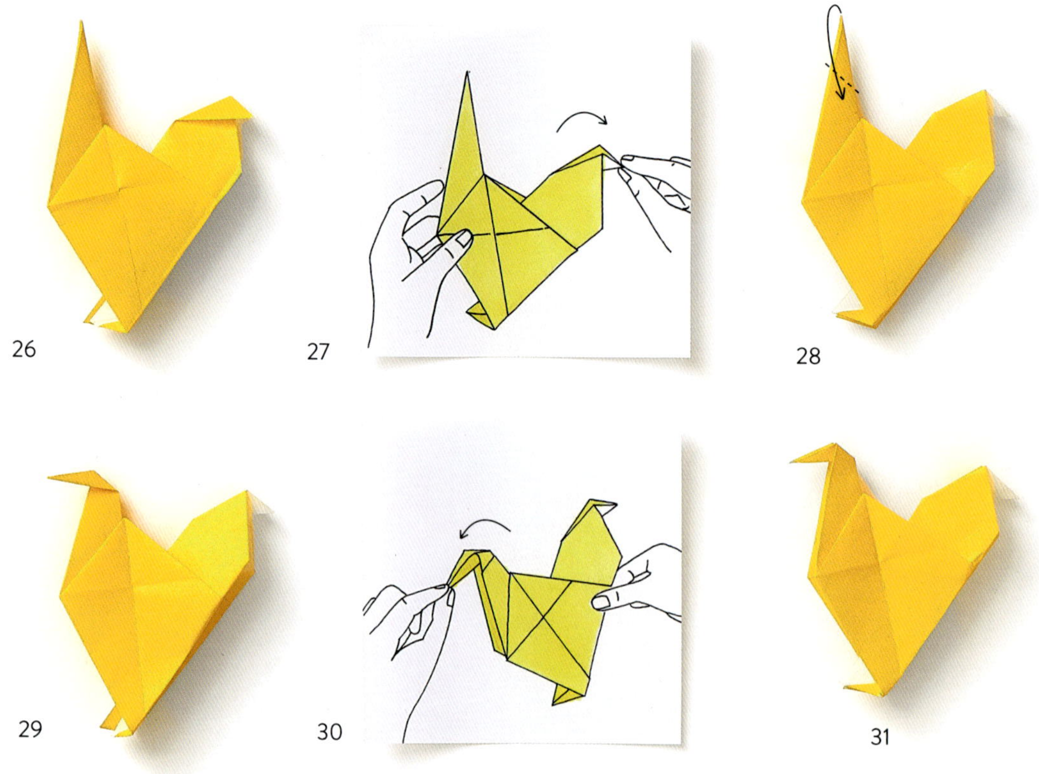

26. 27. Unfold, open out and invert. Squash flat. You have formed the tail. **28.** Fold along the dotted line.
29. 30. Unfold, open out and invert. Squash flat. You have formed the head. **31.** Your cockerel is complete.

Seated crane

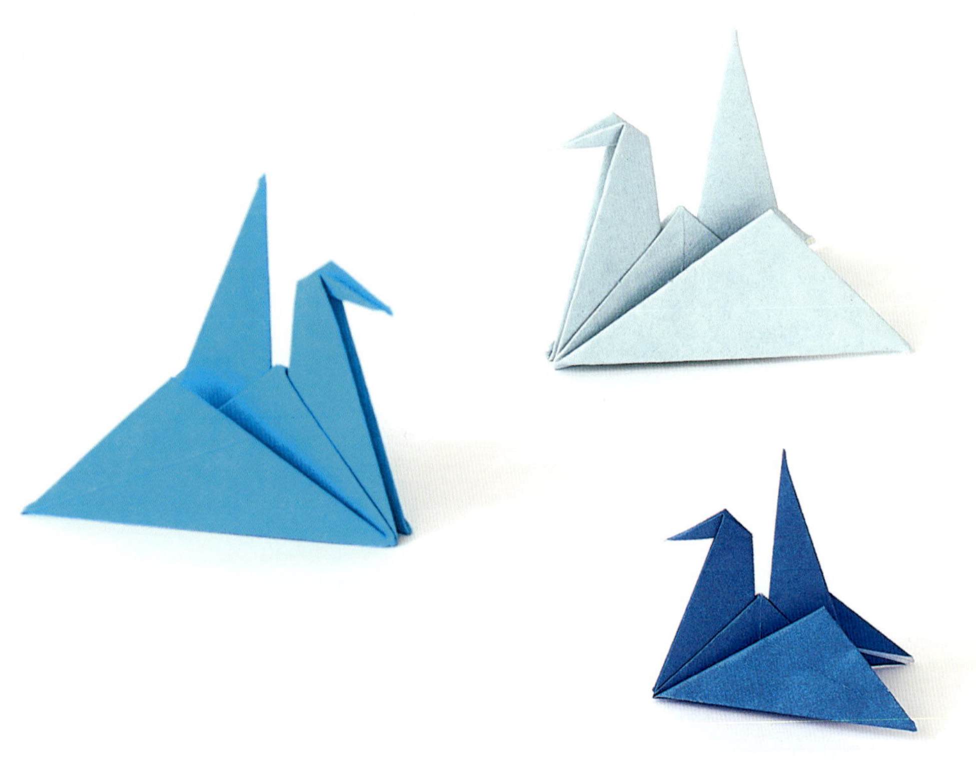

Level ●●●●○

Size

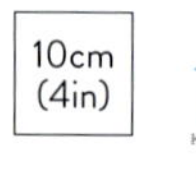

10cm (4in) — 5cm (2in) — 5.5cm (2¼in)

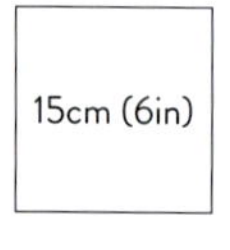
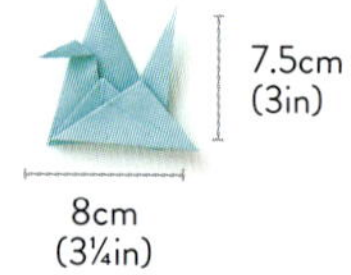

15cm (6in) — 7.5cm (3in) — 8cm (3¼in)

20cm (8in) — 9.5cm (3¾in) — 10cm (4in)

Tip

This design will stand up by itself, and can be used as a place card.

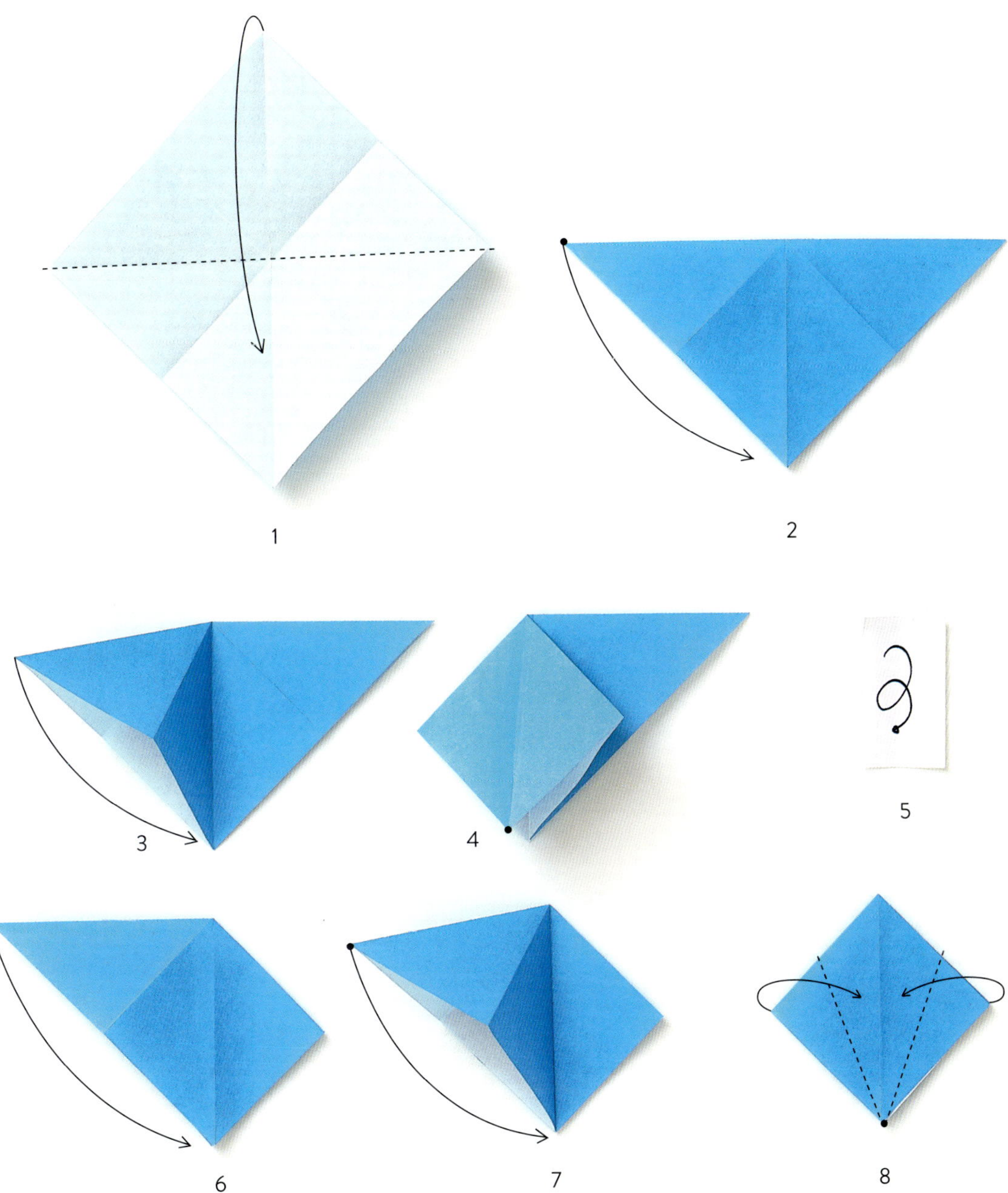

1. Place your square white side up. Mark the creases of the central diagonal, horizontal and vertical lines. Rotate on to one corner and fold in half to form a triangle. **2. 3. 4.** Fold the LH point to the bottom, opening out the fold to form a diamond. Squash flat. **5.** Flip over. **6. 7.** Fold the LH point to the bottom, opening out the fold to form a diamond. Squash flat. **8.** Fold to the central line along the dotted lines.

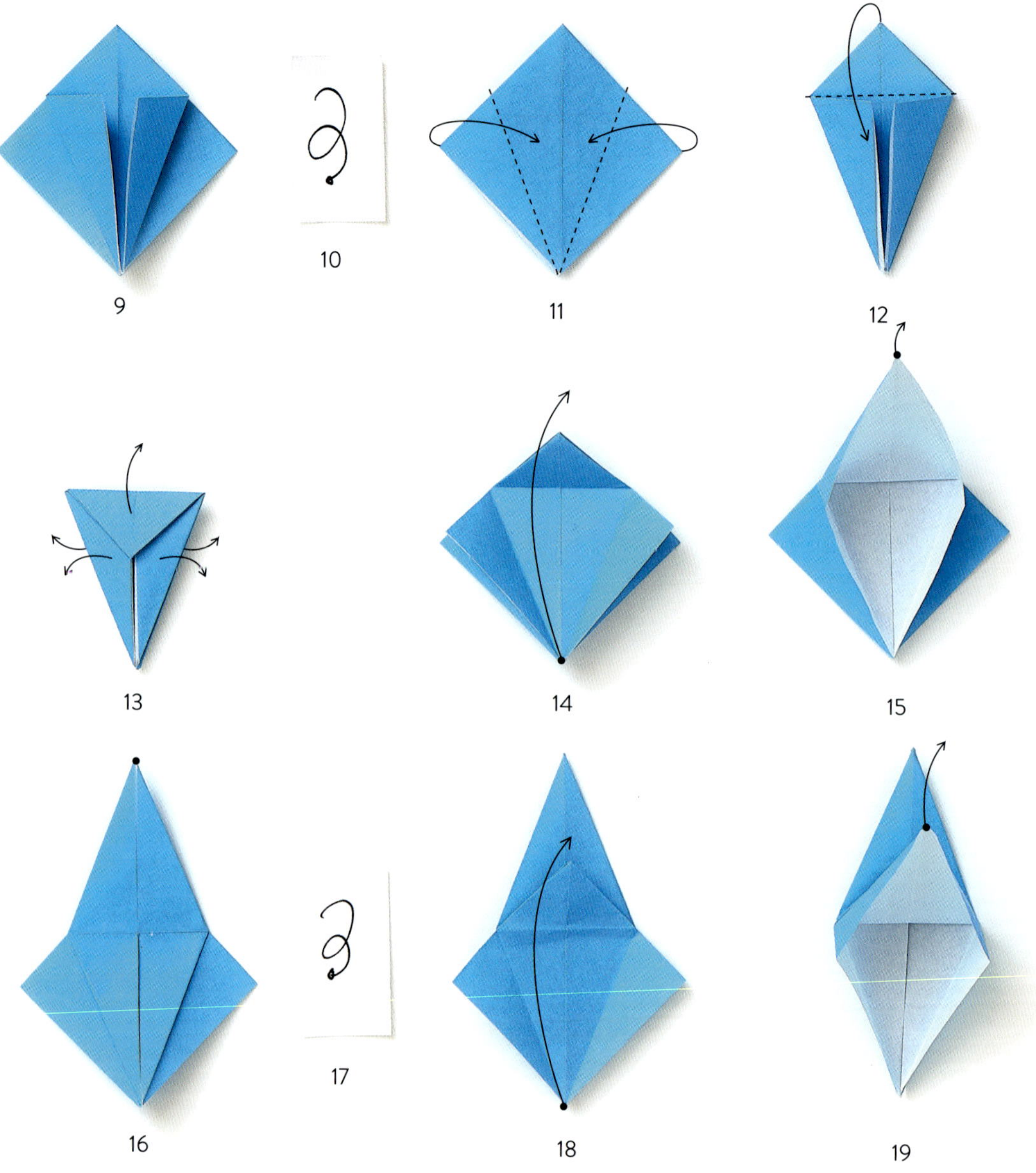

9. You now have this shape. **10.** Flip over. **11.** Fold to the central line along the dotted lines. **12.** Fold the top point along the dotted line. **13.** Unfold the flaps on the front and back. **14. 15. 16.** Pinch the bottom corner and pull it upwards carefully. Squash flat. **17.** Flip over. **18. 19.** Pinch the bottom corner and pull it upwards carefully. Squash flat.

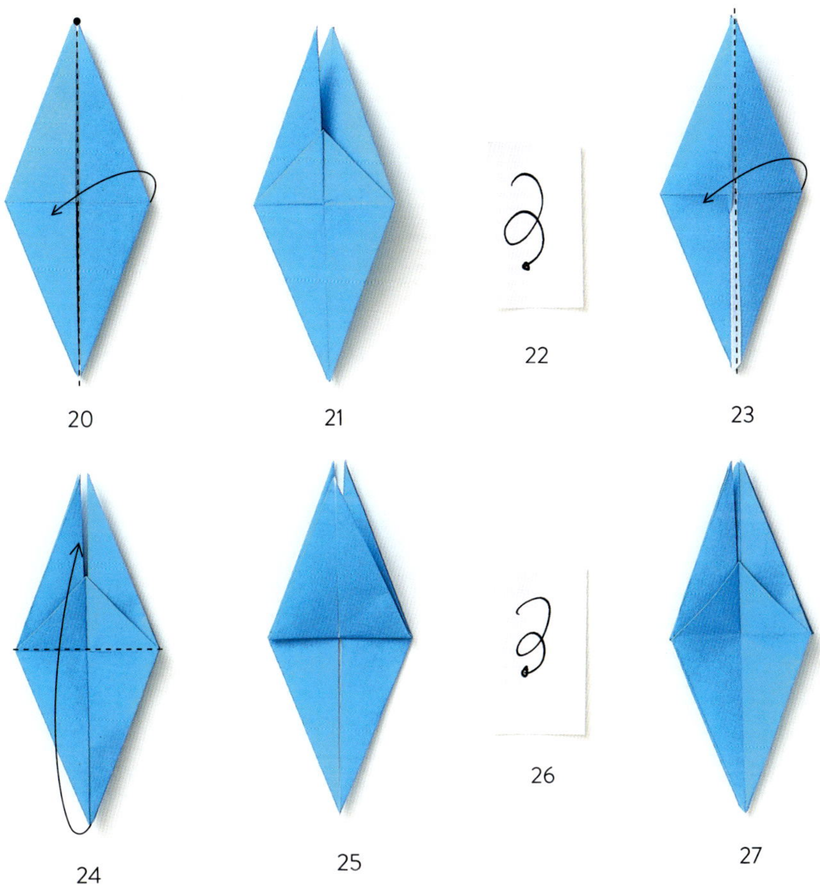

20   21   22   23

24   25   26   27

20. 21. Fold the RH flap on the top layer to the left. Squash flat. You now have this shape. **22.** Flip over.
23. Fold the RH flap on the top layer to the left. Squash flat. **24. 25.** Fold the bottom point of the top layer upwards and squash flat. You now have this shape. **26. 27.** Flip over. You now have this shape.

Version 1

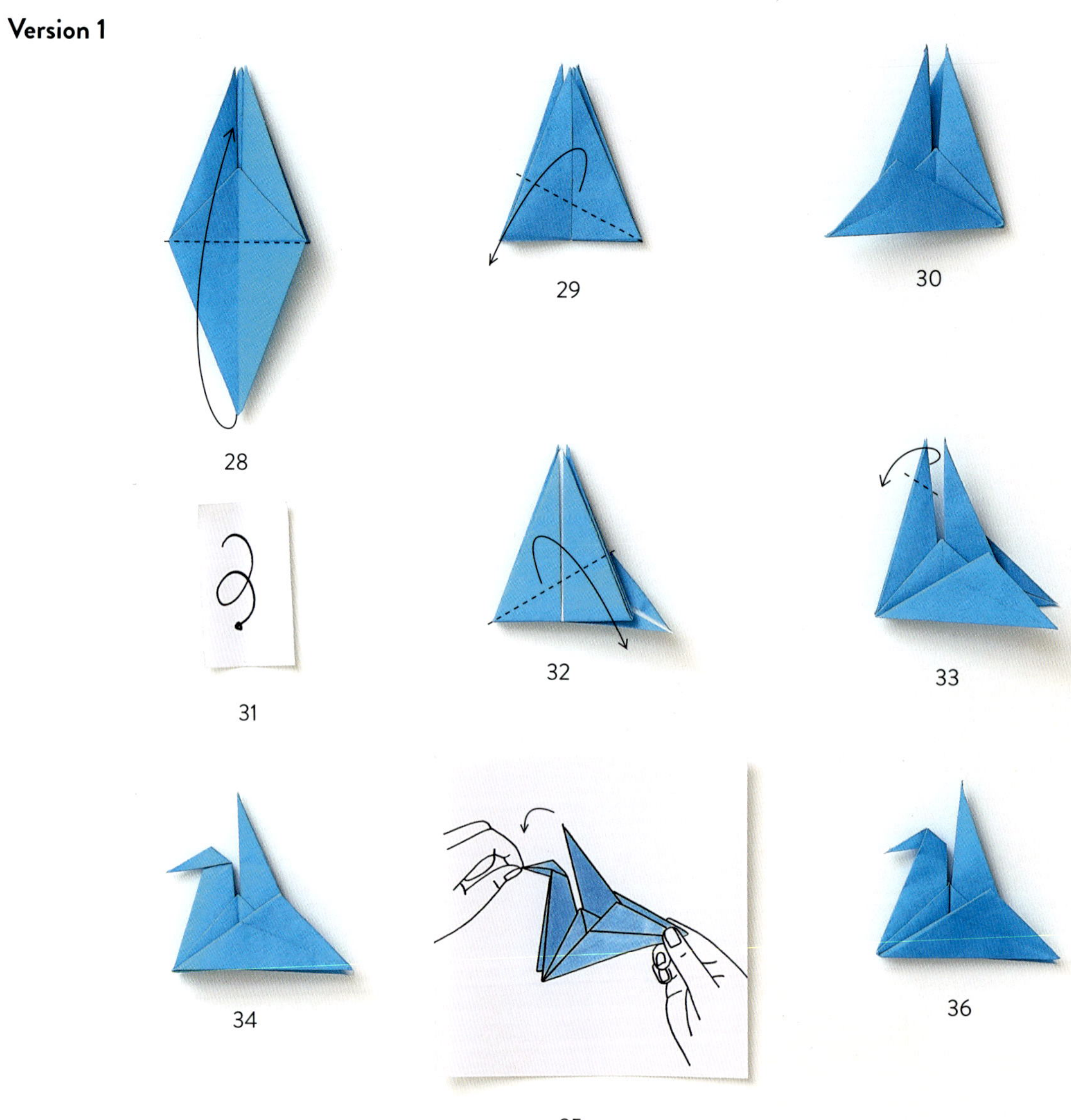

Version 1: 28. Fold in half along the dotted line. **29. 30.** Fold the top layer along the dotted line. Squash flat. You now have this shape. **31.** Flip over. **32.** Fold the top layer along the dotted line. Squash flat. **33.** Fold along the dotted line. **34. 35. 36.** Open the fold and invert. Squash flat. You have now formed the crane's beak. **37.** Your seated crane is complete (see opposite).

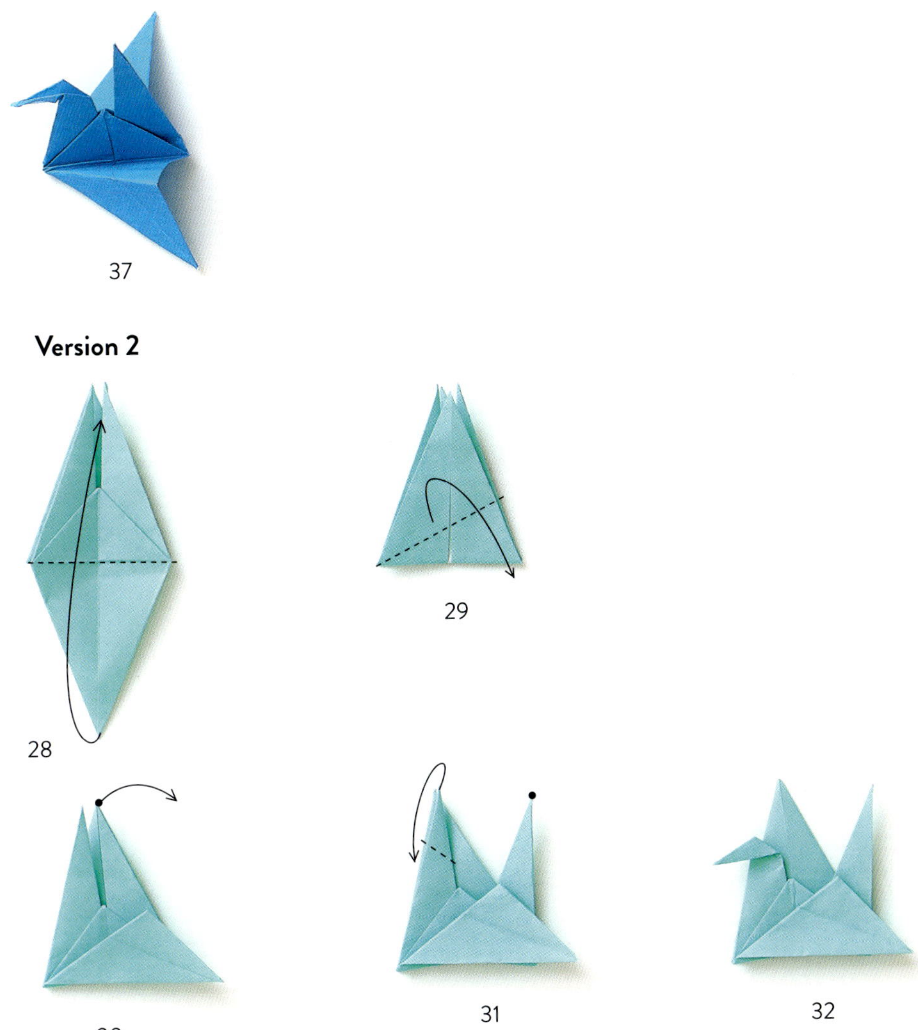

Version 2

Version 2: Starting from step 28 (opposite), fold in half along the dotted line. **29.** Fold the top layer along the dotted line. Squash flat. **30.** Pinch the point at top right and pull it to the right. **31.** Fold the point at top left along the dotted line. **32.** Your seated crane is complete.

Dragonfly

Level ● ● ● ● ○

Size

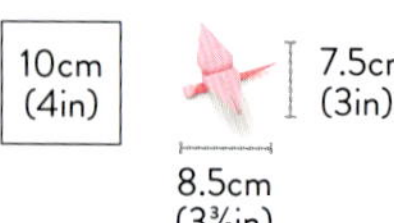

10cm (4in)

7.5cm (3in)

8.5cm (3⅜in)

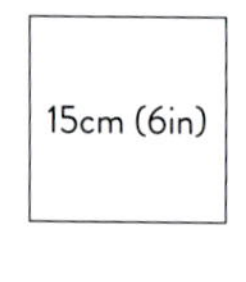

15cm (6in)

11cm (4⅜in)

12.5cm (5in)

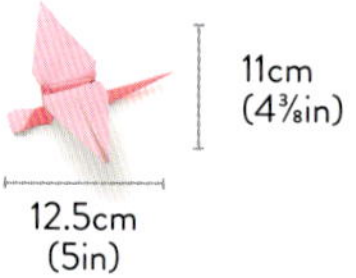

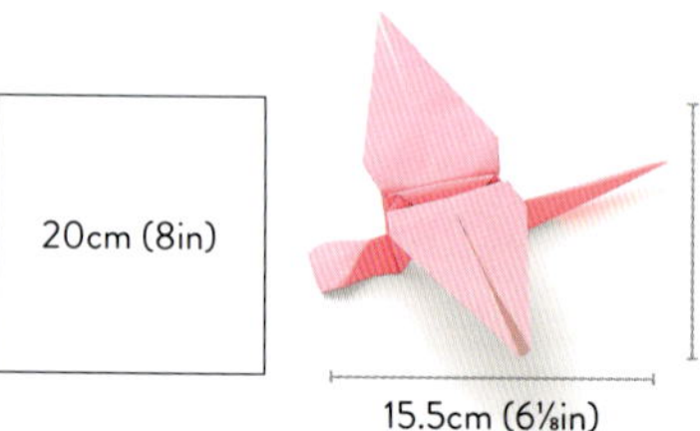

20cm (8in)

14cm (5½in)

15.5cm (6⅛in)

Tip
You will need a pair of scissors.

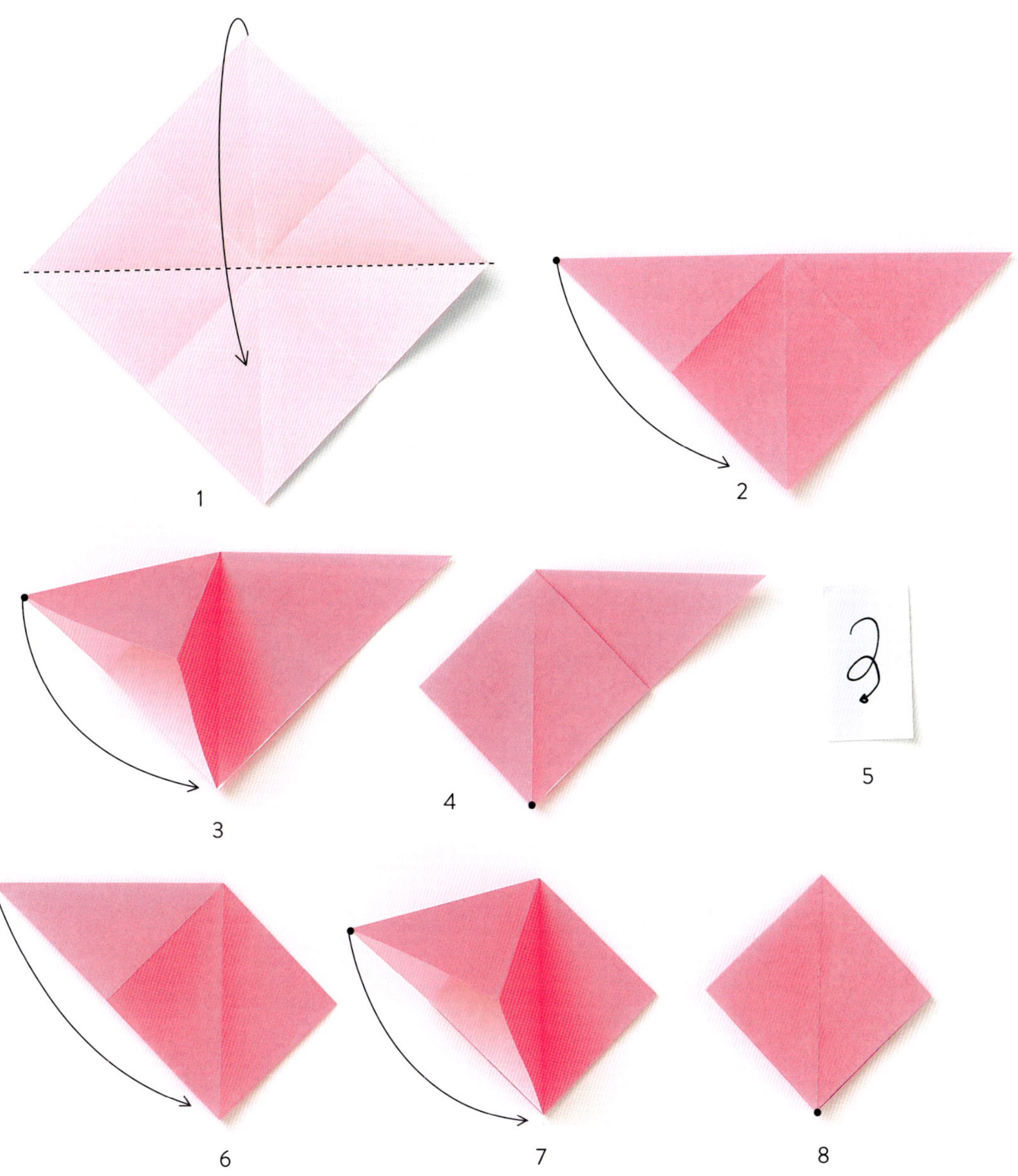

1. Place your square white side up, mark the creases of the central diagonal, horizontal and vertical lines. Rotate on to one corner and fold in half to form a triangle. **2. 3. 4.** Fold the LH point to the bottom, opening out the fold to form a diamond. Squash flat. **5.** Flip over. **6. 7. 8.** Fold the LH point to the top, opening out the fold to form a diamond. Squash flat.

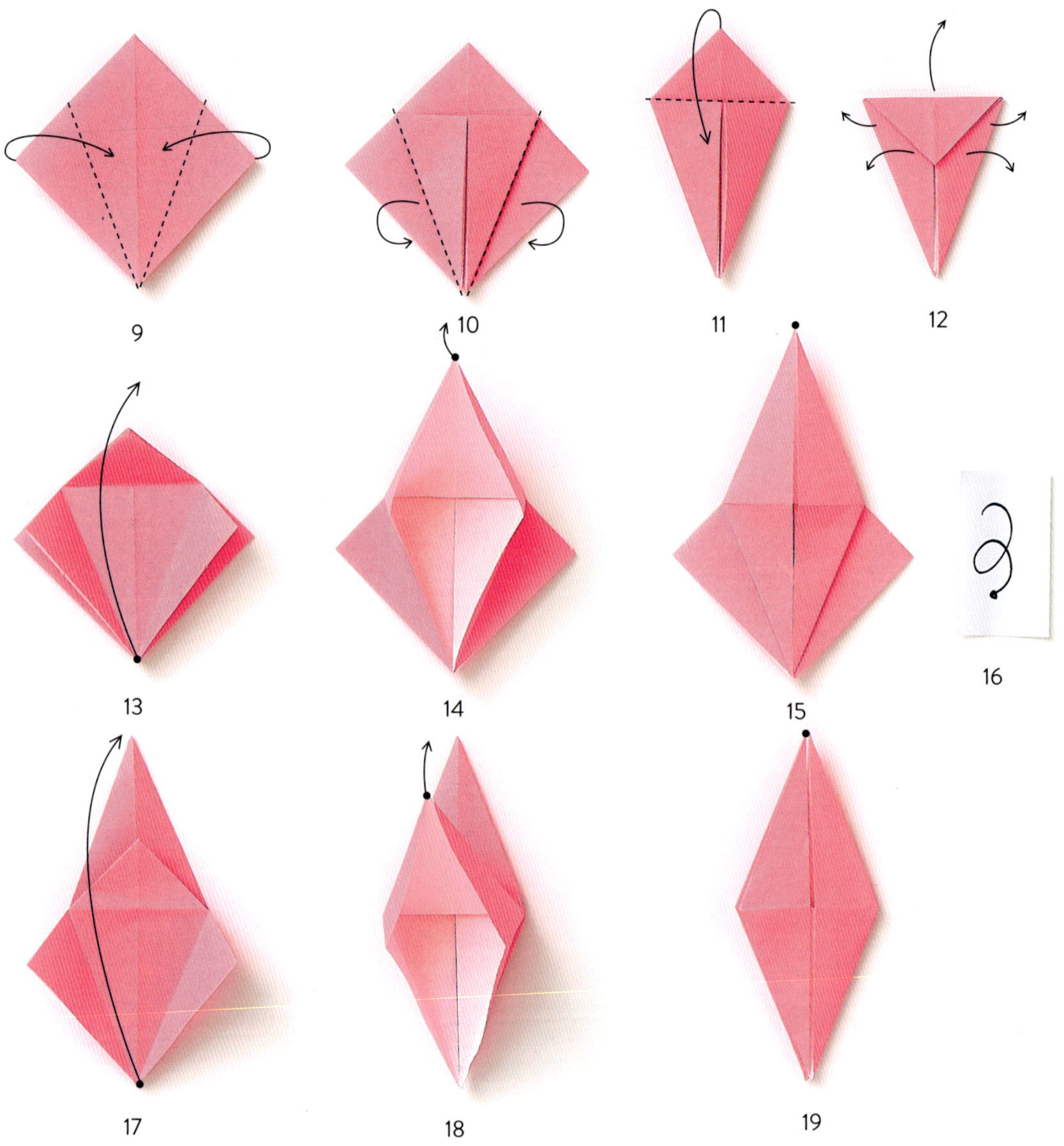

9. Fold the RH and LH points of the top layer to the central line along the dotted lines. **10.** Fold the flaps on the underneath layer behind. **11.** Fold the top point along the dotted line. **12.** Open all the flaps on front and back. **13. 14. 15.** Pinch the bottom corner and pull it upwards carefully. Squash flat. **16.** Flip over.
17. 18. 19. Pinch the bottom corner and pull it upwards carefully. Squash flat.

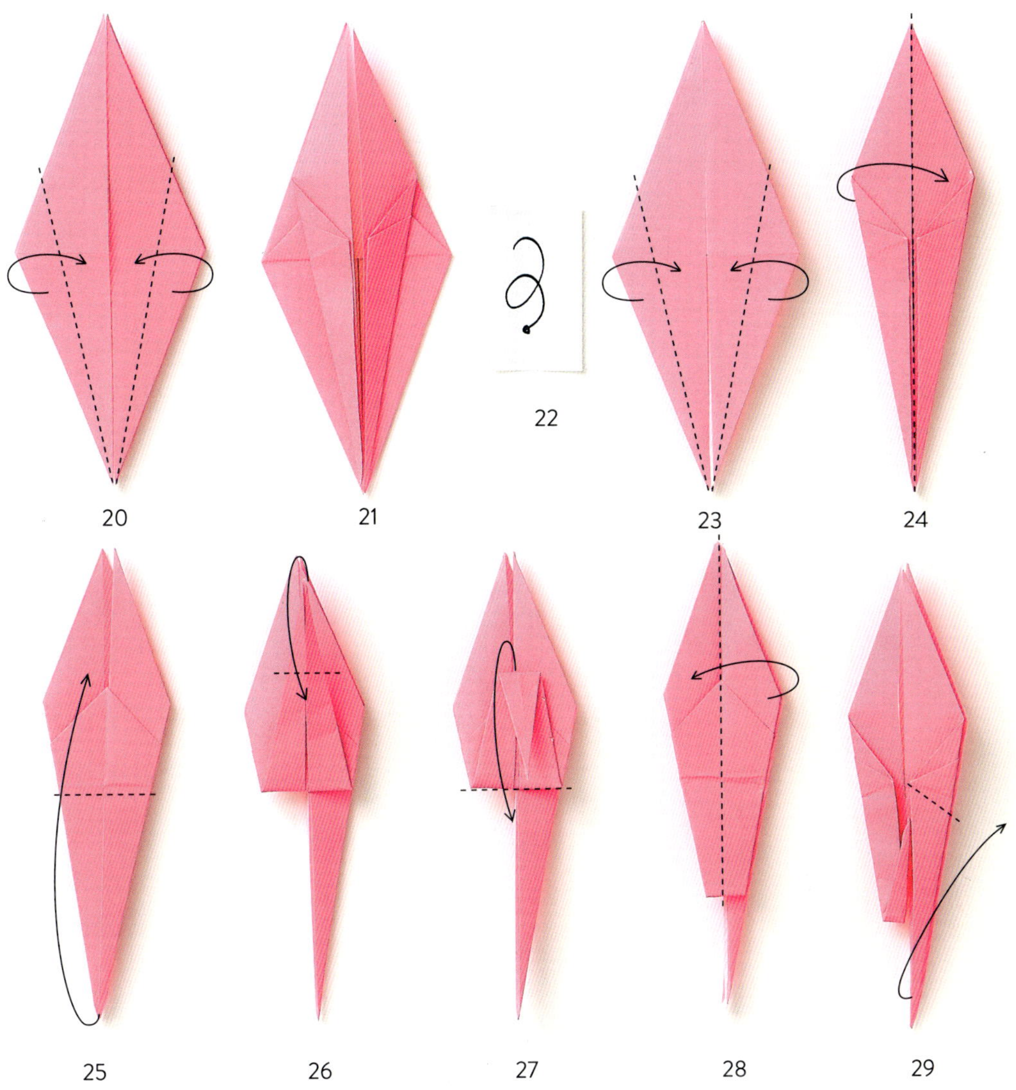

20. 21. Fold the RH and LH flaps on the top layer to the central line along the dotted lines. You now have this shape. **22.** Flip over. **23.** Fold the RH and LH flaps to the central line along the dotted lines. **24.** Fold the LH flap to the right along the dotted lines. **25.** Fold the top layer upwards along the dotted line. **26.** Fold in half along the dotted line. **27.** Unfold along the dotted line. **28.** Fold the RH flap on the top layer to the left. **29.** Fold to the outside along the dotted line.

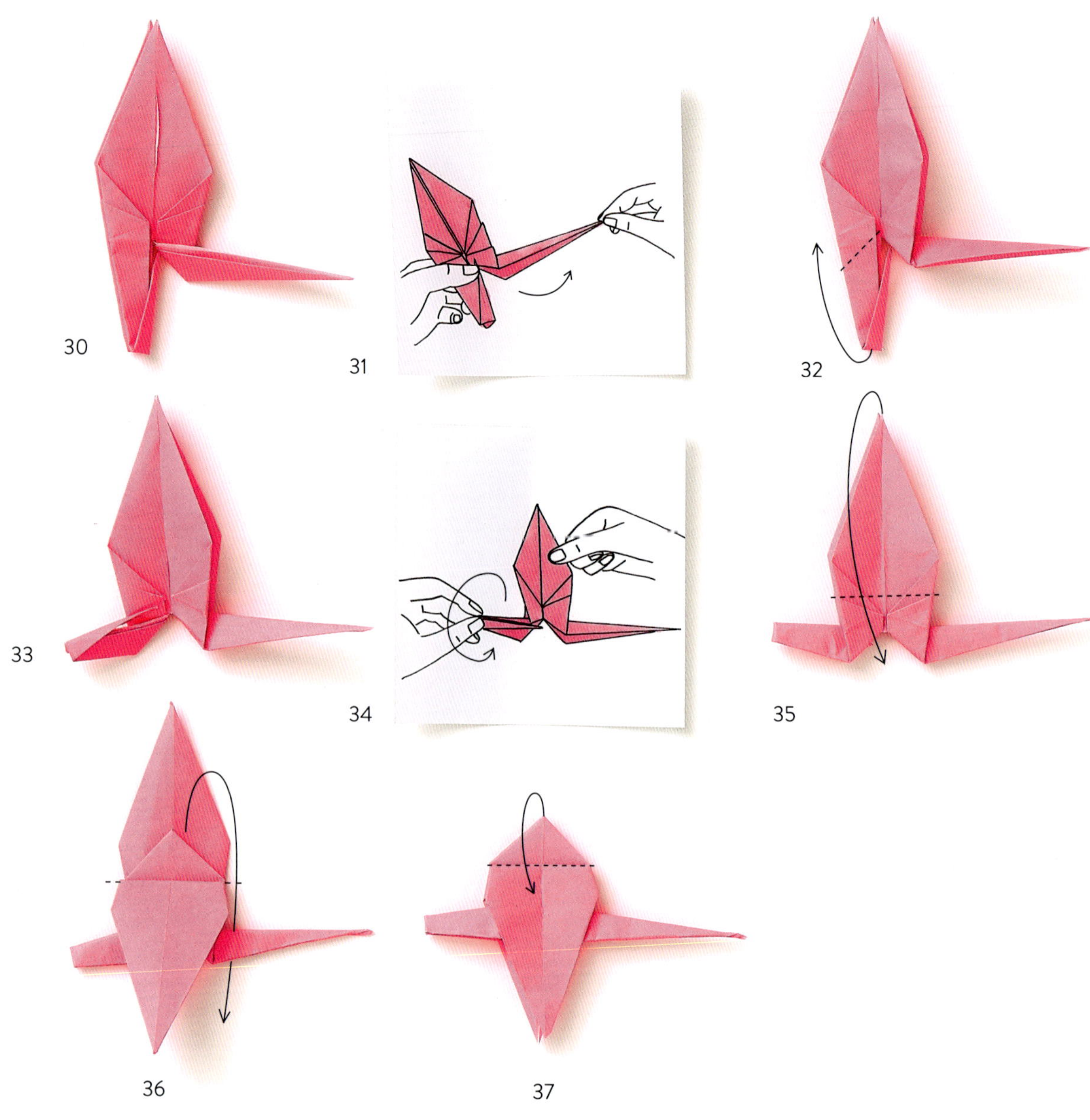

30. 31. Unfold, invert and squash flat. **32.** Fold to the outside along the dotted line. **33. 34.** Unfold, invert and squash flat. **35.** Fold the flap on the top layer to the front along the dotted line. **36.** Fold the underneath flap behind along the dotted line. **37.** Fold the top point along the dotted line.

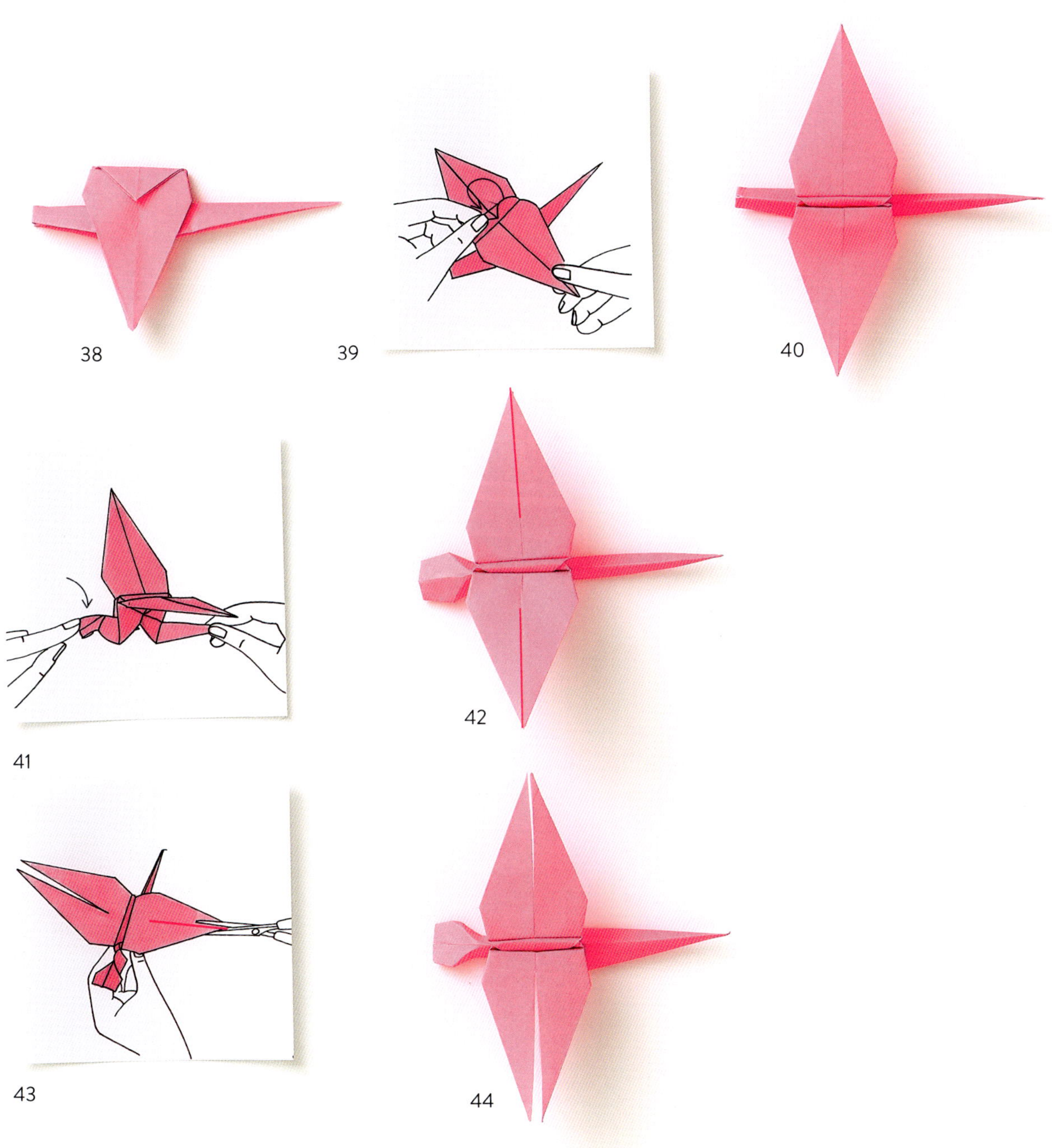

38. 39. 40. Pulling gently on the front wing, tuck the little triangle inside. **41. 42.** Form the head by pressing downwards. You now have this shape. **43. 44.** Cut along three quarters of the central line of each wing. Your dragonfly is complete.

Marguerite

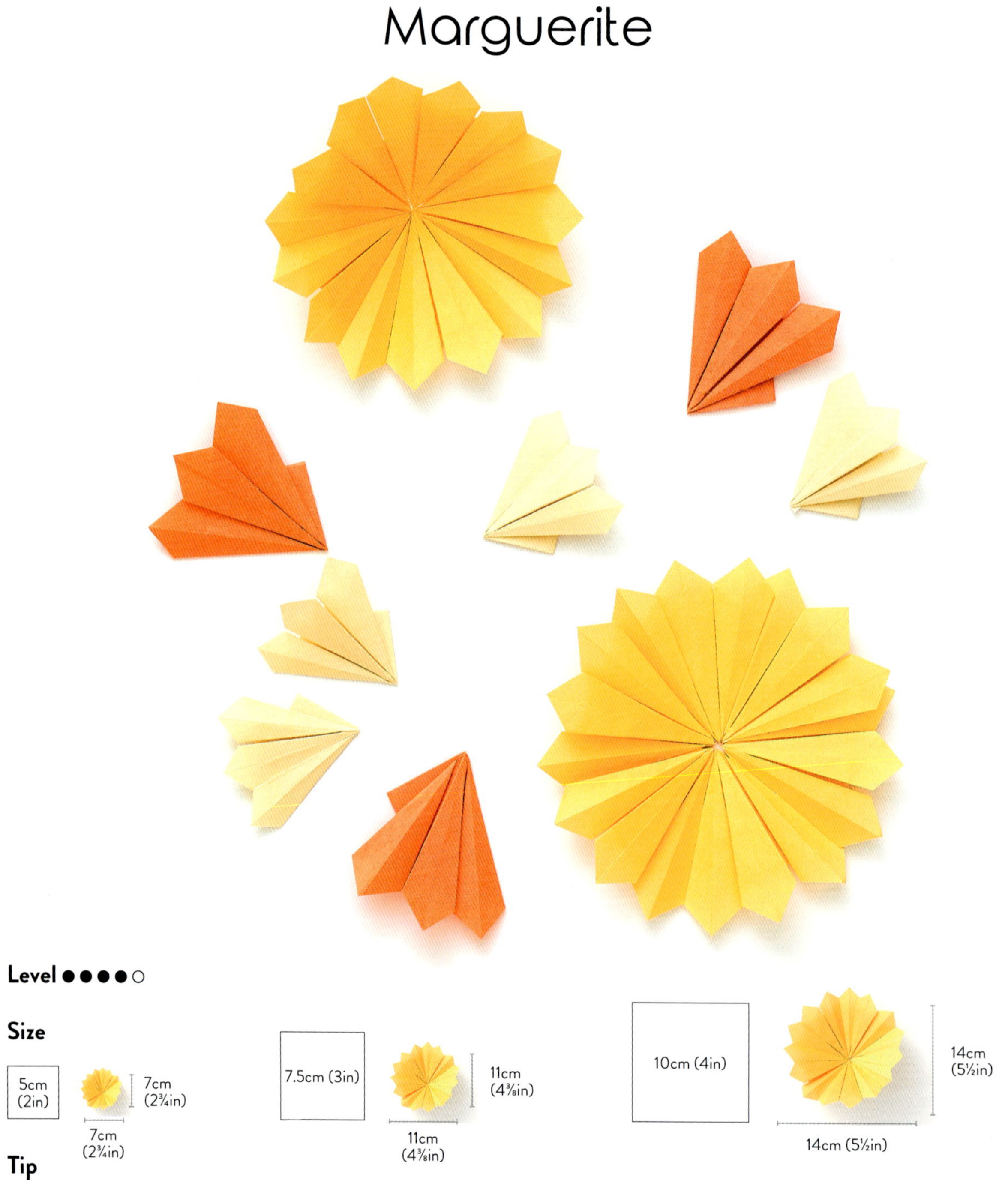

Level ●●●●○

Size

5cm (2in)	7cm (2¾in)	7cm (2¾in)
7.5cm (3in)	11cm (4⅜in)	11cm (4⅜in)
10cm (4in)	14cm (5½in)	14cm (5½in)

Tip

You will need some quick-drying glue. You can make two versions of this flower: a three-dimensional flower made up of five sections and a two-dimensional flower consisting of six sections.

1. 2. Place your square white side up. Mark the creases of the central diagonal, horizontal and vertical lines. Fold in half along the dotted line. **3. 4.** Fold LH point to the right, opening out the fold to obtain a triangle. Squash flat. **5.** Flip over. **6. 7.** Fold the LH point to the right, opening out the fold.

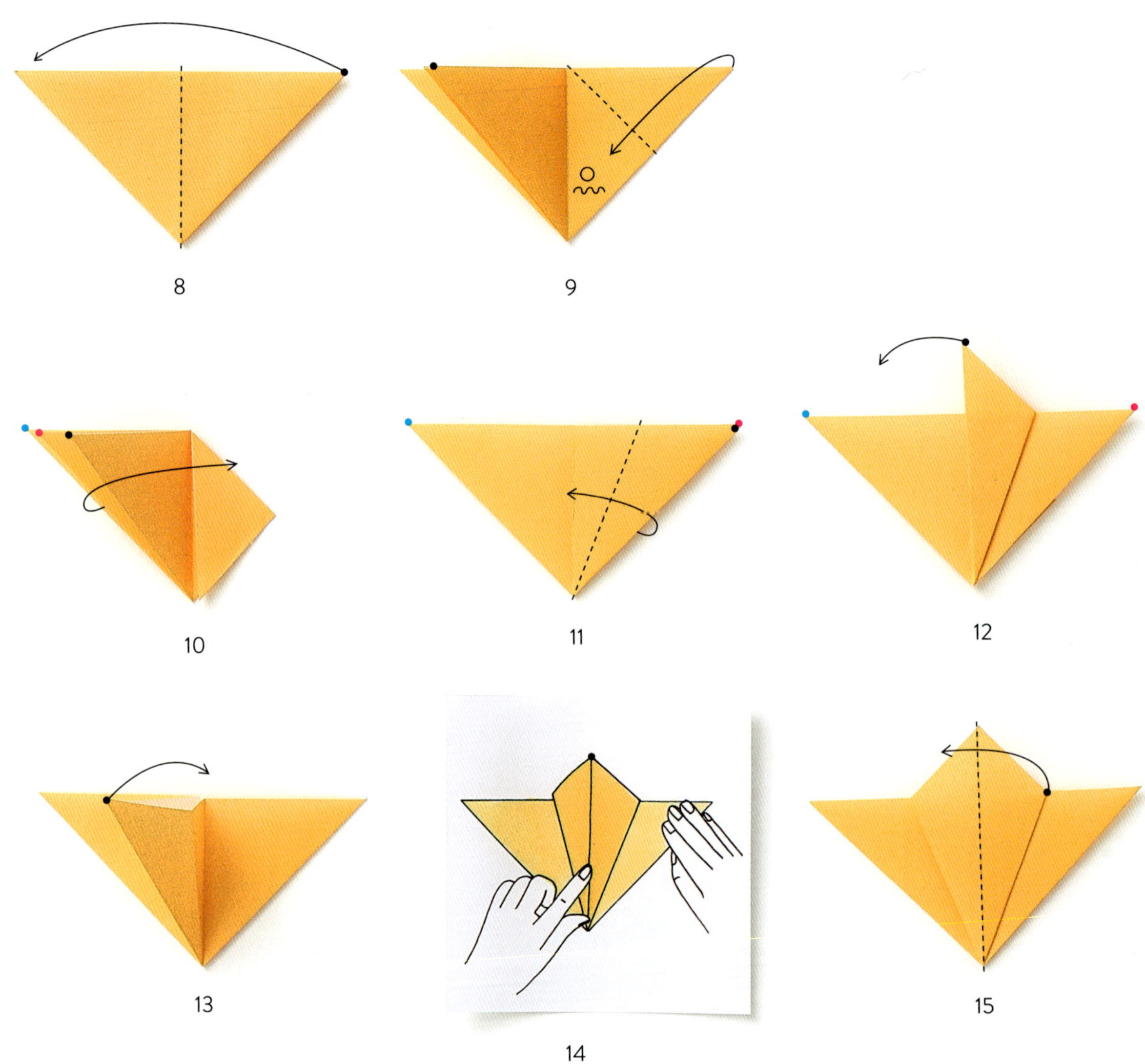

8. You now have a triangle. Fold the top layer on the right to the left. **9.** Take the point on the right to the central line and glue as shown. **10.** Pinch the two uppermost flaps on the left together and fold them to the right. **11. 12.** Fold the uppermost RH flap to the central line along the dotted line, and squash flat. You now have this shape. **13. 14.** Pinch the point, open out the fold and squash flat to form a triangle. **15.** Fold the RH flap to the left.

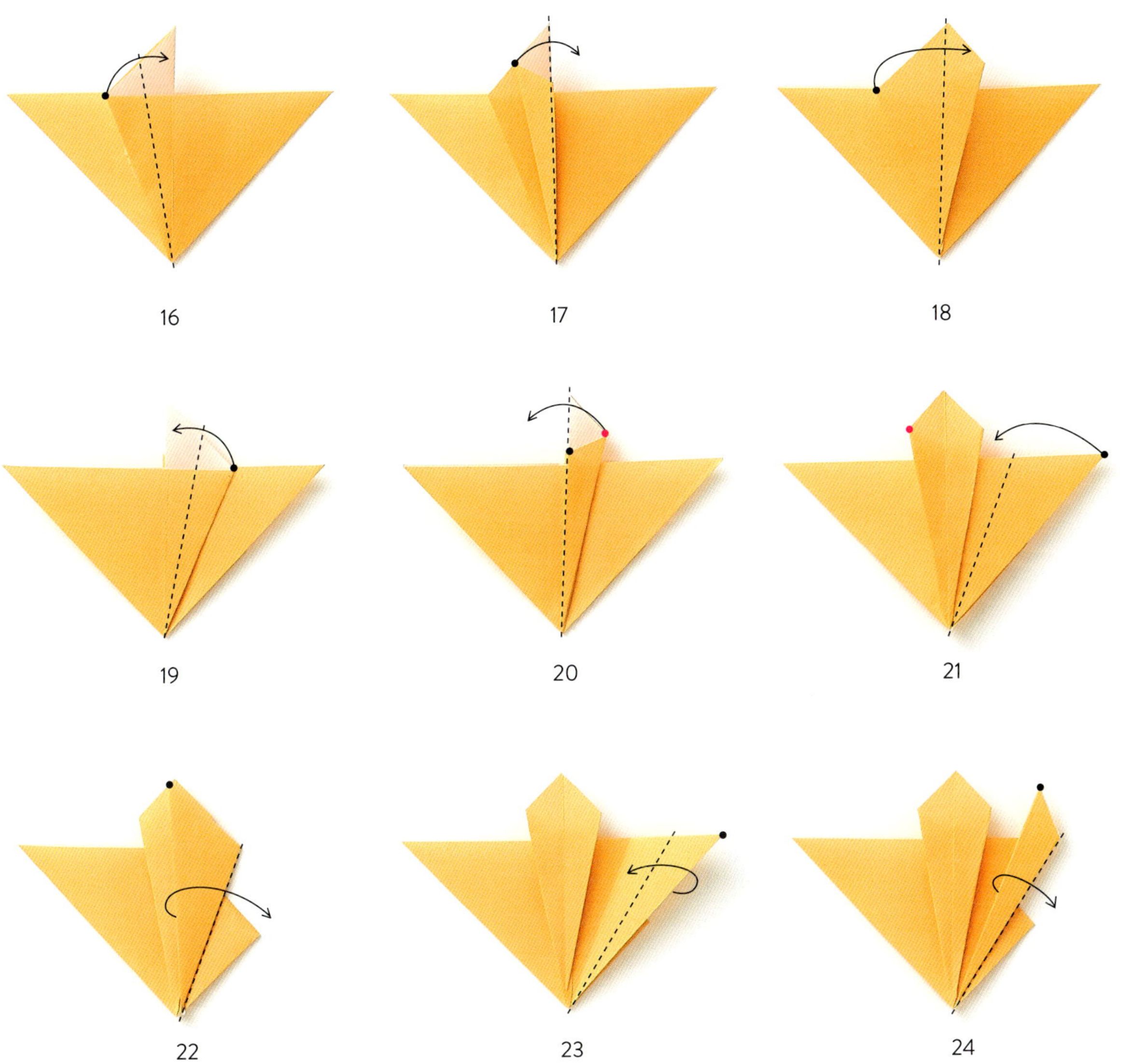

16. Fold the uppermost LH flap in half. **17.** Fold the uppermost LH flap to the right. **18. 19.** Fold the uppermost RH flap in half. Squash flat. **20.** Fold the uppermost RH flap to the left. **21.** Fold along the dotted line. **22.** Unfold. **23.** Fold along the dotted line. **24.** Unfold.

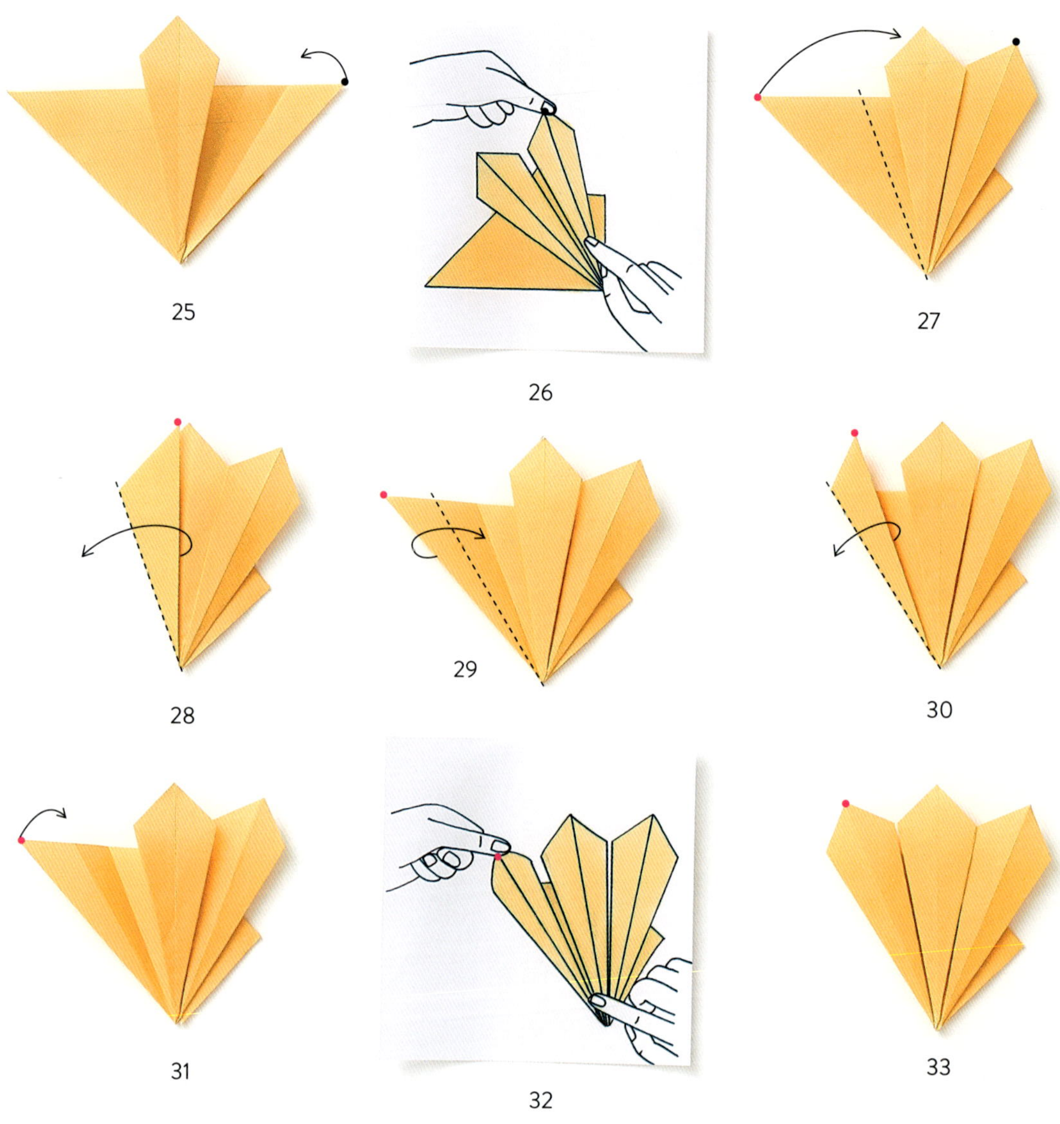

25. 26. Pinch the dot on the right and open out the fold. Squash flat. **27. 28. 29. 30. 31. 32. 33.** Repeat steps 21 to 26 on this side. Squash flat.

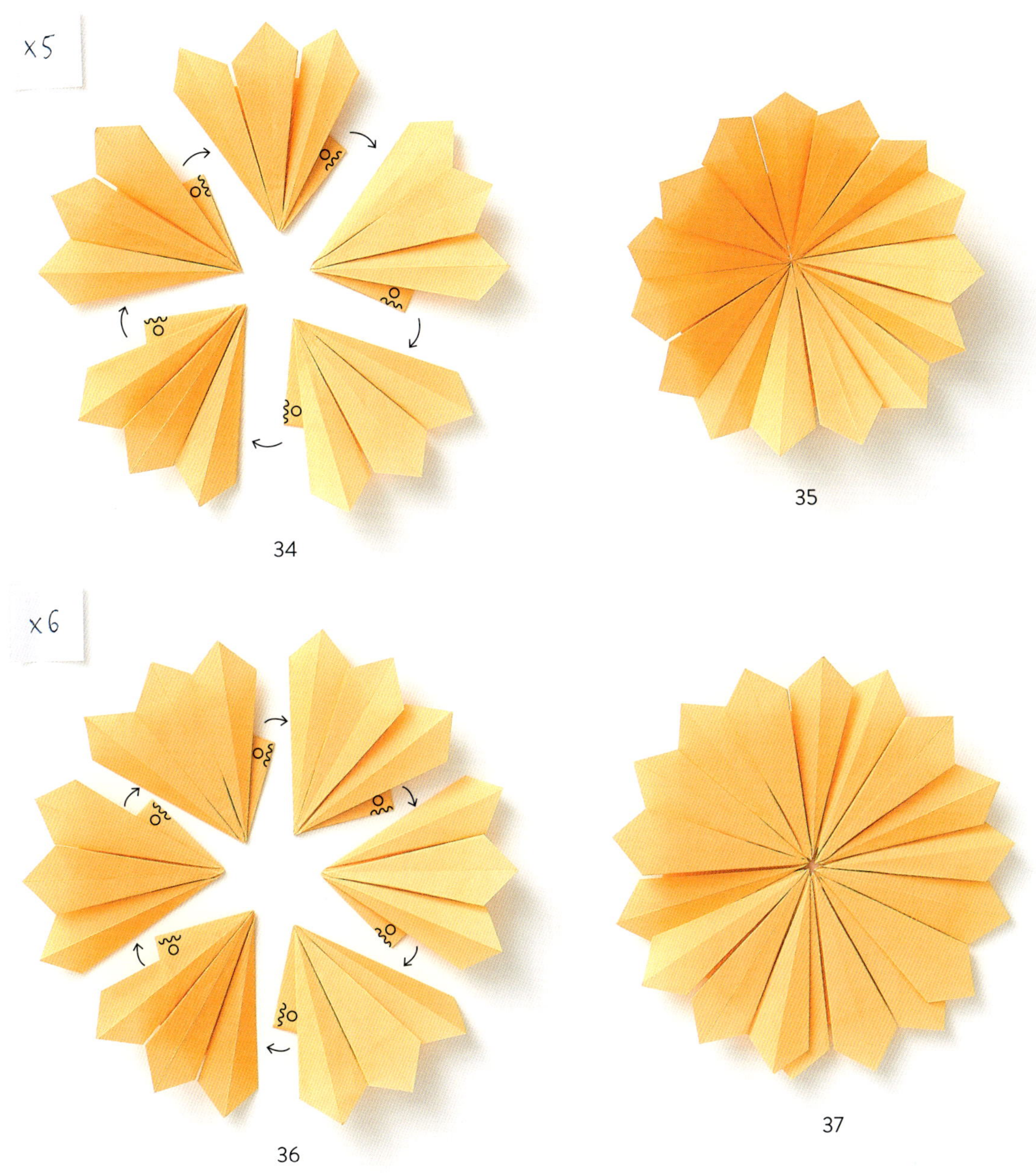

34. Repeat steps 1 to 33 so you have five identical flower sections. Apply a dab of glue to each fold at the point marked and stick together to form a three-dimensional flower. **35.** Your five-petal marguerite is complete. **36. 37. Variation:** You can also make six identical sections to make a fuller, flat marguerite with six petals.

Christmas tree

Level ● ● ● ● ●

Size

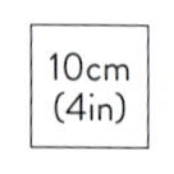

10cm (4in)

7.5cm (3in)

4.5cm (1¾in)

15cm (6in)

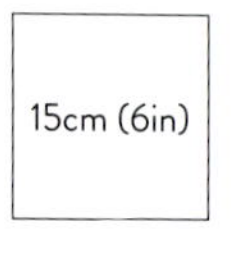

11cm (4⅜in)

6.5cm (2½in)

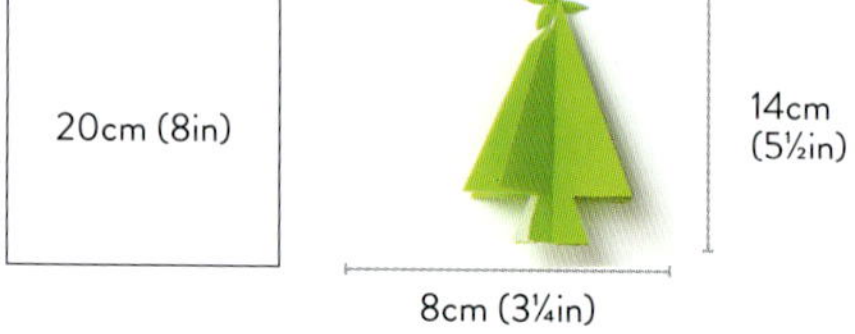

20cm (8in)

14cm (5½in)

8cm (3¼in)

Tip

You will need some quick-drying glue, a pencil and a pair of scissors to make the star on top of the Christmas tree.

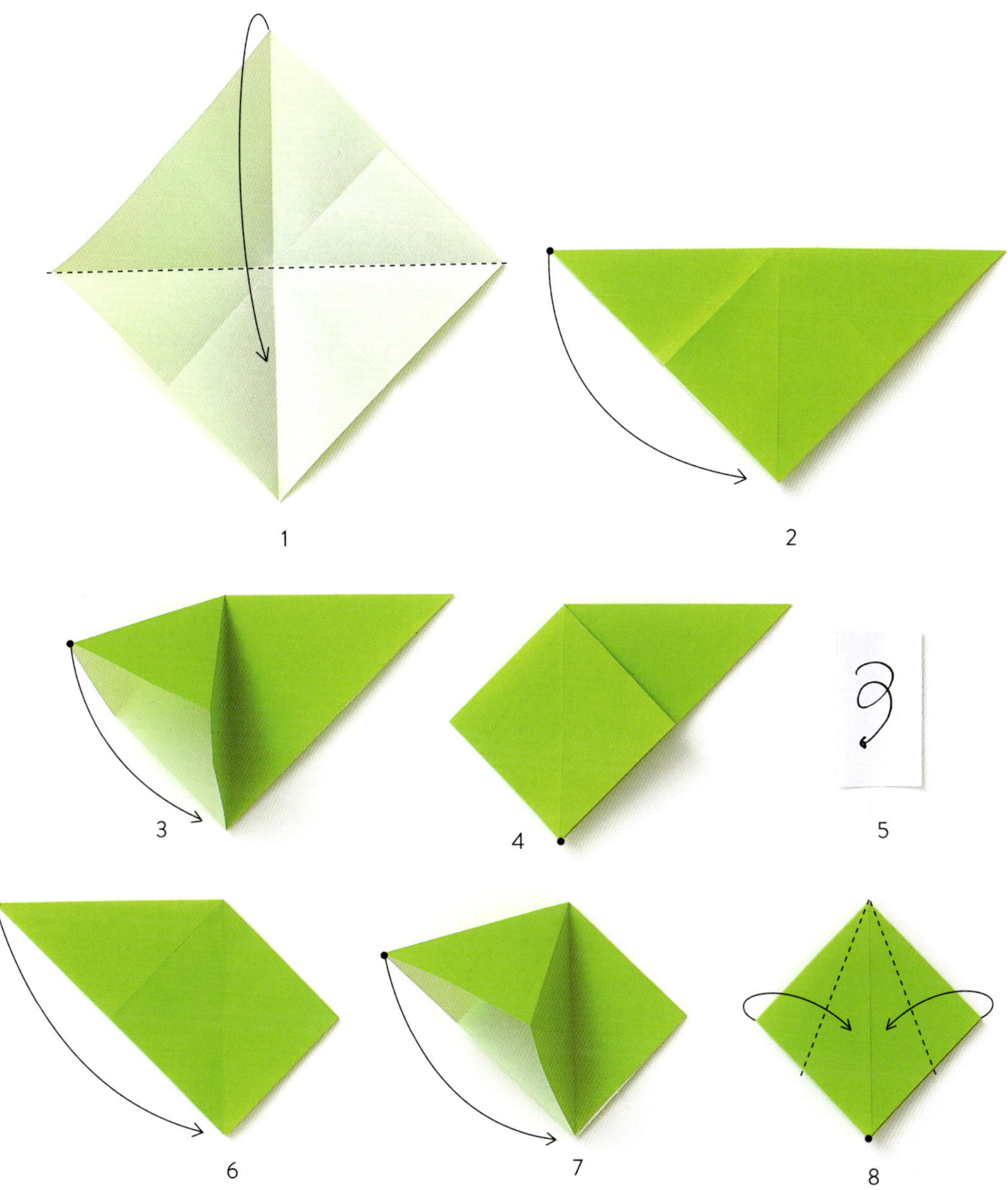

1. Place your square white side up, mark the creases of the central diagonal, horizontal and vertical lines. Rotate on to one corner and fold in half to form a triangle. **2. 3. 4.** Fold the LH downwards, opening out the fold to form a diamond. Squash flat. **5.** Flip over. **6. 7.** Fold the LH point downwards, opening out the fold to form a diamond. Squash flat. **8.** Fold the flaps on the top layer along the dotted lines.

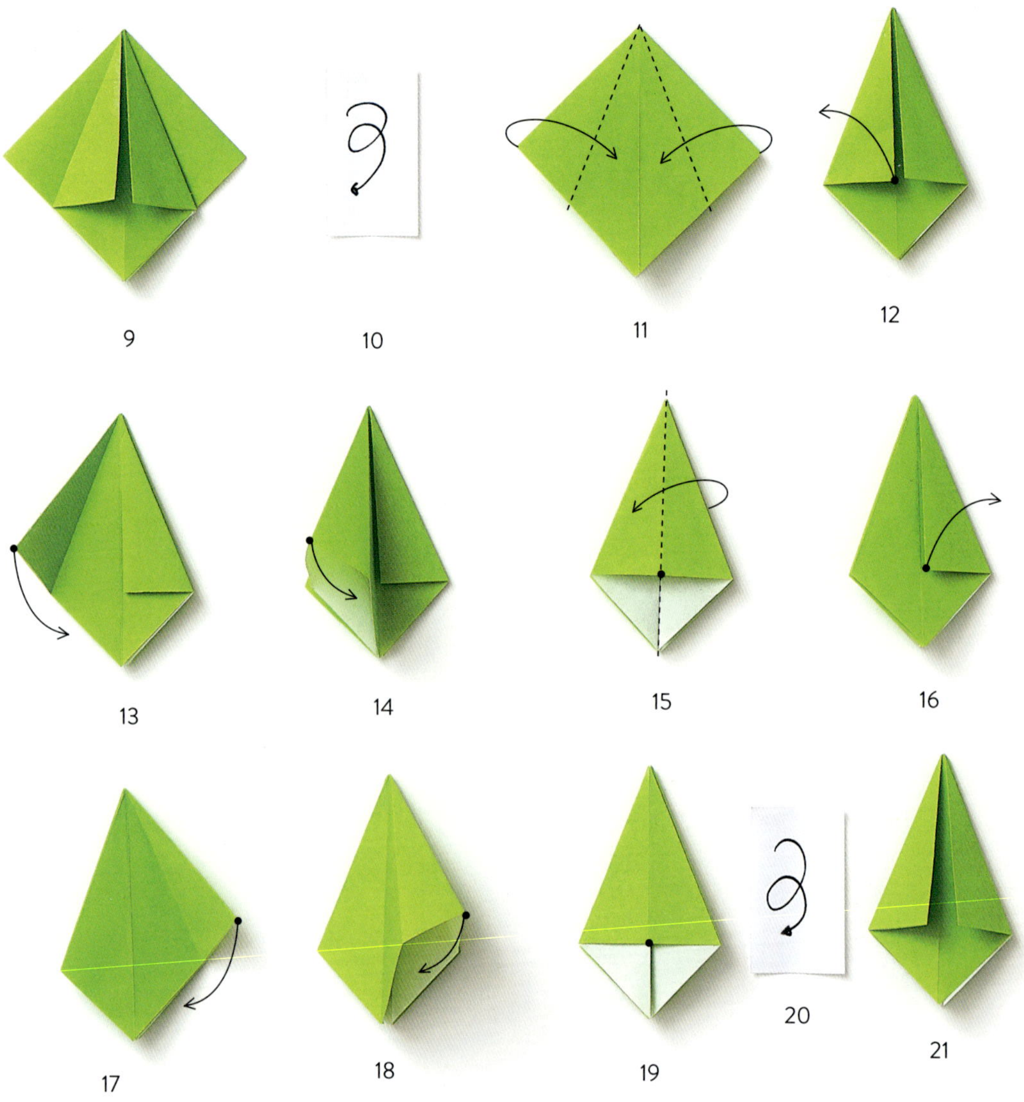

9. You now have this shape. **10.** Flip over. **11.** Fold the flaps along the dotted lines. **12. 13. 14.** Unfold the LH fold, open out the fold and squash flat. **15.** Fold the RH flap on the top layer to the left along the dotted lines. **16. 17. 18. 19.** Unfold the RH fold, open out and squash flat. **20.** Flip over. **21.** You now have this shape.

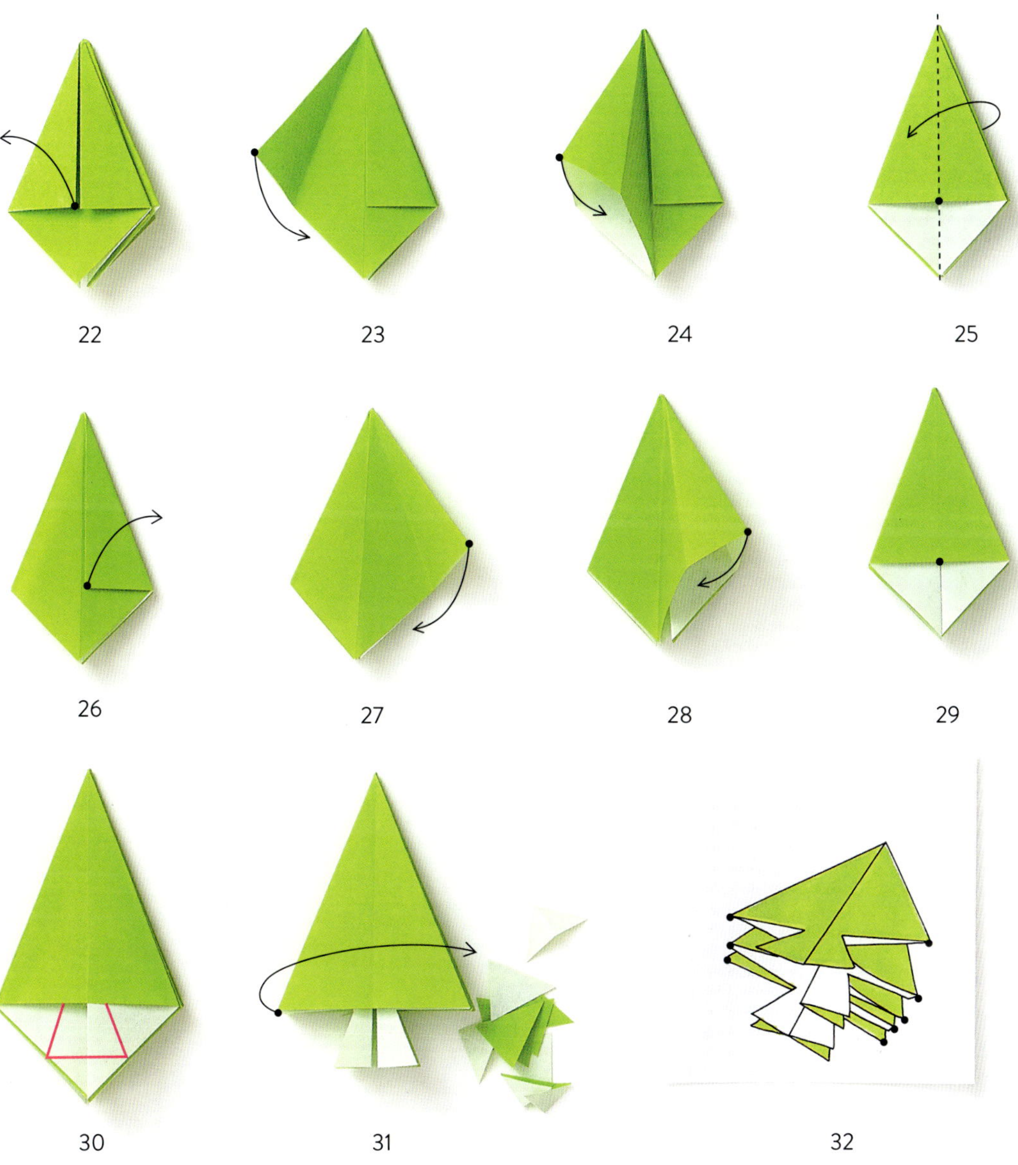

22   23   24   25

26   27   28   29

30   31   32

22. 23. 24. Repeat steps 12 to 14. **25.** Fold the RH flap on the top layer to the left. **26. 27. 28. 29.** Repeat steps 16 to 19. **30. 31.** Draw and cut through all the thicknesses as shown. Fold the LH flap on the top layer to the right. **32.** You now have three folds on the left and five on the right.

33. 34. Apply a dab of glue at the points marked and squeeze together. Hold the folds together as shown.
35. 36. Make a cut in the five folds as shown (make sure you do not cut past the centre line!). You now have this shape. **37.** Carefully unfold the Christmas tree and pull the star into shape. **38.** Your Christmas tree is complete.

Stag

Level ●●●●●

Size

 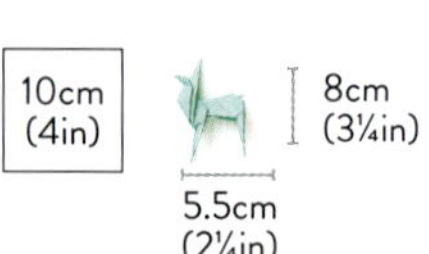 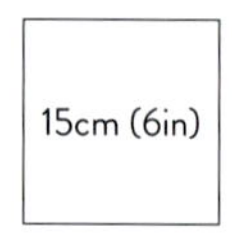 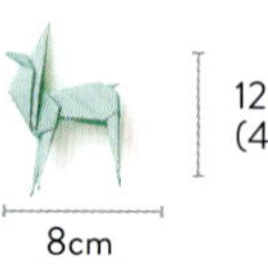 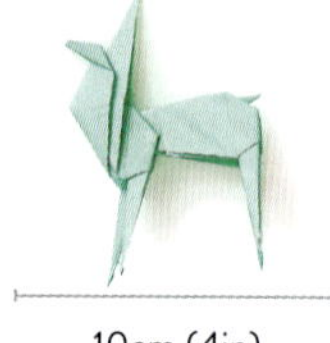

10cm (4in)

5.5cm (2¼in)

8cm (3¼in)

15cm (6in)

8cm (3¼in)

12cm (4¾in)

20cm (8in)

10cm (4in)

15cm (6in)

Tip

For this design, you will need two squares of paper. You will also need some quick-drying glue and a pair of scissors.

1. Place your square white side up, mark the creases of the central diagonal, horizontal and vertical lines. Rotate on to one corner and fold in half to form a triangle. **2. 3. 4.** Fold the LH point to the bottom, opening out the fold to form a diamond. Squash flat. **5.** Flip over. **6. 7.** Fold the LH point to the bottom, opening out the fold and squashing flat to form a diamond. **8.** Fold the RH and LH flaps on the top layer to the central line.

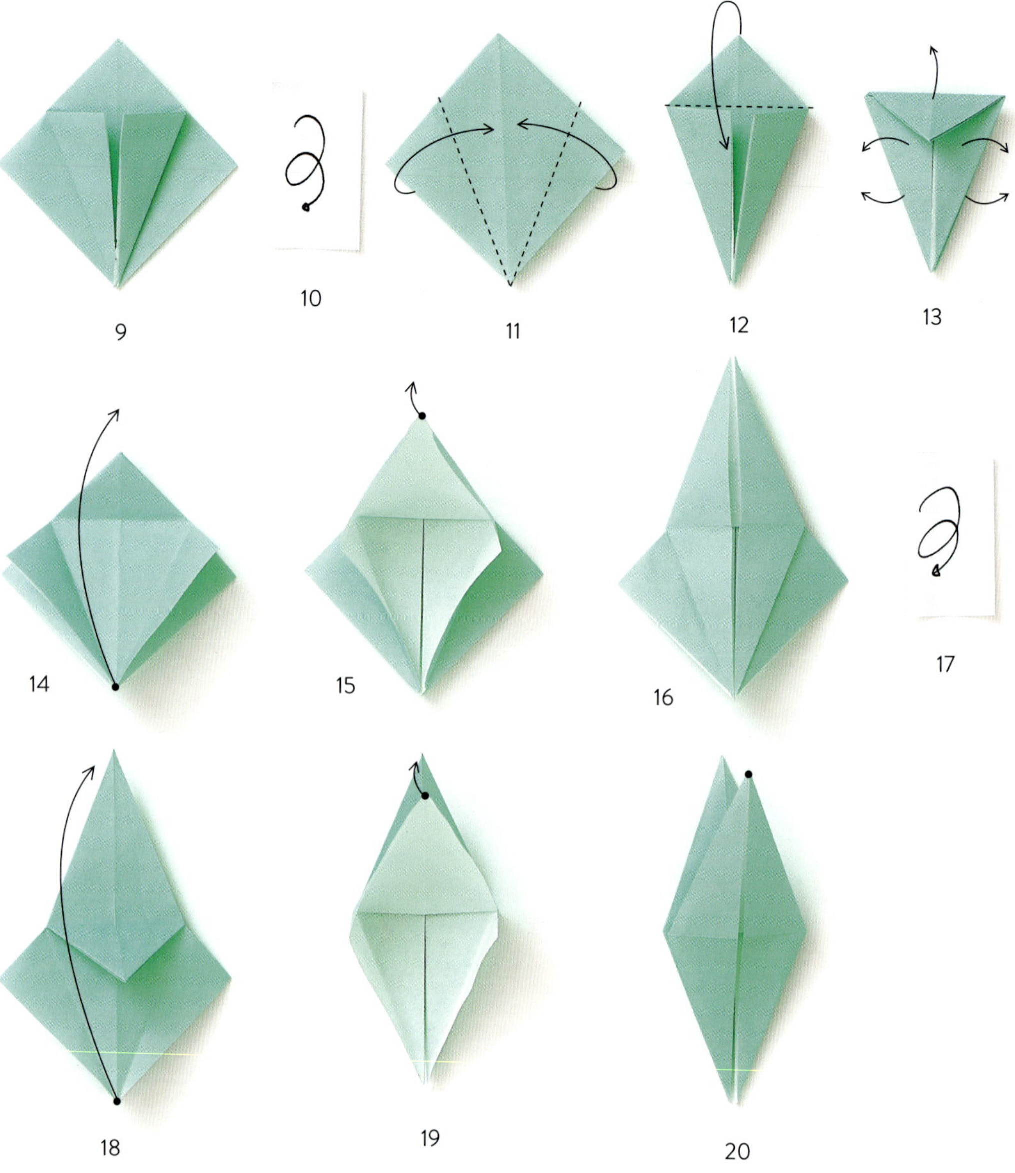

9. You now have this shape. **10.** Flip over. **11.** Fold the two flaps to the central line. **12.** Fold the top section along the dotted line. **13.** Unfold all the flaps on the front and back. **14. 15. 16.** Pinch the bottom point, pull upwards gently and squash flat. **17.** Flip over. **18. 19. 20.** Repeat steps 14 to 16 on this side. You now have this shape.

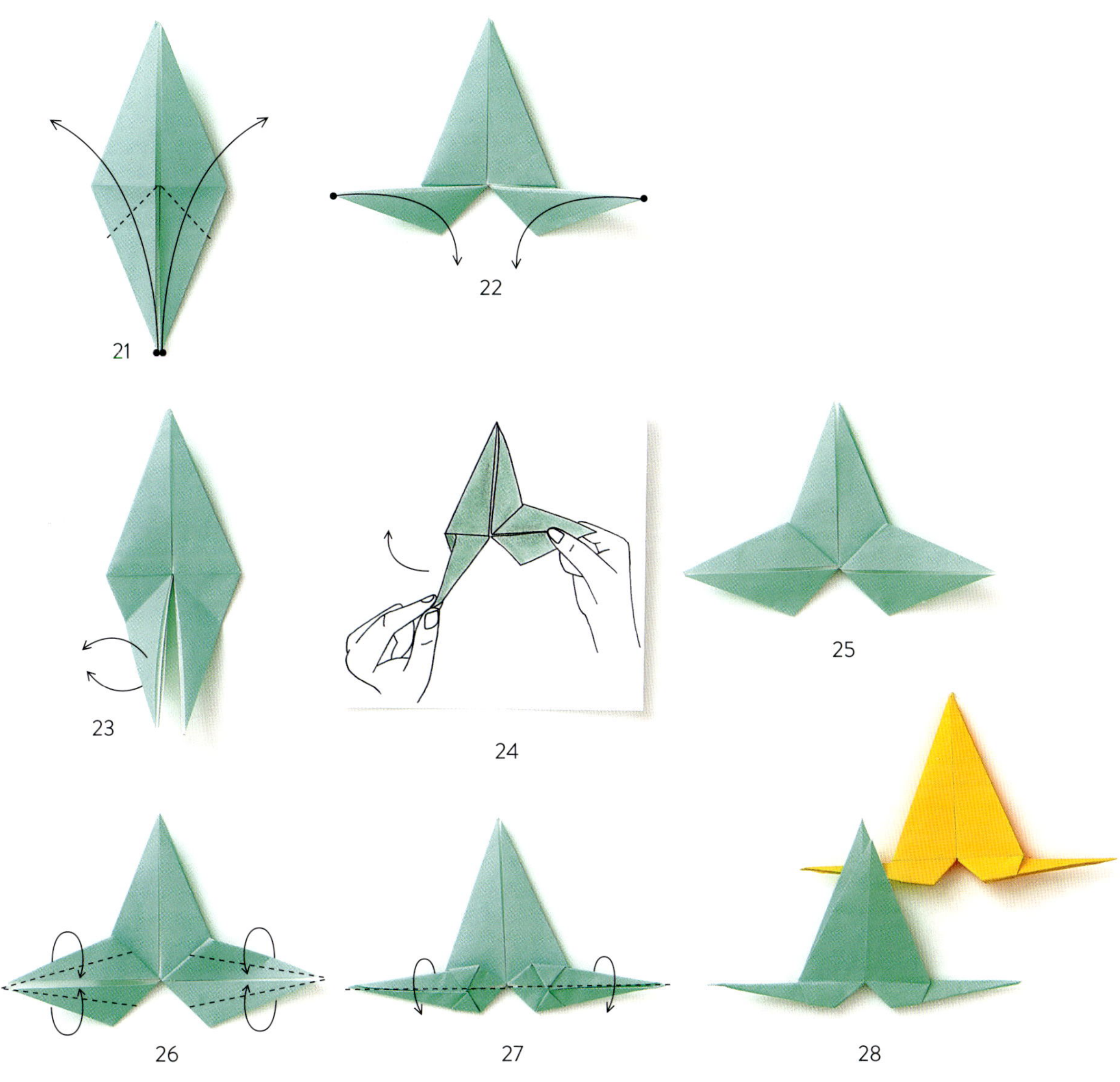

21. 22. Fold along the dotted lines and then unfold. **23. 24. 25.** Open out the LH fold and squash flat. Do the same with the RH fold. **26.** Fold on the left and the right along the dotted lines. **27.** Fold in half along the dotted line. **28.** Repeat steps 1 to 27 with another piece of paper so you have the two parts for the base of the stag.

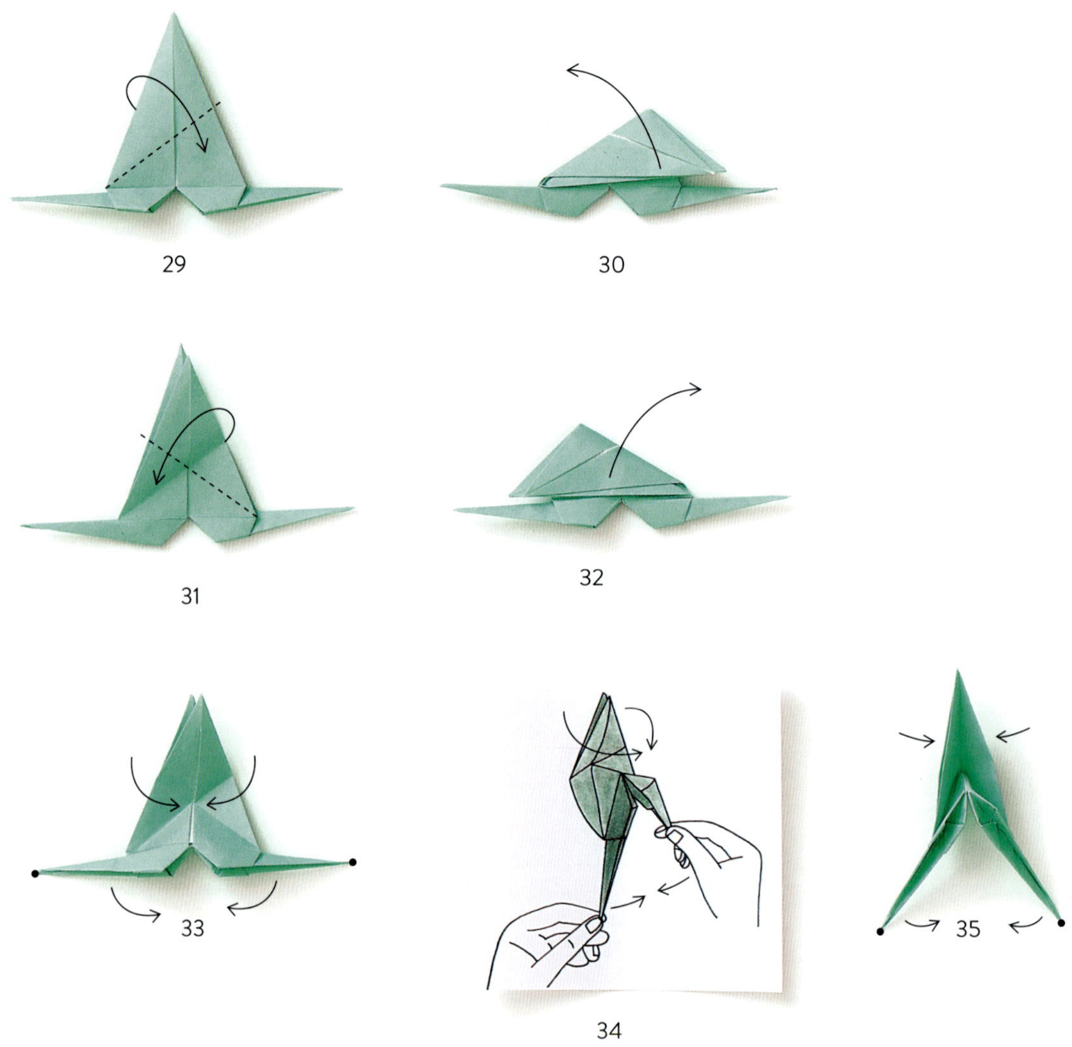

29. 30. Continue the first section by folding the two flaps to the right along the dotted line and then unfolding. **31. 32.** Fold the two flaps to the left along the dotted line and then unfold. **33. 34. 35.** Bring the two dots together to fold in half. Squash flat.

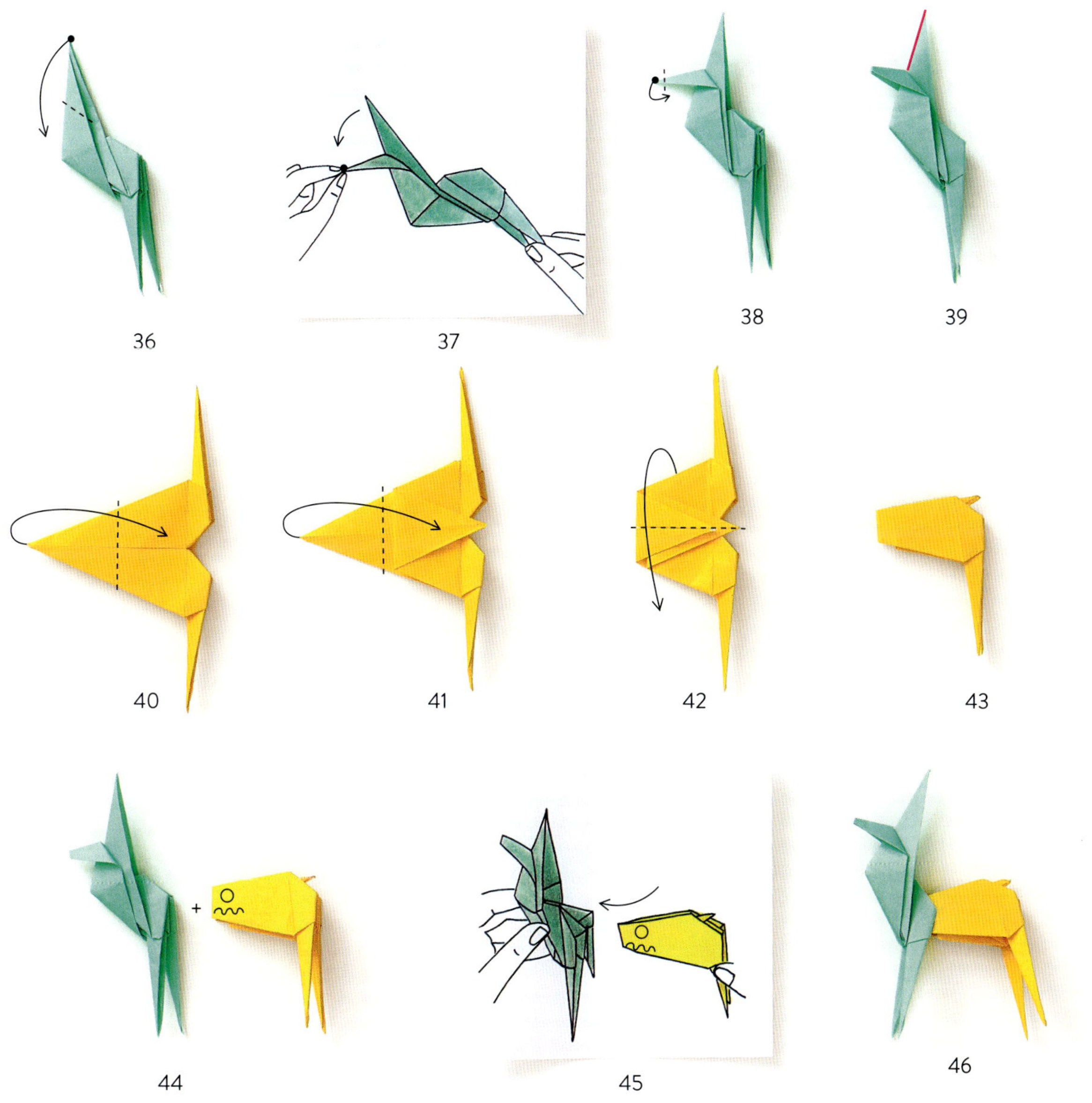

36. Fold along the dotted line. **37.** Pinch the point of the top layer delicately and invert the fold, forming an outside reverse fold. Squash flat. **38.** Fold along the dotted line, invert the fold and hide the point inside the muzzle. You have formed the head. **39.** Cut along the pink line to create the stag's antlers. **40.** Fold the point on the top layer of the second section, to just beyond the RH edge. **41.** Fold the other point, not quite as far as the first. **42.** Fold in half. **43.** You now have this shape. You have made the stag's body. **44. 45.** Apply two dabs of glue to the body and slip it inside the first section. **46.** Your stag is complete.

Majestic crane

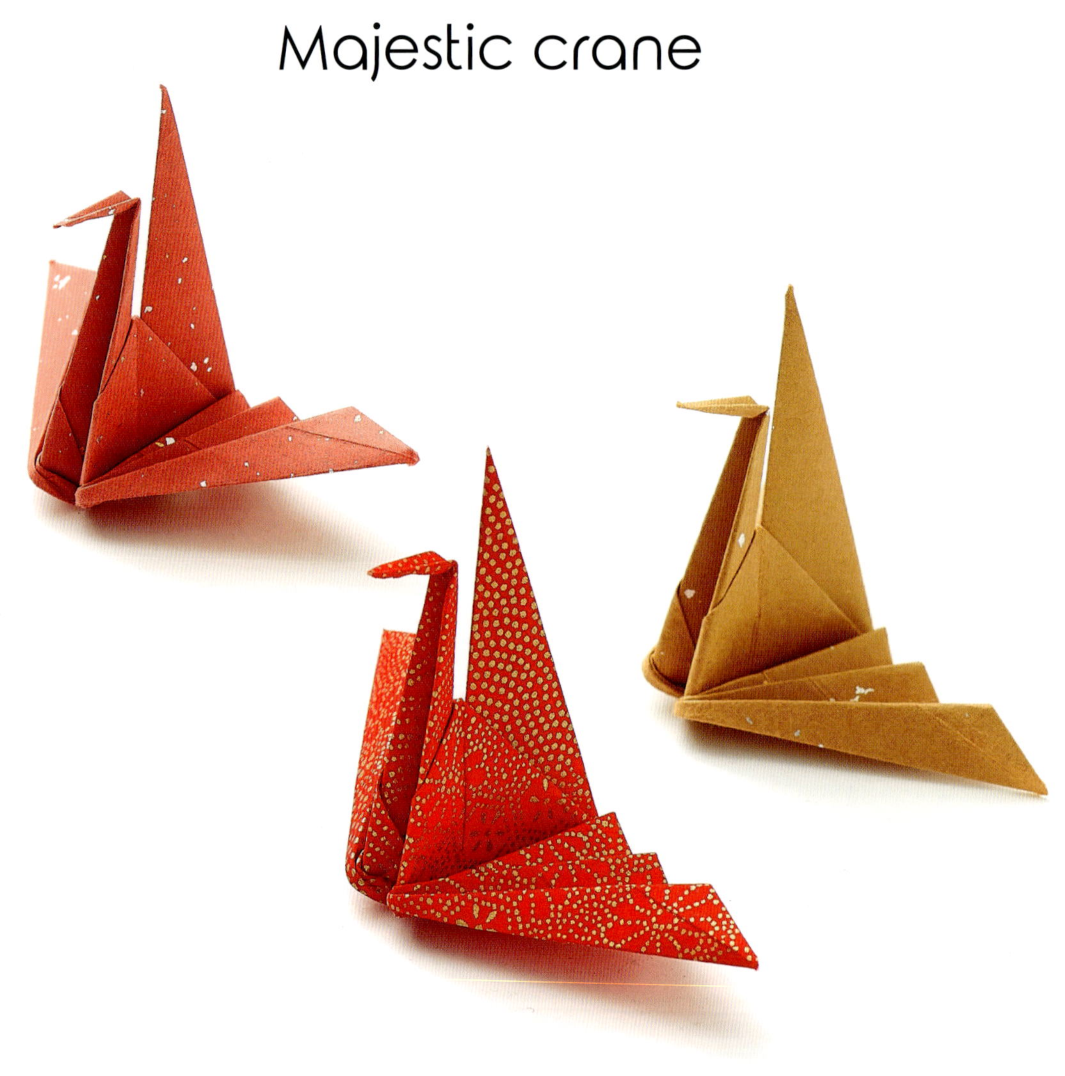

Level ●●●●●

Size

10cm (4in) — 6cm (2½in) — 5cm (2in)

15cm (6in) — 8.5cm (3⅜in) — 7cm (2¾in)

20cm (8in) — 10.5cm (4⅛in) — 9cm (3½in)

Tip

This design will stand up by itself, and it can be used as a place card.

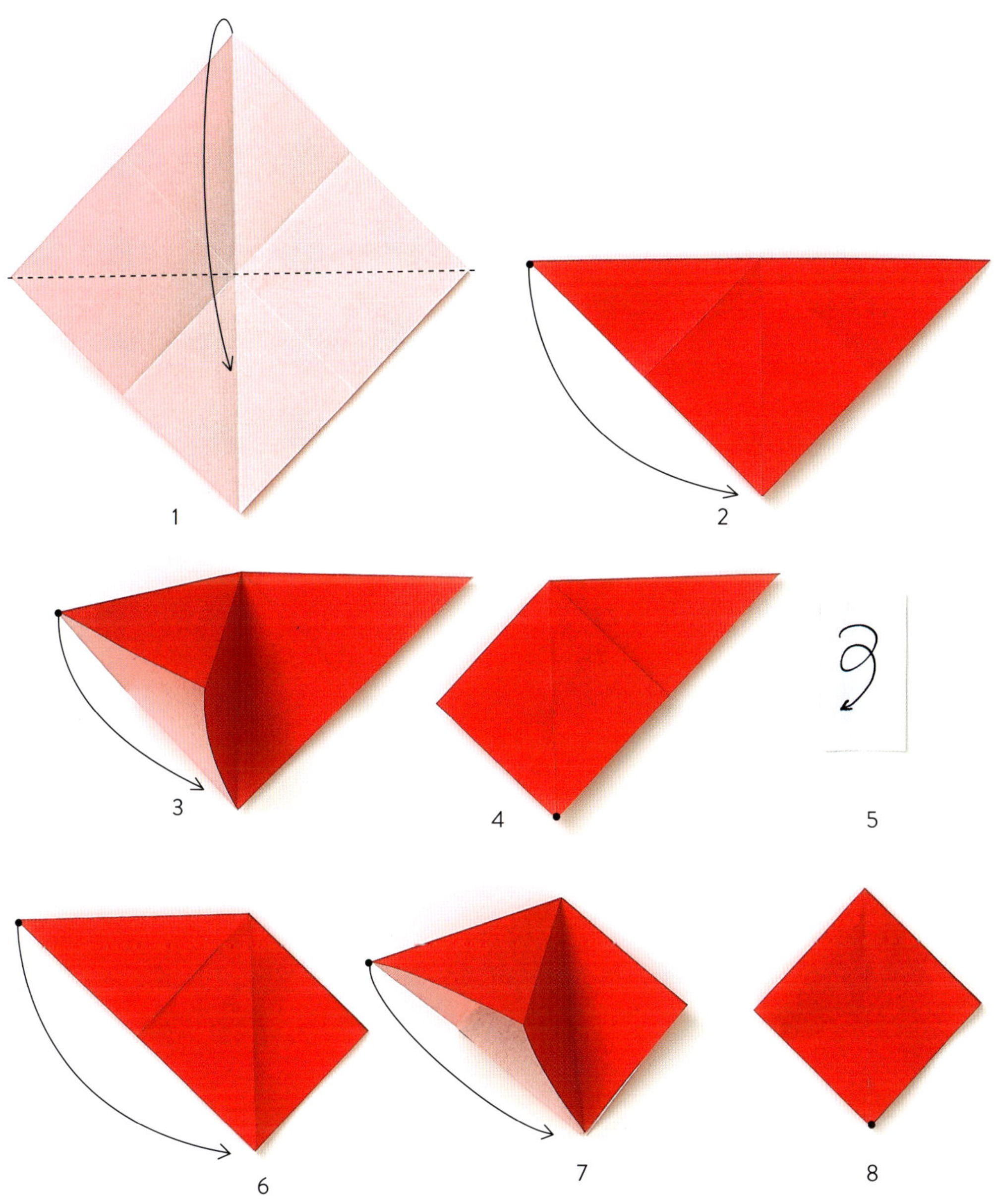

1. Place your square white side up, mark the creases of the central diagonal, horizontal and vertical lines. Rotate on to one corner and fold in half to form a triangle. **2. 3. 4.** Fold the LH point to the bottom, opening out the fold to form a diamond. Squash flat. **5.** Flip over. **6. 7. 8.** Fold the LH point to the bottom, opening out the fold to obtain a diamond. Squash flat.

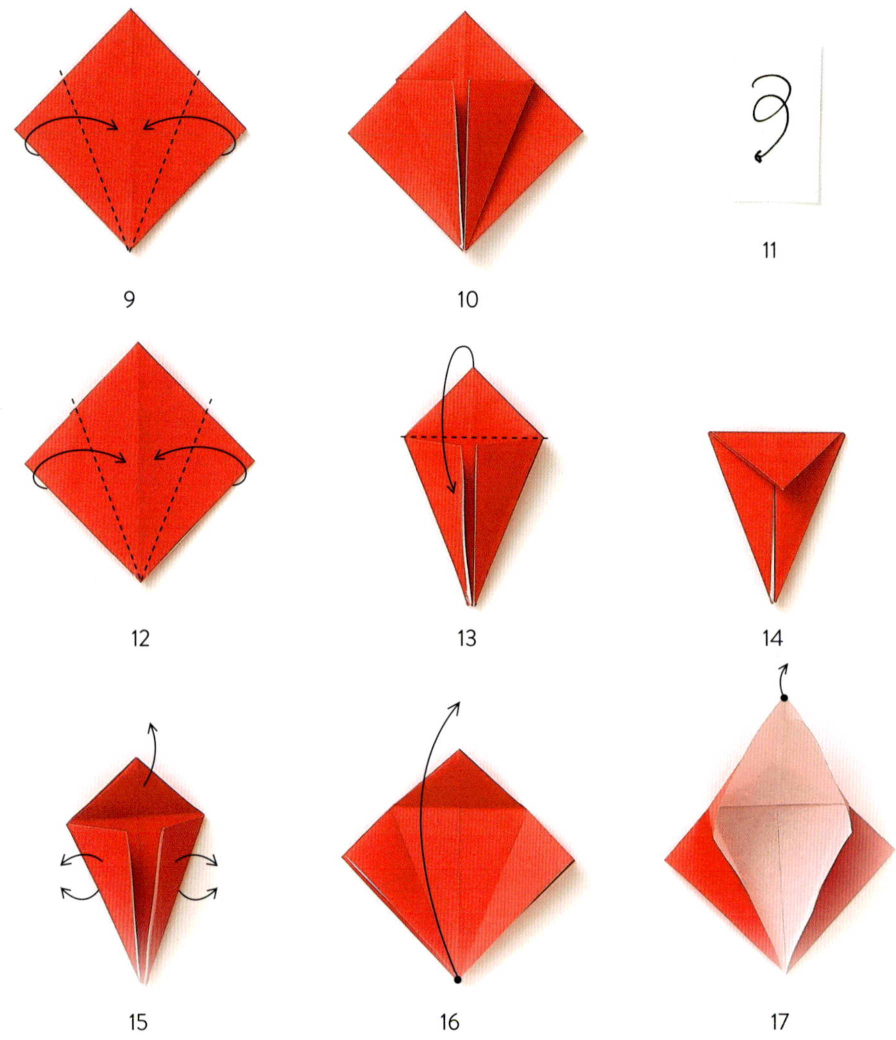

9. 10. Fold to the central line along the dotted lines. You now have this shape. **11.** Flip over. **12.** Fold to the central line along the dotted lines. **13. 14.** Fold the top point along the dotted line. You now have this shape. **15.** Open all the flaps on front and back. **16. 17.** Pinch the bottom corner and pull it upwards carefully.

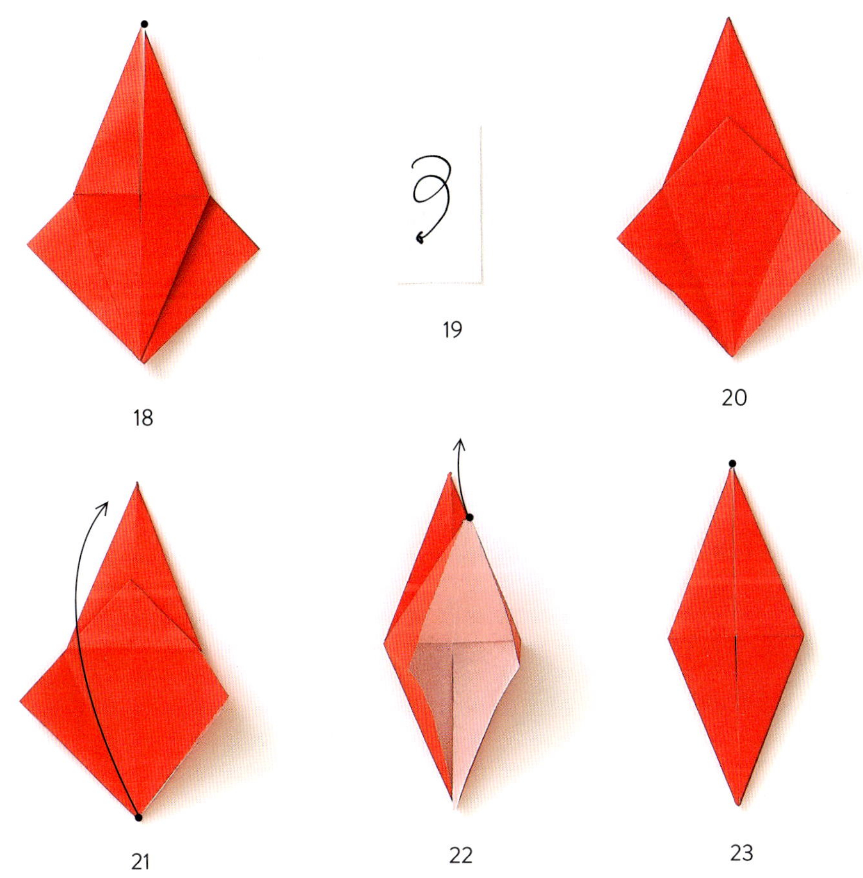

18. Squash flat. **19.** Flip over. **20.** You now have this shape. **21. 22. 23.** Pinch the bottom point and pull it upwards carefully. Squash flat. You now have this shape.

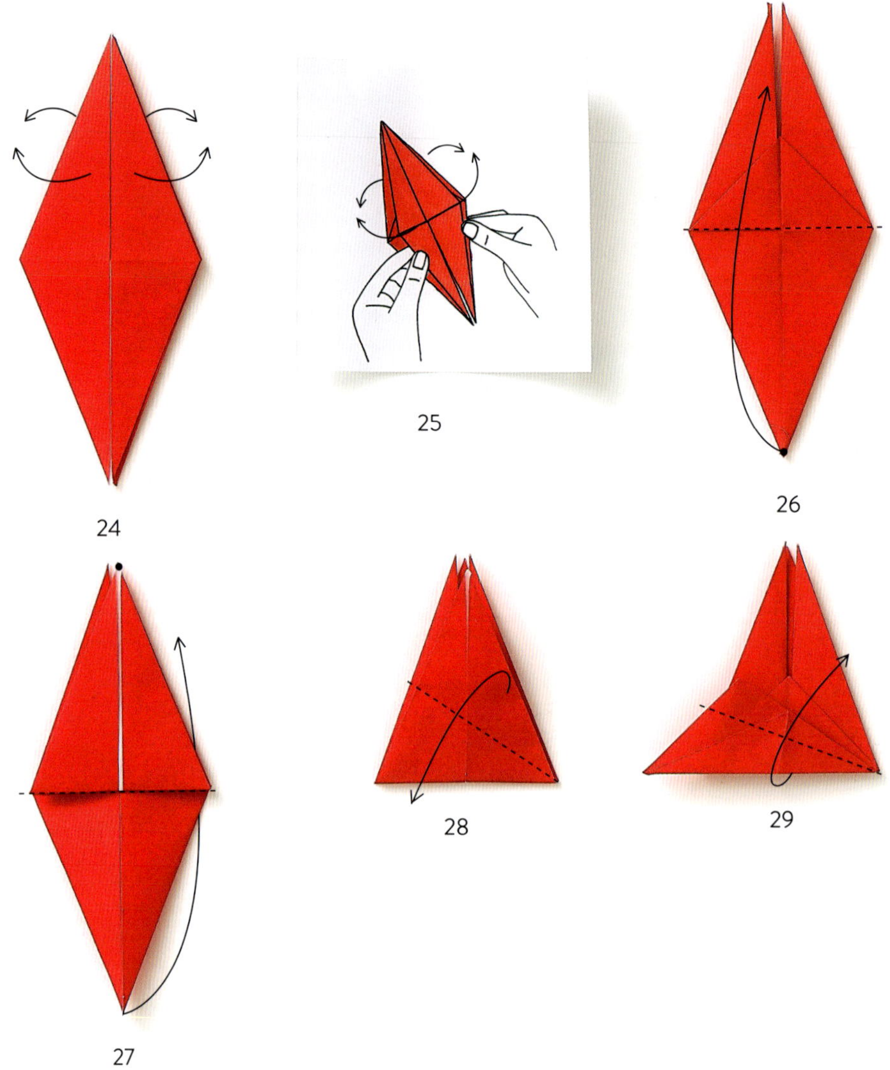

24. 25. Fold the two front flaps against each other and the two back flaps against each other. Squash flat. **26.** Fold the flap on the top layer in half upwards. **27.** Fold the flap on bottom layer in half behind. **28.** Fold the uppermost flap along the dotted line. **29.** Fold the flap along the dotted line, aligning it with the edge of the lower triangle.

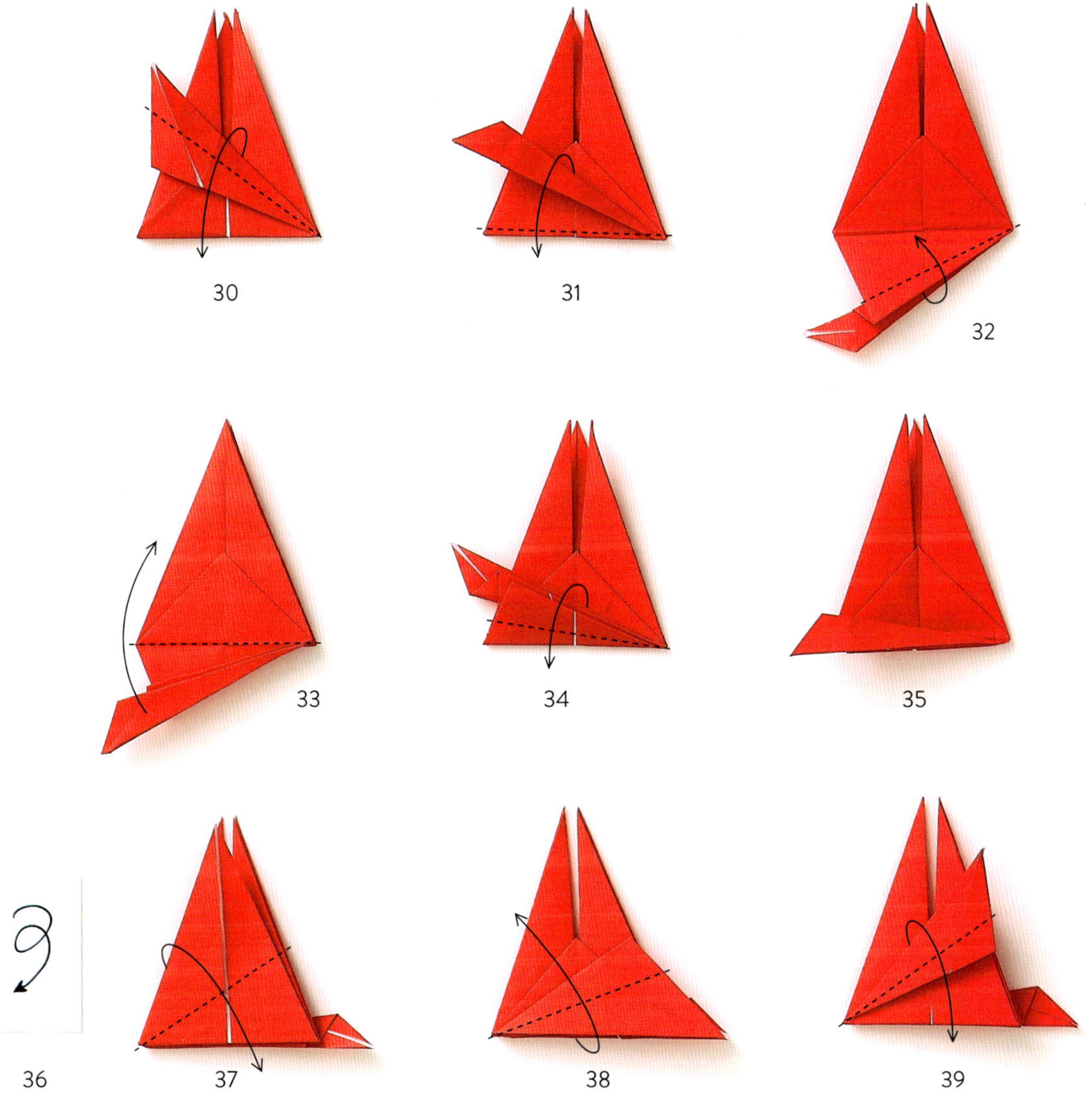

30. Fold the flap on the top layer in half. **31.** Fold along the dotted line. **32.** Fold along the dotted line.
33. Fold upwards along the dotted line. **34. 35.** Fold in half along the dotted line. You now have this shape.
36. Flip over. **37.** Fold the uppermost flap along the dotted line. **38.** Fold the flap along the dotted line, aligning it with the edge of the lower triangle. **39.** Fold the flap on the top layer in half.

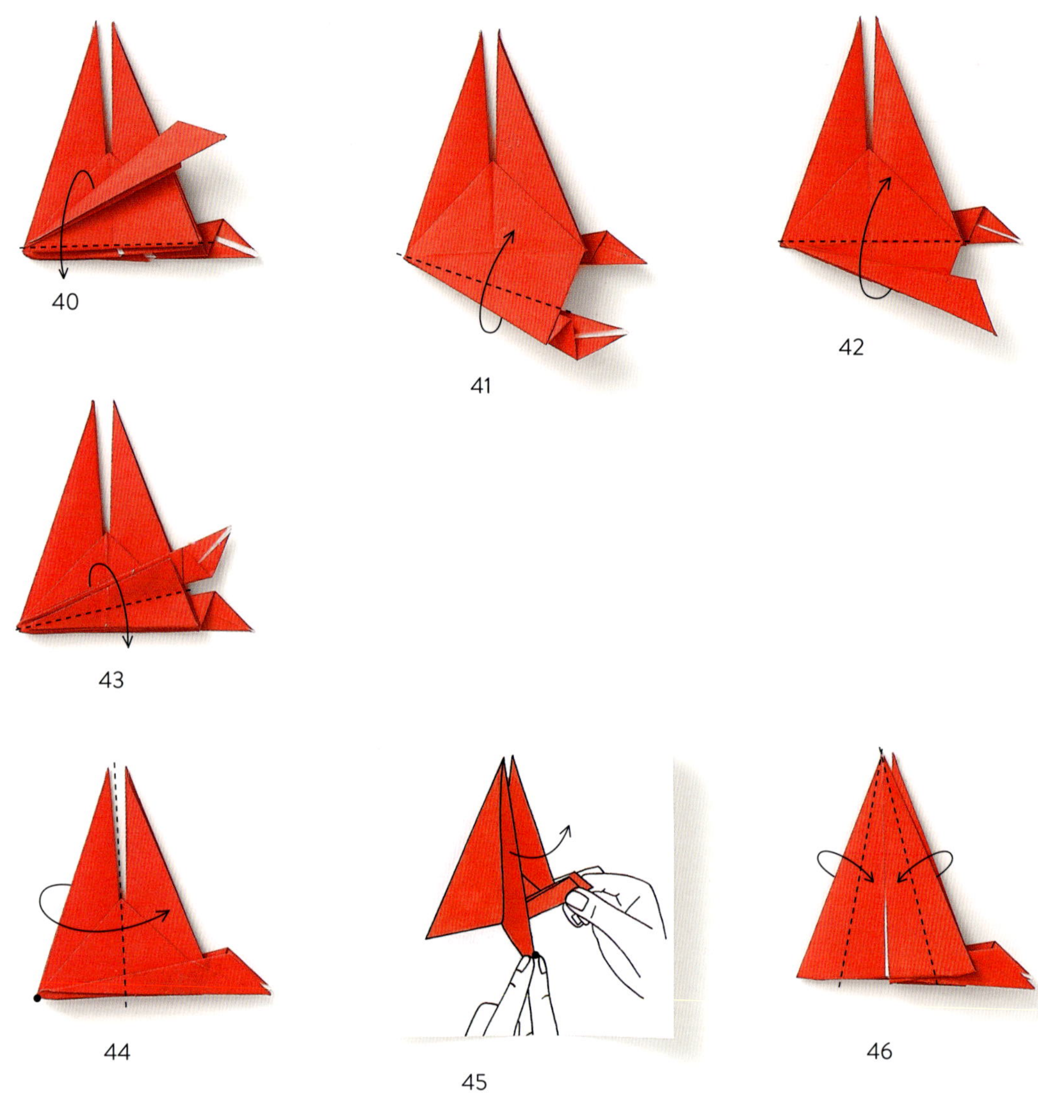

40. Fold along the dotted line. **41.** Fold along the dotted line. **42.** Fold upwards along the dotted line. **43.** Fold in half along the dotted line. **44. 45.** Fold the LH flap on the top layer to the right. You now have this shape. **46.** Fold the RH and LH flaps in half.

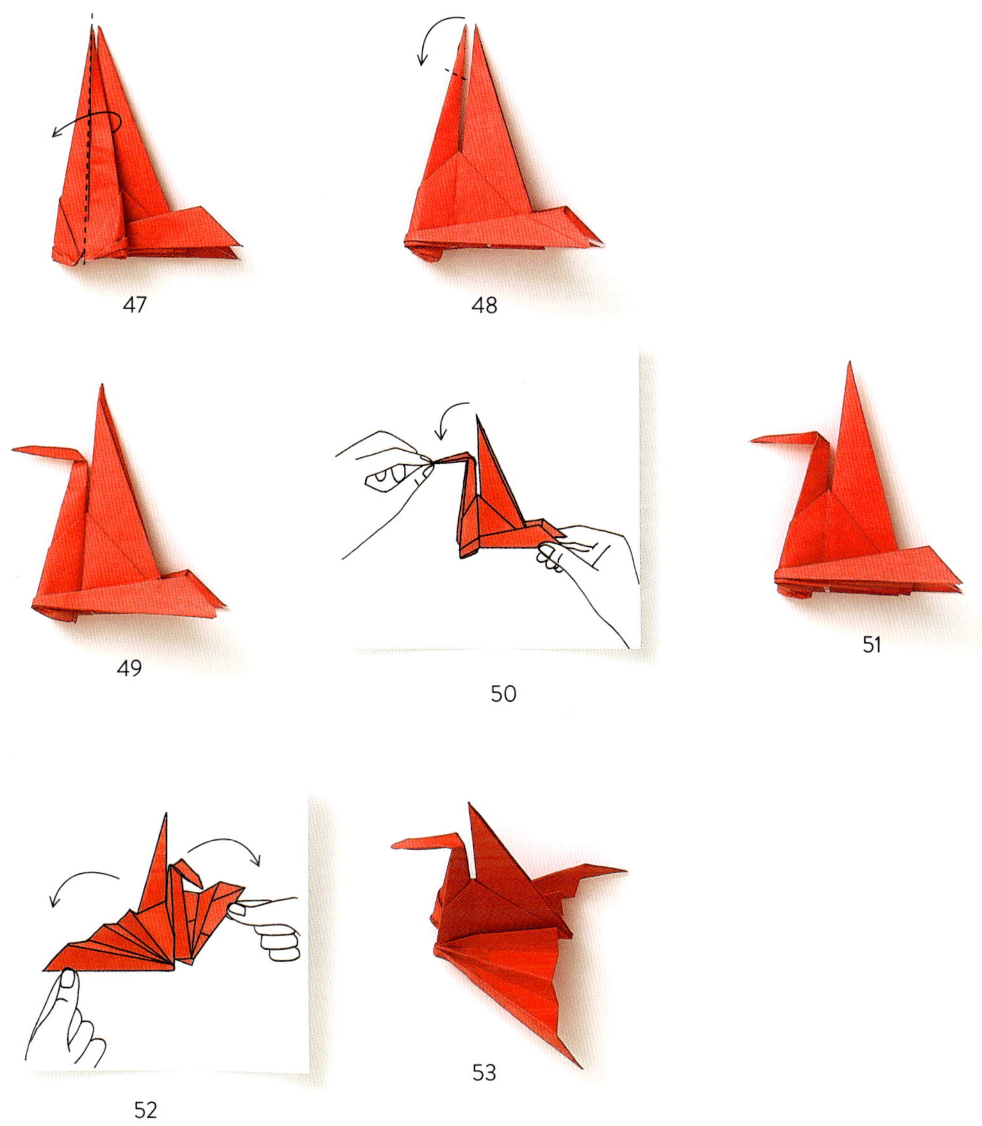

47. Fold the RH flap over the LH flap. **48.** Fold at an oblique angle along the dotted line. **49. 50. 51.** Unfold, invert and squash flat. You have formed the head. **52.** Open out the wings, pulling gently outwards. **53.** Your majestic crane is complete.

Lily

Size

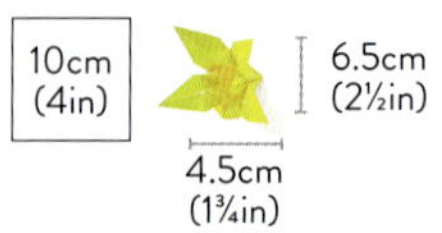

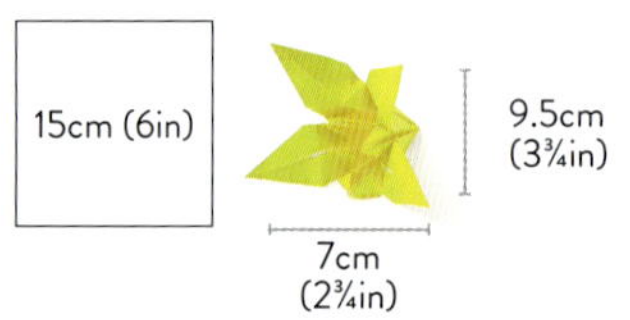

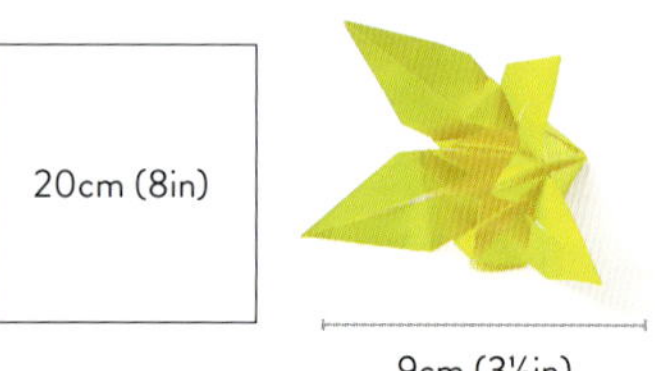

Tip

You can attach this flower to a stem and make a bouquet.

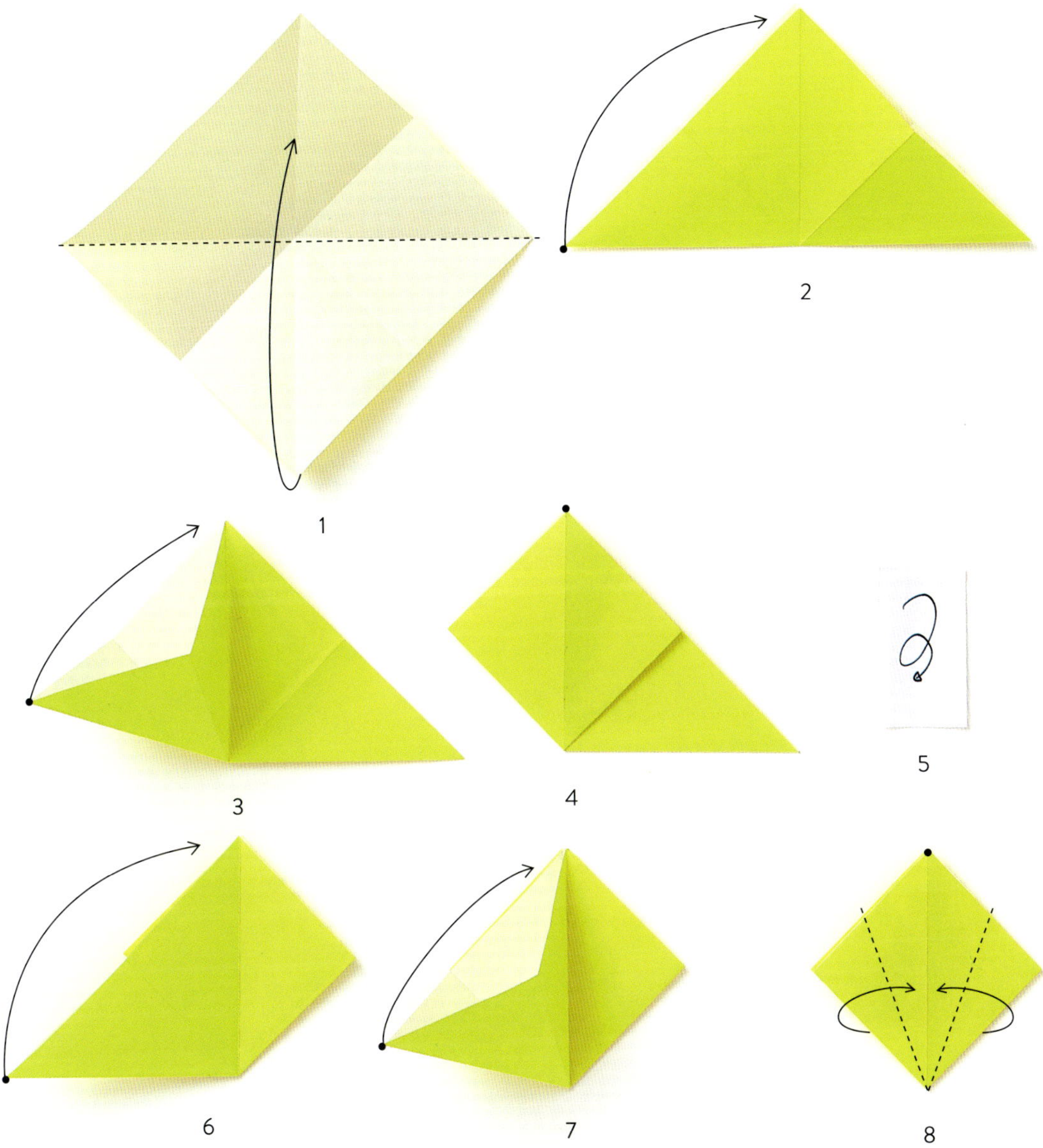

1. Place your square white side up. Mark the creases of the central diagonal, horizontal and vertical lines. Rotate on to one corner and fold in half to form a triangle. **2. 3. 4.** Fold the LH point to the top, opening out the fold to form a diamond. Squash flat. **5.** Flip over. **6. 7.** Fold the LH point to the top, opening out the fold to form a diamond. Squash flat. **8.** Fold the flaps on the top layer along the dotted lines.

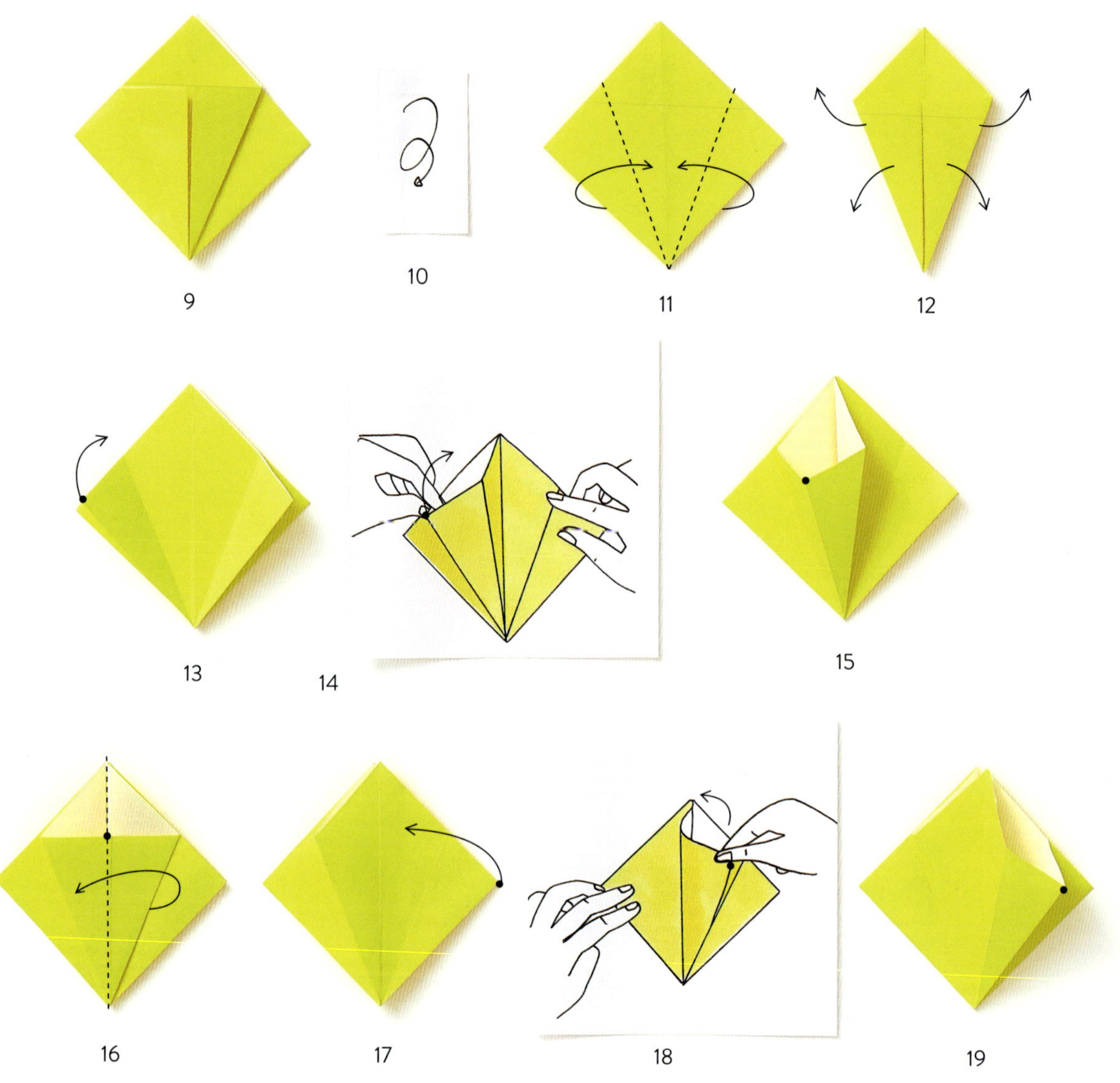

9. You now have this shape. **10.** Flip over. **11.** Fold to the central line along the dotted lines. **12.** Open all the flaps on front and back. **13. 14. 15.** Fold the LH point to the central line, opening out the fold and squashing flat. **16.** Fold the RH flap to the left along the dotted line. **17. 18. 19.** Fold the RH point to the central line, opening out the fold and squashing flat.

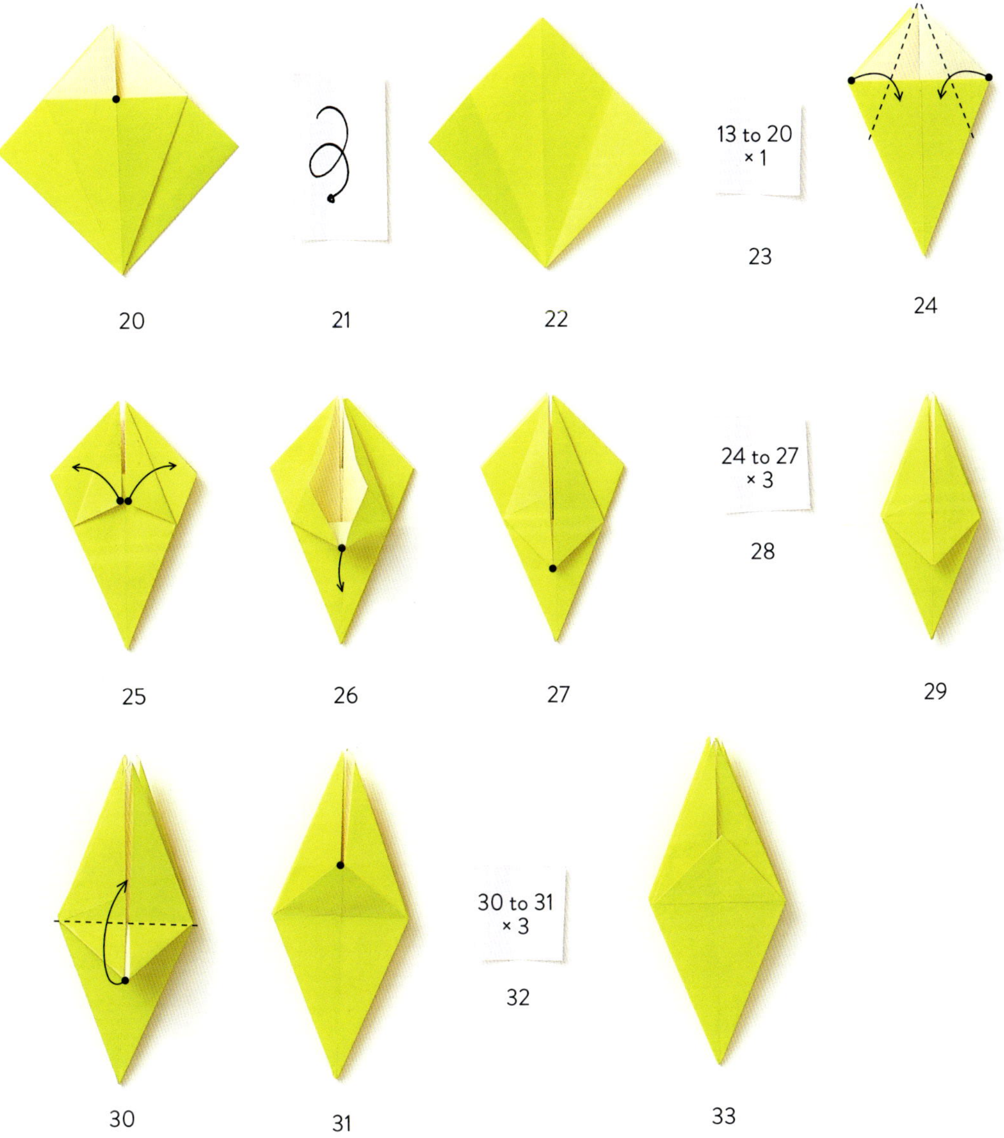

20

21

22

13 to 20
× 1

23

24

25

26

27

24 to 27
× 3

28

29

30

31

30 to 31
× 3

32

33

20. You now have this shape. **21.** Flip over. **22.** You now have this shape. **23.** Repeat steps 13 to 20 on this side. **24.** You now have this shape. Then fold the top layer along the dotted lines. **25.** Open the folds outwards. **26. 27.** Pinch the black dot and pull it gently downwards to open out the fold. Squash flat. **28.** Flip over and repeat steps 24 to 27. Fold the two RH flaps to the left and repeat steps 24 to 27. Flip over. Fold the two RH flaps to the left and repeat steps 24 to 27 three times. **29.** You now have this shape. **30. 31.** Lift the black dot and fold along the dotted line. You now have this shape. **32.** Flip over. Repeat steps 30 to 31. Fold the two RH flaps to the left and repeat steps 30 to 31. Flip over. Fold the two RH flaps to the left and repeat steps 30 to 31 three times. **33.** You now have this shape.

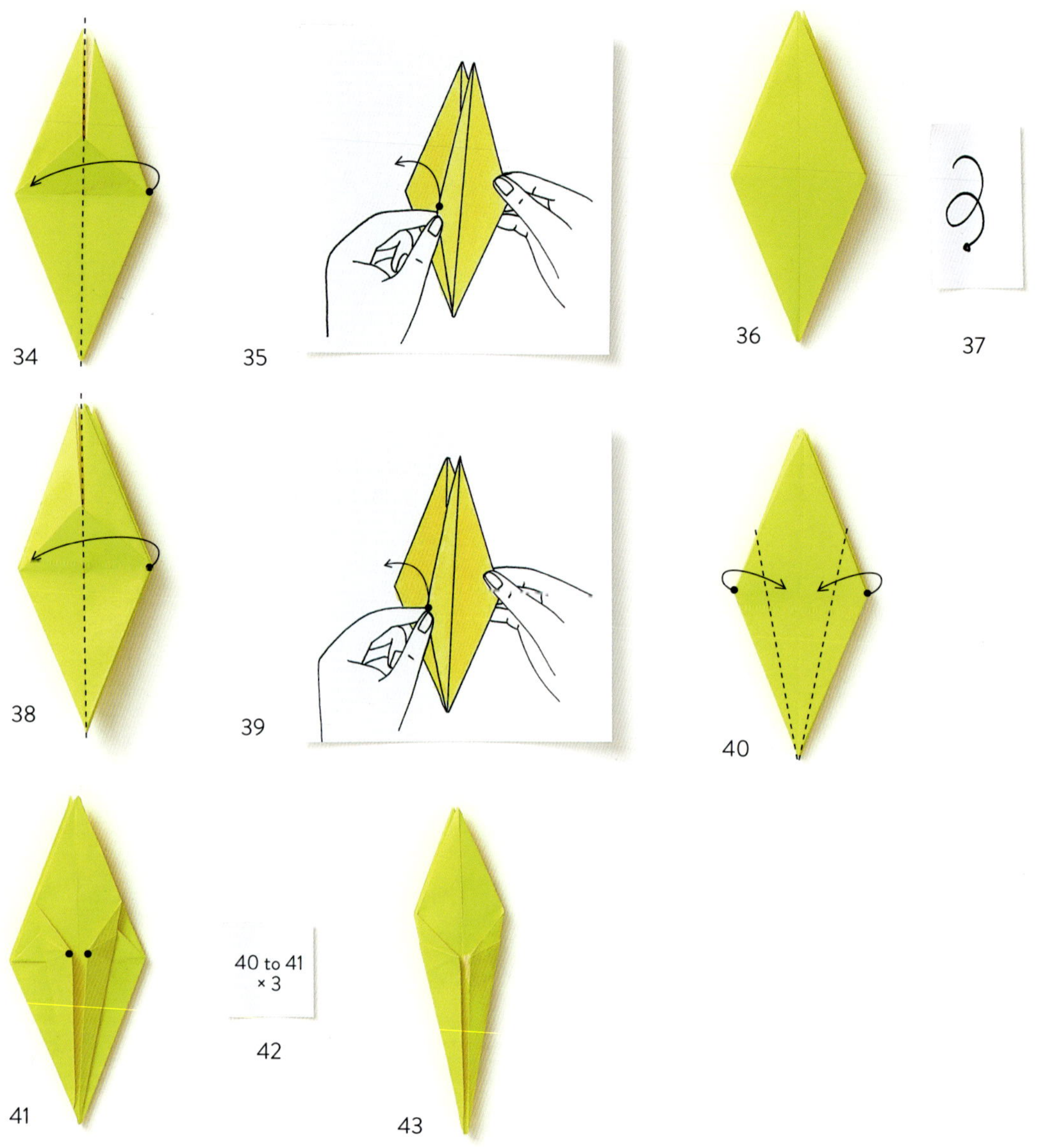

34. 35. 36. Fold the RH flap on the top layer to the left. You now have this shape. **37.** Flip over. **38. 39.** Fold the RH flap on the top layer to the left. **40. 41.** Fold the RH and LH flaps along the dotted lines. **42.** Flip over and repeat steps 40 and 41. Fold the two RH flaps to the left and repeat steps 40 to 41. Flip over. Fold the two RH flaps to the left and repeat steps 40 to 41 three times. **43.** You now have this shape.

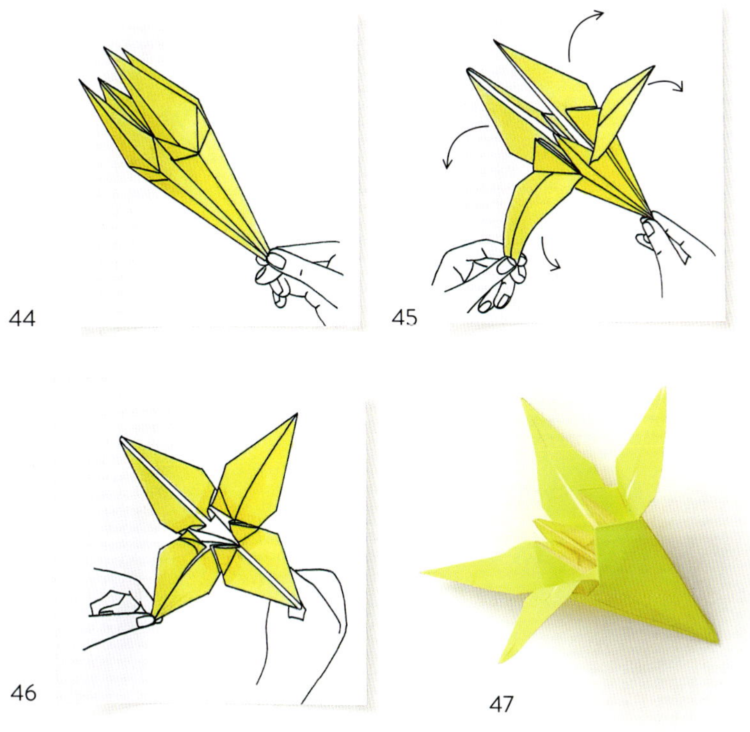

44. 45. 46. Holding the base between your fingers, gently open the petals, pulling them outwards.
47. Your lily is complete.

Difficulty guide

The black dots show the difficulty of the design, from easier for beginners (●)
to more difficult (●●●●●) for more experienced folders.

Birds

Parrot	●●○○○	56
Turtle dove	●●○○○	60
Owl	●●●○○	96
Dove	●●●○○	104
Cockerel	●●●●○	164
Seated crane	●●●●○	170
Majestic crane	●●●●●	200

The garden

Butterfly	●○○○○	32
Tulip	●○○○○	36
Daisy	●●○○○	54
Autumn leaf	●●○○○	72
Four-leaf clover	●●○○○	80
Hydrangea	●●●●○	122
Cherry Blossom	●●●●○	140
Ginkgo leaf	●●●●○	152
Morning glory	●●●●○	156
Campanula	●●●●○	160
Dragonfly	●●●●○	176
Marguerite	●●●●○	182
Christmas tree	●●●●●	188
Lily	●●●●●	208

Water

Goldfish	●○○○○	28
Turtle	●●○○○	62
Scallop shell	●●●○○	112
Frog	●●●○○	130

Animals

Cat	●●○○○	40
Hedgehog	●●○○○	44
Fox	●●○○○	50
Panda	●●●○○	66
Lion	●●○○○	92
Snail	●●●○○	134
Mouse	●●●○○	144
Rabbit	●●●○○	148
Stag	●●●●●	194

Decoration

Cup	●○○○○	30
Fan	●○○○○	48
Tatou envelope	●●○○○	76
Heart	●●○○○	84
Star	●●●○○	88

Clothing

Shirt	●●●○○	100
Ceremonial kimono	●●●○○	108
Dress	●●●○○	116
Simple kimono	●●●○○	126

Acknowledgements

Special thanks to Eriko. You have been an exemplary assistant and paper folder throughout this project, showing the same attention to detail and commitment as always.

A warm thank you to you, Séverine, for your invaluable help, for your vision and advice, for the layout work, your many proofreadings and corrections, and your kindness throughout this project.

Thanks to you, Lucy. I am delighted that your illustrations are once again featured in the step-by-step guides of this book.

Thank you, Richard, for your serenity and your photographic talents. Shooting with you is always a real pleasure.

Thank you, Stella, for always being a ready ear, for your support and friendship, which have also made this project possible.

Because you are once again the fairy godmothers of this beautiful adventure, I thank you with all my heart: Hiromi, Licinia, Karine and Julie.

Thank you to Laurence, Emmanuelle, Muriel and Dominique, for your precious help and willingness to listen.

Thank you again, Pascale, for your trust. I feel lucky to have had you as editor for all these years.

Thank you to my two loves, Cedric and Ulysse, for giving me inspiration and joy in my daily life.

Finally, a big thank-you to all my readers who have shared this love of paper with me. I hope you enjoy the colourful creations in this book, which I have had so much fun making.

Adeline Klam

 www.instagram.com/adelineklam/

Discover a whole world of Japanese
paper and origami at Adeline's shop at
54 Boulevard Richard-Lenoir in Paris
or at the site: www.adelineklam.com

Nana Takahashi

nanahoshi.com

 www.instagram.com/_nanahoshi_/

Nana Takahashi is a Japanese artist who lives and
works in Japan. She is an illustrator and paper artist
who excels in the art of origami and has published
numerous books in Japan. She illustrates most of her
designs with flowers and animals, creating a dreamlike,
poetic world of her own.
"You will find three of my favourite designs in this book.
Thank you, Nana!" – A.K.

First published in the UK in 2026 by
Search Press Limited
Wellwood, North Farm Road,
Tunbridge Wells, Kent TN2 3DR

1 2 3 4 5 6 7 8 9 10

Originally published as *L'Origami Comme Par Magie 2*

Copyright – © Hachette Livre (Marabout) 2022

Proofing and adaptation: Dominique Montembault
Technical drawings: Lucy Tezier
Graphic design: Muxx
Page-setting: Frédéric Voisin

English translation from the original French by
Tankerton Translations.

ISBN: 978-1-80092-383-6
eBook ISBN: 978-1-80093-362-0

Bookmarked Hub
For further ideas and inspiration, and to join our free online
community, visit www.bookmarkedhub.com

Publishers' notes
Metric measurements are used in this book; the imperial
conversions are rounded to the nearest ¼in. Always use either
metric or imperial measurements, not a combination of both.

The Publishers and author can accept no responsibility for any
consequences arising from the information, advice or instructions
given in this publication.

For errata, please visit our website (www.searchpress.com) or
the Bookmarked Hub (www.bookmarkedhub.com).

GPSR information can be found at www.searchpress.com
Printed in China, RRD022026